Alt-Right

D0062634

Alt-Right

From 4chan to
the White House

Mike Wendling

PLUTO PRESS

First published 2018 by Pluto Press
345 Archway Road, London N6 5AA

www.plutobooks.com

British Library Cataloguing in Publication Data
A catalogue record for this book is available from the British Library

ISBN   978 0 7453 3795 1   Hardback
ISBN   978 0 7453 3745 6   Paperback
ISBN   978 1 7868 0236 1   PDF eBook
ISBN   978 1 7868 0238 5   Kindle eBook
ISBN   978 1 7868 0237 8   EPUB eBook

This book is printed on paper suitable for recycling and made from fully
managed and sustained forest sources. Logging, pulping and manufacturing
processes are expected to conform to the environmental standards of the
country of origin.

Simultaneously printed in the United Kingdom and United States of America

Contents

Acknowledgments

This book would not be possible without the efforts of a large group of people who helped me immensely along the way.

Even before I started writing, I was able to rely on a number of trusted sources and advisors, and I would especially like to thank the outstanding team at Pluto Press.

Broadcasting is a team game and I had a tremendous amount of assistance gathering and reporting much of the material for this book from BBC Trending radio producers, bloggers, video journalists and other Beeb colleagues. Our studio managers and technical staff keep us on air and make me sound and look much better than I do IRL, and credit for logistical and moral support goes to the unsung heroes who are our production co-ordinators.

I'm also lucky to have worked with a number of extremely sharp editors and commissioners who have given me jobs, put me to work on written pieces and radio programmes, helped focus my reporting and more than occasionally indulged my obsessiveness. The BBC's Editorial Policy department read a draft of this manuscript and gave some extremely valuable advice.

Outside the BBC, I'm indebted to a large group of journalists, editors and researchers who lent me their time, expertise, skills and promotional efforts.

I'm incredibly grateful to a number of my friends and family members who've been supportive in all kinds of ways. And finally, and most importantly, a huge thank you to R for her patience, tolerance, editing skill, shrewd advice, and much else besides.

Introduction: Is it OK to Punch a Nazi?

Richard Spencer had reason to crow. As one of Donald Trump's most fervent "alt-right" supporters, walking through the streets of Washington on Inauguration Day in January 2017, he was celebrating not only the victory of one of his favorite politicians, but the start of what he thought would be a cleansing revolution. It was the beginning of the end, he thought, for globalism, liberalism, political correctness and multicultural democracy.

In the middle of the crowds, Spencer enjoyed the attention of Trump supporters, protesters and the media in his role as the leader of this new, slightly mysterious fringe movement in American politics. It was a contrast with the recent past. He had spent the years of the Obama administration writing for esoteric websites, bickering with his neighbors in a tiny Montana town,[1] and working out how to spin his twenty-first-century version of white nationalism—and a new nationalist ethno-state world order—into something fashionable, edgy and cool. But now, in Donald Trump, he had found a leader he could follow.

"I think we were in love with him," Spencer told me later.

> He was the man, he was changing everything, he was doing things for us, he couldn't be stopped. I was definitely excited. The alt-right felt unified with average Trump supporters. I could walk around with a Trump hat on ... and get a slap on the back and a pat on the back from an average person. For what I'm doing, which is quote "far-right" politics, that's not something that normally happens.

Suddenly, Spencer felt like he was no longer on the fringes, but in the middle of the slipstream of history. "I never got into any of this to become a marginal figure," he said. "I think we're going to win. Our biggest problem is that we haven't dreamed big enough." And President Trump was the alt-right's first big dream that came true.

But it wasn't just the president that alt-righters counted as being on their side. The inaugural stage would also be graced that day by Stephen Bannon, former executive chairman of the online tabloid Breitbart. Breitbart was a site with a distinct mission, even in America's increasingly partisan media environment. Its staple news diet consisted of stories about immigrants spreading crime and disease, mendacious Democrats, and outrage-inducing examples of political correctness. Breitbart was the new media outlet of choice for the Trumpian right and had become—though perhaps not through deliberate design—the chief popular media amplifier of alt-right ideas.[2] It had previously described Spencer, in laudatory terms, as one of the intellectual founders of the movement,[3] and Bannon himself once bragged to a reporter: "We're the platform for the alt-right."[4] He was about to become the president's chief strategist.

Wandering among the Inauguration Day crowds, Spencer found himself giving an interview amid a small throng at the corner of 14th and K Streets in downtown Washington.[5] Video posted online shows him shrugging off the opponents surrounding him.[6] "I've given conferences for ages, and we usually expect some protesters," he said to the reporter.

But the conversation soon deteriorated into a free-for-all. In the video, people behind Spencer held signs which read "White lives matter too much" and "Fight for socialism over barbarism." Protesters began interjecting with questions. *Do you like black people? Are you a neo-Nazi?*

"Neo-Nazis don't love me, they kind of hate me," he responded.

The reporter asked him about a cartoon frog pinned to his lapel—the now-infamous green amphibian Pepe that had become the mascot of the alt-right movement.

Just as he started to answer—"Pepe's become kind of a symbol..." he began—a man rushed at Spencer and punched him in the face.

*   *   *

Spencer was perhaps the most recognizable leader of a movement that is in some ways unlike any other political force of modern times. The alt-right is an incredibly loose set of ideologies held together by what they oppose: feminism, Islam, the Black Lives Matter movement, political correctness, a fuzzy idea they call "globalism," and establishment politics of both the left and the right.

It's a movement that for most of its relatively short history has existed almost entirely online and one which, despite its lack of organization, formal political channels, official candidates or party membership, burst into mainstream consciousness in 2016, in tandem with the Trump candidacy. With amazing speed after his election victory, the term "alt-right" transformed from an obscure idea into a commonly used—if sometimes ill-defined—label.

As the movement gained attention, it presented a unique set of challenges to journalists, to progressives, and to conservatives who found themselves in the alt-right firing line. What was the best way to deal with this phenomenon, and its outpouring of a mixture of authentic and ironic hate? Where did it come from? What did it stand for? Who were these people, and what did they want?

This book is an attempt to answer some of those questions. It's also an attempt to move beyond exhausted "call out" tactics. These suggest that simply labelling the alt-right racist (or sexist, or homophobic or xenophobic, etc.), or reducing their movement to white supremacism or a rebranded version of the Ku Klux Klan will scare people off.

Let's be clear. These epithets are certainly accurate—many of the alt-right's self-declared members are indeed, by any standard definition of the terms, racist or sexist. Many of them won't even quibble with being labeled as such. They believe in a racial pecking order, and strictly prescribed gender roles. Taken collectively, race is the movement's top obsession—only just nudging out topics such as gender, anti-feminism, free speech, Western civilization and video gaming.[7]

But for those concerned about the alt-right's growing influence, casual label-tossing plays directly into the movement's hands. Some activists are actually proud of being called "racist." Others brush the word off as meaningless, correctly if misleadingly pointing out that, online, such insults are routinely lobbed at people who are nothing of the sort. And, in one of the favorite pastimes of alt-righters, insults are hurled back at their enemies, for almost nothing pleases them more than pointing out hypocrisy, and appealing to the classic logical fallacy, "You do it too!"[8] And so if an alt-righter is accused of being racist or sexist, they're likely to fight back by pointing out some egregious example of similar behavior by someone on the left. It's not really that they care about equality—their movement is profoundly anti-egalitarian. They care about winning arguments, pointing out logical inconsistencies and verbally bludgeoning their opponents into submission, which they routinely do online.

Imprecision allows even the most extreme alt-righters—and many of them hold views far out of step with any recognizable mainstream political party or movement—to avoid being pinned down, and to accuse their accusers of misrepresenting them.[9] Thus to call the alt-right "racist" or an offshoot of the KKK and leave it at that is to step into their trap, where activists can either refute the claim with selective facts or embrace it—but either way claim victim status—and tweet out a few Pepe memes in triumph. The internal logic of the alt-right quickly breaks down under scrutiny—and the fissures that have already started to kill it off become glaringly obvious—but in order for this to happen, it must be properly examined and exposed.

* * *

Getting a handle on the alt-right is difficult. It is, as mentioned, an oppositional force with no real organizational structure. It's a creature of the internet, where many of its members, even some of the most prominent, are anonymous or tweet under pseudonyms because they are afraid of the impact of their political activities on their jobs and relationships. It's a movement with several factions which shrink or swell according to the political breeze and the task at hand.

It's hard to get an overall sense of its size and scope. Numerical estimates are useless and perhaps a bit beside the point. The alt-right is not like the KKK—hate-tracking groups can't provide reasonable estimates of the number of people who belong to local or national organizations, because there are virtually none. Website membership, readership figures and Twitter follower counts are inexact measures, regularly inflated by those running the sites, and swelled by the curious, clictavists, pranksters and the relatively uncommitted, as well as a huge cohort of committed opponents keeping tabs on the movement.

But even if metrics were available, they would probably be misleading in the opposite direction. Some of the movement's ideas are shared by a host of people, including mainstream politicians who wouldn't identify themselves with the alt-right tag, and some who only have a dim idea of what the alt-right actually is. Meanwhile others with alt-right sympathies and whose agendas overlap with the movement are outraged at the term, and even threaten legal action to extract apologies from news outlets who use it to describe them.[10]

In fact, some of the people most identified with the movement shun the label, a trend which accelerated after the election of

Trump, as the alt-right garnered attention and was given a bad name in much of the mainstream press. And the alt-right as a widespread phenomenon is new—so new that as late as August 2016, in the home stretch of the US Presidential campaign, I wrote a much-clicked-on story for the BBC News website with the simple headline: "Trump's shock troops: Who are the 'alt-right'?"[11]

But while the term "alt-right" and the movement's coalescence as a result of the current political climate is a relatively recent phenomenon, there are definitive identifiable strands of alt-right thought, some of which reach far back into history (or which alt-righters grandiosely *imagine* reach far back into history). There are some broad observations and useful conclusions to be drawn about the overall nature and philosophy of the alt-right, and some specific conclusions that can be made about the various wings of the movement.

To begin with, there are what might be called the alt-right's forefathers. The movement's most identifiable leaders have for years been active in the white ethno-nationalist scene, working towards an elusive goal: to make their brand of far-right politics palatable to a mainstream audience. It's a hard sell in the United States, a country mostly populated by the descendants of immigrants from around the world, where pluralism is a broadly accepted concept across both major political parties and the phrase "E Pluribus Unum"—*out of many, one*—is printed on every coin.

And yet they found traction as their online efforts melded with the current fever pitch of anti-elitism, and found a willing audience in a concentrated generational backlash of young men. These foot soldiers feel aggrieved by the successes of feminism and the progress made by ethnic minorities, and have also felt rising anxiety as former certainties about race, sexuality and gender crumble. At the same time, some are puzzled and scared—as are many people from the more traditional right as well as the left—by the censorious atmosphere of many university campuses today, a confusing, sometimes barely comprehensible minefield of trigger warnings, privilege checking, safe spaces, and complicated sexual politics. For the alt-right, all of these fall under the umbrella of one of the ideas they loathe the most: political correctness.

They are also opposed to feminism. While some begrudgingly give credit to second-wave feminists and concede that legal equality between the sexes is a valid goal, others argue against any such notions. Some even say that giving women the franchise was a terrible mistake. Many embrace the old conservative lament that "these days" things have "gone too far" and call for a reaffirmation of traditional values. At the same time, other alt-righters are obsessed with porn and the promise of sexual freedom offered by "pick-up artists."[12]

When it comes to religion there are equally baffling contradictions. The alt-right counts many committed atheists in its ranks and many in the movement scorn monotheistic religious thought. Some embrace a purely cultural notion of Christianity—they prefer cathedrals and incense to church communities and prayer—or even adhere to a pre-Christian paganism. You will also find a few churchgoers and many others who, like Steve Bannon, are fond of talking about the "Judeo-Christian West."[13]

Most importantly, alt-righters see no unity in the Abrahamic religions. Anti-Semitism is rife and goes well beyond sketchy reports of Bannon's comments about Jews.[14] Nazi imagery and "jokes" about gas chambers are one of the alt-right's defining tropes, and debate revolves not around the question of what should or shouldn't be said, but rather about what most irritates its opponents.

As for Islam—as a whole, and not just in its radical extremist form—it is viewed as an existential threat to Western civilization. Some of the less worldly alt-righters in America view Europe as already lost to the invading hoards from the East, despite Muslims making up only 6 percent of the continent's population.[15]

Tied to their opposition to Islam is the alt-right's sharp rebuke of immigration and their belief that, despite centuries of American history to the contrary, gradual assimilation is nothing but a pipe dream. Given these main tenets, you can see how the candidacy and then presidency of Donald Trump prompted cheers and swooning among the alt-right faithful.

* * *

So who exactly are the people who make up the alt-right? Here again the nature of the movement and its life online make it extremely hard to pin down the characteristics of the individuals involved. It's safe to assume that many are men, and most are white, but there are notable exceptions. The conventional wisdom, created in part by alt-right sympathizers, has established that this is a youthful movement, and while there may be an element of truth in that description, the movement probably doesn't skew as young as it thinks it does.[16] I've encountered a number of middle-aged alt-righters, people established in professions or completely alienated from the world of work, who have come together in their resentment of what they consider the establishment elite.

Alt-righters are scattered throughout the United States, with significant concentrations in other English-speaking countries, particularly Britain, Canada and Australia, and adherents throughout Europe. Despite their anti-immigrant stance, more than a few alt-righters are immigrants, or children of immigrants. It does seem that a significant cohort are university students or recent students, who bear a particular grudge against the forces of political correctness. It's unclear if any particular socioeconomic backgrounds are particularly over- or under-represented.[17]

Central to the alt-right's conception of itself is that it represents something fundamentally countercultural—activists have compared their movement to punk rock or the hippies of the 1960s. The comparison stems not from shared political values but from the alt-right's claim to "outsider" status. Like the

8

hippies and the punks, alt-righters rail against what they see as an oppressive establishment. The difference is that their establishment is made up of academia, the Washington "swamp," and influential leftists in the media, rather than the corporate world and free-market politicians. In the words of one alt-righter, the movement "is basically political punk rock: loud, abrasive, hostile, white, back to basics, and fun."[18]

But the argument that the alt-right represents a "counterculture" comes almost entirely from the movement itself and rings hollow when properly examined. It has received little scrutiny in the media—the anonymity of most activists being a key barrier to testing the proposition. In actual fact, the alt-right is quite a culturally sterile space—producing a bunch of Photoshopped images ("memes"), tweets, propaganda videos and in-jokes, sure, but very few original songs, bands, films, or other cultural artefacts of the type that flourish in real countercultural communities. This is a movement with no soft power, and which immediately found it hard to keep up oppositional pretenses after their hero was elected president.

There are a few other things crucial to understanding the movement. As a creature born and raised on the internet, it values trolling and internet pranks not just as sideshows or light diversions, but as key forms of political action. Pranking takes a variety of forms, from memes to campaigns of tweeted nastiness or disinformation, often loosely coordinated, but designed to knock liberals and mainstream conservatives off balance. Activists exaggerated their own role in Trump's victory, hyping up chat on 4chan—a freewheeling, confusing-to-outsiders message board which played a key role in the movement's development— and social media skirmishes into "The Great Meme War," which they hoped would be only the first campaign in an online wave of populism spreading across the Western world.[19]

The alt-right does have a few proto-institutions, like Spencer's National Policy Institute, and some media: most notably Breitbart, the /pol/ section of 4chan, numerous accounts on

Twitter, popular Reddit forums and YouTube accounts, and niche websites and message boards devoted to conservative news or topics such as men's rights.[20] While each of these has a particular role to play in the movement, building institutions hasn't been the main focus of most of the people involved—a strategy that, as we'll see, can be both a strength and a weakness.

If it's tough to tell who's involved in the alt-right, pinpointing exactly what these individuals believe in is more difficult still. Because if you move just a step or two away from the handful of core values described above, you find that even self-described and enthusiastic alt-righters have widely different views. Take the issue of white nationalism. Some key alt-right figures run a mile from the concept.[21] Others don't necessarily dismiss the idea out of hand. And some alt-righters are positively proud of the label. One prominent fringe member described his life goal as: "Reestablishing global white supremacy ... blacks have supremacy in Lagos and Asians in Shanghai and whites are uniquely being deprived of their homelands in a global plot to exterminate them from the Earth."[22]

The policy fuzziness can be seen again and again, even when looking at issues that fall squarely within the movement's key obsessions: race, sexuality, and gender relations. Some on the alt-right are intensely anti-Jewish, others—to paraphrase a Breitbart headline about Stephen Bannon—are friends of the Jewish people. Some call gay people "degenerate," others are themselves gay, and many couldn't care less about the sexual orientation of their fellow activists. And, as noted, their views on feminism, and on particular women, vary wildly. Several young women could credibly be called leaders of the alt-right, while some (male) supporters have views on the role of women in society that are more or less indistinguishable from the fundamentalist Muslims they hate.

Economic concerns are secondary, and amongst the alt-right you can find every viewpoint from Russia-worshiping statists to techno-utopian libertarians.

And as if all that weren't confusing enough, any sense of a coherent ideology is painted over with a thick layer of irony and oodles of the activists' own enthusiastic coded language, used both to communicate amongst themselves and to deploy insults against opponents. Words like "cuck," "degenerate," and "virtue signal" serve both as, well, *signals*, in that grand internet tradition, to the snobby, geeky in-group, but also as subtle and sometimes successful ways to worm alt-right ideas into the mainstream consciousness.

Their fondness for jokes and pranks, pushing boundaries and twisting language, mean that it's often not possible to tell whether, for instance, the anons slinging racial and gay slurs on 4chan actually hold extreme beliefs, or think that shouting "nigger" and "faggot" is funny, or are just trying to shock or offend for effect.[23]

Language is crucial to understanding the movement. The alt-right style, as it plays out online, mirrors that of their sworn enemies, the "social justice warriors" of the identity politics left. As they mock and trick, they claim victim status for men and white people, flip left-wing arguments on their head, and consistently harangue their enemies for being inconsistent. In a later chapter I'll lay out some of the most common alt-right terms and trace their origins, from far-right conspiracy theories to genetic pseudoscience, philosophy, pornography, pop culture, and various internet subcultures.

To begin with, it's useful to divide the movement into two broad groupings: the so-called "alt-light" and a harder core. The former group might disagree with some of the movement's broader ideas, reject anti-Semitism, begrudgingly admit feminism may have once had a point, and dismiss the influence of extremists. Some of the movement's most popular figures are also drawn from the ranks of the "alt-light"—they are in some ways the "acceptable faces." The hard core, meanwhile, includes people who are devoted to the idea of ethno-nationalism, and encompasses bloggers and activists who claim to embrace peace, along with real, unironic, and sometimes violent neo-Nazis.

These groupings are crude and I won't try to guess at the numerical breakdown or the percentages in each wing—although several in the movement have tried to do so, on the basis of scant evidence and usually in the hope of minimizing the influence of white supremacists.

The two groups are fluid and have plenty of disagreements within themselves. But they provide a valuable framework through which to start thinking about the movement. The alt-light plays down the extremists; the hard core uses the relatively more attractive and "moderate" wing to draw people further towards its side. The latter group includes an element—small but significant—prepared to use violence to achieve the movement's ends. I'll refer back to this division at several points throughout the book.

* * *

The video of Richard Spencer being punched on Inauguration Day became instant internet art. It was set to hip-hop and Springsteen, mashed up with the *Bee Movie* and *Raiders of the Lost Ark*.[24] An earnest conversation began about the morals of violence in an age of extremism. Stories with some variation of the headline "Is it OK to Punch a Nazi?" appeared in the *New York Times*, *Vice*, *The Nation*, *Haaretz*, and other outlets.[25]

A hastily coded video game riffed on the theme. Players could use a computer in conjunction with a smartphone to simulate hitting Spencer, before moving on to further bouts, culminating in a climactic fight with Adolf Hitler.[26] Inside the game, the far-right targets weren't given the ability to fight back. But online there was plenty of counter-punching by the right. One alt-right-friendly website ran a story with the headline "Is it Okay to Punch a New York Times reporter?"[27] And a crowdfunding website run by Chuck Johnson, another alt-right personality, raised more than $5,000 in a "bounty"—a reward which would go to anybody who could identify the person who attacked Spencer.[28]

For the movement's supporters, it was a case of supposedly liberal journalists revealing their hypocrisy and displaying their moral weakness by appearing to condone or at least consider the legitimacy of street violence. And, at the same time, the mainstream media (it was alleged) failed to understand this supposedly youthful, ostensibly edgy movement. Because, strictly speaking, Spencer was correct in drawing (as he was attempting to do just before he got smacked in the face) a line between himself and neo-Nazis. Technically, Nazis want to kill and enslave what they see as inferior races. Ethno-nationalists like Spencer—those who believe that political entities should be properly divided along racial and ethnic lines—don't go that far. Instead, they preach separation, with dedicated homelands based on tribal groupings, including large swathes of the planet reserved for white people.[29]

For many that might seem like a minor quibble, but this is a movement made for minor quibbles—and for making the most of every possible quibbling opportunity that can be used to attract publicity. And casual observers might have easily made mental Nazi associations by the way in which Spencer first came to broad public attention.

Less than a week after the US presidential election, he presided over the annual conference of his rather dull-sounding National Policy Institute. Early publicity hinted that even Spencer didn't have much faith in a Trump win. The NPI website made scant reference to a possible victory by the Republican candidate, instead simply stating that the gathering was happening at "a time when more people joined our movement then [sic] ever before and when our ideas began invading the mainstream."[30]

But the mood at the conference was decidedly more upbeat after Trump's surprise triumph. After Spencer delivered the keynote address, he shouted "Hail Trump, hail our people, hail victory!" Some delegates responded by thrusting their right hands in the air.[31] The footage received worldwide attention. Spencer claimed to a reporter that the outburst was "clearly done in a spirit of irony and exuberance" and later called the gesture of some of the participants a "Roman salute" rather than a Nazi one.[32]

In any case, he got what he wanted, and described the conference as a public relations success.[33] Creating controversy—in the language of the movement, "triggering" people by "trolling"—was the whole point.

*   *   *

The heady days between Trump's victory and his inauguration were the high-water mark for the popularity and cohesiveness of the alt-right. Soon after, it began to fracture and crumble. But its ideas have left a mark on American politics and its success has tracked that of right-wing populist and nativist movements around the world. This strain of thought won't be going away anytime soon, and anyone concerned about reactionary extremism would do well to study the alt-right's methods and be on the lookout for what comes next.

I first began to notice the movement while reporting for BBC Trending, a unit inside the British Broadcasting Corporation devoted to reporting on the world of social media. In one sense I didn't come to the alt-right—they came to me, bubbling up in attacks against "establishment media" and their own perception of a universally dominant, politically correct, liberal-leaning media. Prior to my work at Trending, I had made a number of radio documentaries about US extremists, society and technology, and American identity movements. But none of the alt-righters hurling stock insults at me and my colleagues could have guessed how much I knew about the kinds of environments in which their movement had developed. I grew up in a suburb of a post-industrial city, and from a young age I was fascinated with computers and the freewheeling, connective power of the internet. I went to university in the Midwest, where among other things I studied countercultural and fringe movements.

As their voices became louder during the Trump campaign, one question nagged me. If it was true that the alt-right was made up mostly of white males from middle America—a world I was from and instantly recognized—what was making some of them turn to a sharply reactionary, often baffling, extreme movement?

In the following chapters I'll lay out a story based on original sources and interviews, the voluminous, mind-crushing online output of alt-righters themselves, along with my own reporting experiences and those of my colleagues.

To start with, I'll outline and explore the main strands of thought that came together to form the movement. Chapter 1 will introduce the small cluster of intellectuals who gave the alt-right its name and its basic shape. Chapter 2 will focus on the racial arguments that underpin the alt-right's thoughts and actions. In Chapter 3, I'll explain more about the online hangouts—the movement's home turf—particularly the /pol/ section of 4chan. org. Chapter 4 traces anti-feminist and "pick-up artist" groups, and the catalytic influence they had on the alt-right through the drama that was "Gamergate."

Chapter 5 provides a comprehensive list of the most commonly used alt-right activist terms and a description of the movement's rhetorical style, while Chapter 6 demonstrates how its core ideas spread through a select few online media outlets.

In Chapter 7, I explore the influence of neo-Nazi propaganda in the movement and the uneasy relationship between the alt-right's extreme and hyper-extreme wings. In Chapter 8 we'll learn more about the ordinary people at the heart of the movement and explode the myth that the alt-right is made up mostly of hip youngsters with countercultural sensibilities. Chapters 9 and 10 focus on the extremist fringes and the people who are prepared to take direct, sometimes violent action—including conspiracy theorists and violent murderers and terrorists.

Chapter 11 will tie together all of these disparate strands using the cause that brought them together—the Donald Trump campaign and opposition to Hillary Clinton. And finally, in Chapter 12, I'll explain why the movement began to fray even before Trump took office, and ask what might be next for the far right.

Through careful examination of the alt-right's online presence—including the sometimes difficult to swallow words of its leaders—and its influence on real-world events, I aim to bridge the existing knowledge gap about the alt-right's understanding and origins, and pin down hard evidence of the movement's real viewpoints.

As we'll see, there are some startlingly clear events, manufactured conspiracy theories, propaganda victories and warning signs that point to the danger of the alt-right. On the other hand, there are deep fractures and contradictions in the movement which have been exacerbated rather than healed by Trump's victory.

The alt-right garnered a huge amount of media attention after Richard Spencer got punched and Donald Trump officially ascended to office, with wave after wave of renewed interest after the violent scenes in Charlottesville, Virginia and elsewhere. But so far what's been lacking in most day-to-day media accounts is a definitive account of who they are—their leaders and their foot soldiers, what motivates them and guides their beliefs, their intellectual antecedents, and the hard truth about the risk they pose to politics and society today, in the United States, Europe and elsewhere.

This is an attempt to define, demystify and declaw the alt-right, to find out where the movement came from and where it might be going.

1

The Intellectuals

In November 2008, a professor named Paul Gottfried stood up in front of a few dozen people at the first gathering of his newly formed H.L. Mencken Club. It was an event that, at the time, made almost no impression on the general public. It attracted no press coverage or scholarly attention. In fact, before a reporter phoned him up in 2016, Gottfried himself says it had slipped his mind that, through his speech, he had inspired the name of a nascent political movement.[1]

Gottfried's club was named after one of America's most famous early twentieth-century journalists and was inspired by Mencken's constant questioning of the "egalitarian creed, democratic crusades, and welfare statism with which American democracy was already identified during his lifetime."[2]

It was not a good time for the right in America. Less than a month before, Barack Obama had been elected president, and Democrats had tightened their control on Congress. The presidency of George W. Bush was about to end amidst economic calamity and historically low approval figures.[3]

Gottfried—bald, jowly and bespectacled—looked like a central casting version of what he was: a philosophy professor at a small college in Pennsylvania. He described himself as a "paleoconservative"—a term which, according to some sources, he also invented.[4]

Paleoconservativism—a Stone Age-y play on "neoconservativism"—is a branch of thought that's had a rump of a following on the right in America for many years. Paleos dislike immigration and multiculturalism. In contrast to neoconservatives, they are skeptical of free trade and foreign military adventures. They look to the past and are strict traditionalists when it comes to gender, ethnicity, race and social order.[5] It was a movement which held the seeds of the alt-right, and one that had been confined to the political fringes for decades. Before Trump, the most high-profile politician with paleoconservative leanings was Pat Buchanan, who in a presidential run in 2000 scored 0.4% of the popular vote.[6]

Despite the small, subdued crowd, the Mencken Society's first meeting in a Baltimore hotel included some key characters in what would become the brain trust of the alt-right. Peter Brimelow, a British journalist and critic of multiculturalism and immigration, attended and spoke at the conference, as did Jared Taylor, editor of the far-right magazine *American Renaissance*.[7]

Gottfried, standing in front of the audience, announced:

> We are part of an attempt to put together an independent intellectual right, one that exists without movement establishment funding and one that our opponents would be delighted not to have to deal with. Our group is also full of young thinkers and activists, and if there is to be an independent right, our group will have to become its leaders.

He then launched into a ramble taking in Muslim control of the Iberian Peninsula, the last few decades of American conservative thought, Elizabeth I's defeat of the Spanish Armada and Flannery O'Connor.[8]

While it was not headline-producing stuff, Gottfried did manage to identify the broad outlines and deep concerns of what would eventually become the alt-right movement. He gave a nod to the far-right websites Takimag and Brimelow's VDARE.com, from where most of the intellectual energy of the movement would come in the years before the alt-right gained anything like mainstream attention. He put his finger on the outsider nature of the small group and identified the Republican and conservative establishment as enemy number one.

"A question that has been asked of me and of others in this room is why we don't try to join the official conservative movement," he said. "This movement controls hundreds of millions of dollars, TV networks, strings of newspapers and magazines, multitudinous foundations and institutes, and a bevy of real and bleached blondes on Fox News."

He concluded that the establishment—or, as Gottfried put it, the "dark side"—wouldn't have them. He continued, sarcastically:

It has treated us, in contrast to such worthies as black nationalists, radical feminists, and open-borders advocates, as being unfit for admittance into the political conversation. We are not viewed as honorable dissenters but depicted as subhuman infidels or ignored in the same way as one would a senile uncle who occasionally wanders into one's living room.[9]

Although he didn't go into much detail or name names, he hinted at the alt-right's obsession with race-based science and questionable theories about the relative intelligence levels of different ethnic groups, decrying what he described as censorship against anyone outside of what he saw as a neo-conservative and center-left consensus. "This imperial ban has been extended even to brilliant social scientists and statisticians who are viewed as excessively intimate with the wrong people," he said. And in just a few words he encapsulated the stubborn self-righteousness which would come to characterize the alt-right: "We are convinced that we are right in our historical and cultural observations while those who have quarantined us are wrong."

Gottfried never actually put a name on his imagined movement. A decade later, even as he continued to sympathize with some of the alt-right's leading figures, he rued being associated with it.[10] But the title of his address was dramatic and catchy, and it contained the name that, in a shorter form, would stick: "The Decline and Rise of the Alternative Right."

* * *

The Mencken Club continued its quest over the years of the Obama presidency, holding annual conferences and banging the drum for the "independent right." But a group holding meetings in Baltimore hotels with doddery professors behind lecterns wasn't ever going to build a mass movement in the internet age. Others took up the cause and advanced the idea of what was initially dubbed the "alternative right." Chief among them was Gottfried protégée Richard Spencer. Spencer's background included an expensive prep school in Texas and an academic career—Yale, Chicago, Virginia. He dropped out of Duke's Ph.D. program and eventually settled in the small town of Whitefish, Montana.[11] In 2010, he founded the website AlternativeRight. com. It became the first thrust at defining the alt-right and developing a raw online communications strategy.

Spencer and Gottfried would later slightly disagree on who came up with the name "alternative right," with Spencer claiming authorship and Gottfried insisting it was a joint effort.[12] However, Gottfried was made an editor of the new site, and Spencer plucked his inspiration from the professor's words, declaring that the effort marked "an attempt to forge a new intellectual right-wing that is independent and outside the 'conservative' establishment."[13]

AlternativeRight.com was the first of Spencer's alt-right outlets, and, like the Mencken Club, it didn't find a huge audience at first. It was eventually shuttered in 2013. But those early missives give an insight into the formulation of the alt-right argument style. They give the overall impression of a small group of academic-minded people holed up together, lobbing words into the ether and seeing what, if anything, might stick.

Spencer aimed for a freewheeling bloggy style, using short posts to comment on news reports and, in what would later become a hallmark of the alt-right, ranging outside of the world of politics. At the same time, the worldview of AlternativeRight. com was framed in ethnic and racial terms, with posts, for instance, about how white, blonde women are naturally more attractive than black women, or pointing out violent crime against gays in majority-black neighborhoods.[14]

But Spencer's goal was always to appeal to a broader audience—including those who wouldn't even think of showing up at a Mencken Club meeting. Posts dealt with the stock market, state fairs, MC Hammer.[15] One started by quoting a report that the rules of Scrabble would be changed to allow proper nouns and names including, Spencer pointed out, African-American names: "Mattel has failed to account for Americans' creativity in naming their offspring. Indeed, the store of possible names would seem limitless and fluid. There must be three or four different spellings of 'Shaniqua.' Though granted, few Chaniquas play Scrabble."[16]

After a woman was recorded on a London tram shouting racial abuse at other passengers while her toddler played in her lap ("Load of black people and a load of fucking Polish," the woman said), Spencer opined:

> Her language is crude; her feelings are real. Who can deny that her native London has been destroyed? Certainly not the Diversity on the tram, who, mouthing television commentary, can only claim they're doing jobs the Brits won't. This woman has apparently been arrested for "racially aggravated public order offence." If any were in doubt of the true totalitarian nature of Cool Britannia, let Epic Tram Lady stand as an example.[17]

The label "Epic Tram Lady" never really did catch on, however the post was an early display of the alt-right's style of hero worship, where activists elevate ordinary or obscure folks who perform non-politically-correct, illegal or even violent acts into feted champions.

A central tenet of both Spencer's writings and the intellectual arm of the alt-right is the idea of "human biodiversity" (HBD). There is a collection of posts tagged with that label on AlternativeRight.com. The idea is an exaggerated and simplified interpretation of complicated human genetic variation. The HBD crowd argues that because different people have different traits, and some of these traits are linked to genetics, genes—often expressed through sorting people into tremendously broad racial and ethnic groupings—are determinative. In its most basic form: whites have higher IQs than blacks, while East Asians and European Jews have higher IQs than whites. A slice of alt-righters—call them the intellectual utopians—take this even further and argue that the world should be sorted and divided according to ethnic and religious groups. The world, Spencer and others argue, should be broken up into ethnic nation-states.[18] And because he is white, he is primarily concerned with the ethnic nation-state or states devoted to white people. "We're going to have to have hegemony," he told me during an interview. "And that doesn't mean we control the entire planet, but we are going to have to create a realm that is ours and is always safe for white people."[19]

As for how to achieve this, Spencer calls for "peaceful ethnic cleansing." When pressed on how that might happen, he suggests paying people to move. "I think re-immigration is definitely possible," he said, "and I think it could be done entirely humanely and entirely through financial incentives."[20]

In a 2016 speech, Spencer trotted out a rhetorical flourish often and effectively deployed by the alt-right: paint today's radical reactionary ideas as having roots in a long-lost progressive past:

We should remember that in the last century, racially defined nation-building was a major "progressive" cause. We now think that the so-called "liberal elites" have always been dedicated to multiculturalism and race-mixing. This is not quite the case, as liberals have a history of adopting "national determination" and even "ethno-nationalism" as their causes. In 1919, following the Great War, the world's statesman met in Paris to (for lack of a better term) re-map the world after the dissolution of the defeated empires. New countries were invented (the Kingdom of Croats, Serbs, Slovenes), old ones were reborn (Poland), and ethnicities got their day in the Sun (Czechoslovakia). Related to this process was the Balfour Declaration and British mandate for a homeland for the Jews in Palestine. Nationalists of many stripes captured the hearts and minds of political actors. Today, in the public imagination, "ethnic-cleansing" has been associated with civil war and mass murder (understandably so). But this need not be the case. 1919 is a real example of successful ethnic redistribution— done by fiat, we should remember, but done peacefully.[21]

It's odd to call the Treaty of Versailles successful, but more to the point, his posts on AlternativeRight.com raise the question of whether Spencer is as dedicated to the "peaceful" part of his plan as he is to the "ethnic cleansing" part.

A long post from 2011 about the Norwegian mass murderer Anders Breivik, who killed 77 people, starts reasonably enough: "What kind of "ultra-nationalist" murders the children of his own people? The answer is one who is truly deranged."[22] Spencer then mixes in his own brand of racial politics, an endorsement of Breivik's Muslim hate, and a dash of conspiracy theory, to argue that the killer is worth listening to.

"Anders Behring Breivik's work (if this actually is Anders Breivik's work) is rational and argued; he is clearly influenced by many neoconservative authors, but also many from the non-aligned Right," he writes. "We still aren't sure whether Breivik is the man who perpetrated Friday's bloddy [sic] actions

... But we should most definitely study Breivik's 'European Declaration of Independence.'"

Spencer goes on to quote favorably and at great length from another blog post, this one by Kevin MacDonald, an academic whose writings describe Jewish people as characterized by "ethnocentrism, intelligence and wealth, psychological intensity, aggressiveness,"[23] and who has been called "a primary voice for anti-Semitism from far-right intellectuals."[24]

For his part, MacDonald seemed absolutely puzzled that Breivik's manifesto didn't talk more about Jews. "It could well be that his silence on Jewish hostility toward Europe and the West and his rejection of ethnocentrism are motivated by his strategic sense," he wrote.

Still, he went on (remember, this about a mass murderer): "It must be said that he is a serious political thinker with a great many insights and some good practical ideas on strategy."[25]

Spencer was enthusiastic: When it came to the study of Breivik's manifesto, "Kevin MacDonald had made an excellent start."[26]

* * *

Spencer's projected image was an attempt at a break from old-school white nationalism. It came through not only in the style of his arguments and his personal style—he's often pictured in sharp suits and interviewed while eating in fashionable restaurants—but also in the scale of his ambition. When I spoke to him, he was clear on his ultimate goal: "I want what could probably be called a global empire. This isn't going to be like Israel, this is going to be something on a very large scale. And that is a homeland for all white people, whether you're German or Celtic or Slavic or English.

"It doesn't matter if it's achievable in our lifetime, or maybe it's utopian, maybe we're always going to be questing after the ethno-state," he said. "I get almost miffed when people say, all we want is a little nation state like Estonia … a nation-state of that size, or an ethnic enclave, is going to be dominated by bigger powers.

"What I want to create is this bigger civilizational, hegemonic domain."

Spencer envisions an ethnic bloc with a unified foreign policy, a deep skepticism about military action and a common line on immigration.

"I think we need to get over the twentieth century," he said, despite his previous hearkening back to history. "And picking sides in those conflicts, the First or Second World War, we're just being trapped in the past. We just need to recognize that all of it was catastrophic and bad for us. Even for the people who came out on top, it was ultimately bad. I dream we can have a unified foreign policy, there will be one realm.

"It would be one big Roman Empire. It should probably include Near Asia as well. Constantinople is such a profoundly symbolic city. Retaking it, that would be a statement to the world, that would be a statement that we were back."

What would you do, I asked, with the people who were there already—the Turks?

"There's lots of places they can go," he said. "The Middle East or something. Who cares?"

*   *   *

Spencer's project developed over time. He is at pains to distinguish himself from stereotypical white nationalists who march with hoods on their heads and who, he says, get bogged down in paranoia, doomsday scenarios and bad news. He's also very aware of the limitations of explicit racial appeals in the modern world. After AlternativeRight.com, he planned another online venture, Radix Journal, which he hoped would appeal to a broader cross-section of society.

"Sometimes the movement fails when you have websites called whiterights.com or demographicreality.org, when we're focused so intently and brutally on race," he told me, while adding: "I don't want this to sound sinister. I'm very upfront about what I believe."

"What I wanted for Radix," he continued, "is a journal that includes writing that someone who's apolitical or a leftist or someone who's more literary minded could read and not just be put off immediately by the right-wing race stuff.

"It's not that I'm just trying to make this palatable, it's that white nationalism doesn't really have anywhere to go. All of its arguments have been made. And I don't know what new IQ data someone needs to see, or someone needs to say again 'It's healthy to love your race.' I don't know how many more times we need to hear that."

Spencer's work has led to an uneasy relationship with some of his neighbors in the tiny town of Whitefish, with a population of less than 7,000. Whitefish lies in western Montana, in an area of the United States that has had a long and troubled history with white nationalists. Since the 1980s, extremists led by the one-time leader of the Aryan Nations, Richard Butler, have imagined an independent white homeland extending from eastern Washington state, through Idaho and western Montana. (Spencer scoffs at the plan, and told me it lacks ambition).[27]

Local residents are acutely aware of this history. In 2014, the city council passed a resolution to "celebrate the dignity, diversity and inclusion of all its inhabitants and visitors, and condemn ideologies, philosophies and movements that deny equality of human rights and opportunities, and challenge our Constitutional freedoms."

Spencer, perhaps surprisingly, was delighted. He was quoted by the local newspaper, saying the ordinance was a "pleasant surprise"—"in contrast to the 'no-hate' ordinance that some residents had urged the council to adopt, effectively barring

Spencer and his think-tank, the National Policy Institute, from doing business in Whitefish."[28]

* * *

Spencer's brand of ethnic nationalism was not the only intellectual thread that ended up defining the alt-right. In fact, despite his academic bent, his prep-school and elite-university education, and his cultivated image, Spencer almost seems like a no-nonsense to-the-point man of the people compared to another alt-right luminary who wrote the foundation document for a strand of thought dubbed "neoreactionary"—or "NRx" for short.

Curtis Yarvin was a Silicon Valley entrepreneur,[29] but he had a side gig for nine years. This was a blog called Unqualified Reservations, which he wrote under the pseudonym "Mencius Moldbug."

The introduction to the blog gives a flavor of his rhetorical style: "Stubbornness and disrespect, programming languages and operating systems, obsessive epistemology and formalist propaganda, Austrian economics and contemporary verse."[30] Yarvin's actual posts are similarly rambling, highbrow, and obstinate.

"The other day I was tinkering around in my garage and I decided to build a new ideology," was how Yarvin kicked off the first Unqualified Reservations post in April 2007. It continued:

What? I mean, am I crazy or something? First of all, you can't just build an ideology. They're handed down across the centuries, like lasagna recipes. They need to age, like bourbon. You can't just drink it straight out of the radiator. And look what happens if you try. What causes all the problems of the world? Ideology, that's what. What do Bush and Osama have in common? They're both ideological nutcases. We're supposed to need more of this?

Furthermore, it's simply not possible to build a new ideology. People have been talking about ideology since Jesus was a little boy. At least! And I'm supposedly going to improve on this? Some random person on the Internet, who flunked out of grad school, who doesn't know Greek or Latin?[31]

Yarvin's posts go on for miles, discursively and didactically, mixing historical references, and—a bit like Spencer—combining academic-ish analysis and high ideas with pop culture. That first post alone namechecks *The Princess Bride*, *American Idol*, Vienna in 1907, Franklin D. Roosevelt, the *New York Times* and half a dozen philosophers of varying degrees of obscurity.

The blog was, from the beginning, written by a fully formed persona likely to have instant appeal to a certain type of conservative: young, heterodox, erudite, much more likely to get information online than from dusty books or walking the streets. Yarvin was slightly hectoring, a bit aloof and mysterious, with a trenchant libertarian slant, a penchant for false modesty, and Silicon Valley cred. Unlike Spencer, he preferred to deal with ideals and generalizations rather than specific current events or news stories. Yarvin inhabited the same space as his target audience, which was sizeable but never enormous. His most notable posts garnered a couple of hundred comments—decent numbers, but hardly internet-breaking.

On the other hand, he was more entertaining than academic types like Gottfried or MacDonald, and, as the movement developed, he became the alt-right's favorite philosophy instructor. "There is this idea called social justice that a lot of people believe in," he wrote in another post:

The notion is, in fact, fairly universal as of this writing. What it tells us is that Earth is small and has a limited set of resources, such as cities, which we all want as much of as possible. But we can't all have a city, or even a street, so we should share equally.

28

Because all of us people are equal and no one is more equal than anyone else.[32]

This is, of course, a vastly oversimplified—and, some would argue, totally misguided —notion of a huge range of ideas that come under the umbrella term "social justice." But the idea of the oppressive forces of equality forming a dissent-crushing monolith, and Yarvin's self-portrayal as a brave truth-teller (although not so brave, it seems, to put his real name out there from the start), served a useful purpose—it allowed him to dismiss progressive ideas out of hand and sweep away those who defend them as unthinking quislings. This, as we'll see, is a crucial building block for many alt-right arguments.

People have different skills, he argued, so if they are made equal they won't necessarily remain equal; attempts at trying to attain equality will lead to violence, and any wealth redistribution will effectively leave someone less well-off and thus lead to—once again—violence. Yarvin deployed this technique—exaggerate, simplify, burn down the straw man—again and again against both liberal and mainstream conservative ideas.

Another of Yarvin's key contributions to the development of alt-right thought was a searing critique of democracy based on supposed genetic "facts" combined with a dash of intellectual snobbery. One early post was titled "The case against democracy: ten red pills."

Here he used the alt-right's number one metaphor, pinched from the film *The Matrix*, in which Neo (the Keanu Reeves character) is offered the choice between a blue pill and a red pill. The blue pill represents close-minded but blissful ignorance. The red pill, though hard to swallow, liberates people to realize the truth. On 4chan /pol/—the main gathering space for alt right foot soldiers—"red pill" has become a shorthand for "the truth," so much so that the board has a rule (one of very few) asking contributors to avoid obviously banal conversation prompts such as "Red pill me on X."[33]

Describing someone as "red-pilled" implies they are clear-eyed, truth-seeking heroes—by extension, the blue-pilled are the intellectually lazy, scale-eyed, soma-taking masses. The red pill/blue pill idea is another binary concept which would become a cornerstone of alt-right political thinking.

Yarvin's "ten red pills" post is one of his classic long-winded lectures. Here's a small fraction by way of a sample:

Have you ever considered the possibility that democracy is bunk?

I grew up believing in democracy. I'll bet you did too. I spent 20 years of my life in democratic schools. I'll bet you did too.

Suppose you were a Catholic in 16th-century Spain. Imagine how hard it would be for you to stop believing in Catholicism.

You are a Catholic. Your parents were Catholics. You were educated by Catholics. You are governed by Catholics. All your friends are Catholics. All the books you've ever read were written by Catholics.

Sure, you're aware that not everyone in the world is a Catholic. You're also aware that this is the cause of all the violence, death and destruction in the world.

Look at what Protestants do when they get into power. They nail genitals to the city gates. They behead their own wives. Crazy stuff! And let's not even start on the Turks...

Now suppose you're you. But you have a time machine that lets you talk to this 16th-century Spanish Catholic version of you.

How do you convince this guy or gal that the answer to all the world's problems is not "more Catholicism"? How do you say, um, dude, this Trinity thing—the virgin birth—transsubstantiation... ya know...

So you see how hard it is to explain that democracy is bunk.

Of course, I could be wrong. Who the heck am I? No one. And everyone who is someone agrees: democracy is wonderful.

So I'm not telling you that democracy is bunk. I'm just suggesting you might want to consider the possibility.[34]

Picking apart each individual argument seems fairly easy. You could begin by questioning whether it's really fair to compare democracy in all its tropes, forms and economic variants to a religion, or challenge the idea that it's as universal as Catholicism was in sixteenth-century Spain. But Yarvin's metaphors pile up on each other, multiplying like viruses, and refuting them all would probably take multiple books twice the size of this one.

Perhaps a more interesting avenue to wander down is the rather more direct one which leads to Yarvin's point. When he gets to the nub of the argument—which he does, eventually!—he neatly separates his views (the "red pill" version) from what he considers mass delusions (the "blue pill" version):

1. Peace, prosperity, and freedom
   blue pill: Democracy is responsible for the present state of peace, prosperity, and freedom in the US, Europe and Japan.
   red pill: The rule of law is responsible for the present state of peace, prosperity and freedom in the US, Europe and Japan.
2. Democracy, freedom, and law
   blue pill: Democracy is inseparable from freedom and law.
   red pill: At best, democracy is sand in the gears of freedom and law. At worst it excludes them entirely, as in Iraq.
3. Fascism and communism
   blue pill: The disasters of fascism and communism demonstrate the importance of representative democracy.
   red pill: Fascism and communism are best understood as forms of democracy. The difference between single-party and multiparty democracy is like the difference between a malignant tumor and a benign one.[35]

Yarvin carried on writing Unqualified Reservations for years in this didactic way. Over time his posts mixed in poetry[36] and poetic criticism,[37] whisky giveaways,[38] notes about bitcoin, and grandiose personal declarations[39] ("Why I am not a libertarian," "Why I am not an anti-Semite").

His contribution to the alt-right is fundamentally political and specifically anti-democratic.[40] The "neoreactionary" label was originally meant to be something of a dig slung by a critical libertarian blogger, but the name stuck.[41] At points Yarvin summarized his ideas—for instance in a "Gentle Introduction" which, he points out with great effort, is nothing like gentle: "It's like talking about a 'mild DMT trip.' If it was mild, it wasn't DMT."

Nor can it really be called "an introduction." Part 1 alone is 8,000 words long, and there are nine parts. In any case, it's in this series that Yarvin comes closest to pinning down his point:

> The basic premise of [Unqualified Reservations] is that all the competing 20th-century systems of government, including the Western democracies which came out on top and which rule us to this day, are best classified as Orwellian. They maintain their legitimacy by shaping public opinion. They shape public opinion by sculpting the information presented to the public. As part of that public, you peruse the world through a lens poured by your government. Ie: you are pwned[42]

The agent of that pwning—gamer slang for being "owned," beaten, conquered—is "The Cathedral," a blob which Yarvin, through some rhetorical trickery, portrays as the "established church" and which encompasses universities, bureaucrats, government and the press. It's like Donald Trump's "swamp" but much much bigger and more decentralized.

The Cathedral is always pushing left-wing thought, Yarvin argues, and furthermore: "right represents *peace, order and security*; left represents *war, anarchy and crime*."[43] Anarchy,

32

he argues, serves an ever-growing professional-managerial-political-intellectual class: "The left is chaos and anarchy, and the more anarchy you have, the more power there is to go around. The more orderly a system is, the fewer people get to issue orders."[44]

And yet despite all this anarchy out there, at the same time Yarvin insists modern Western society is a "theocracy." He's not using that concept as a metaphor: "We don't just live in something vaguely like a Puritan theocracy. We live in an actual, genuine, functioning if hardly healthy, 21st-century Puritan theocracy. What this means is that you can trust hardly any of your beliefs."[45]

Yarvin's lectures are an intellectual game designed to appeal to people with relatively little experience of intellectual games who are nonetheless young and politically searching. He's clearly extremely well-read and there's at least the surface appearance of logic and solid research. Among other concepts now popular on the alt-right, Yarvin deploys the "Overton Window"—the idea that there is a relatively narrow range of policy prescriptions on any particular issue that the public will accept and politicians will talk about. Chatting about the previously unthinkable will move the Overton Window, the theory says, and ideas that were once radical will eventually shift towards the mainstream.[46]

Yarvin constructs a more or less self-contained and morally clear world—call it the "anti-Cathedral." It's easy to see how going from Facebook or 4chan to his small blog—in the simple format provided by the Google-owned platform Blogger, it has no pictures or graphics—would feel something like walking into the serenity of a Colombia University classroom after weeks wandering around noisy Manhattan.

There's one more Unqualified Reservations post which sticks out and is worth mentioning partly because of the attention it garnered later. The title of the post is "Why I am not a white nationalist." It includes a quote that turned into something of a stick to beat Yarvin with later on: "It should be obvious that, although I am not a white nationalist, I am not exactly allergic to the stuff."[47]

Yarvin goes on to list nine white nationalist blogs and websites, including American Renaissance and VDARE, which he calls "the two central organs of intellectual white nationalism." He's careful to draw a line which includes these sites within the pale, while refusing to link to "out-and-out" racist blogs.

He then goes on to argue: "White nationalism is the most marginalized and socially excluded belief system in the history of the world." This is mostly, he says, because of Hitler. White nationalism isn't dangerous, Yarvin continues, at least compared to other systems: "The worst thing about white nationalism, in my opinion, is just that it's nationalism. Nationalism is really another word for democracy."[48]

It was certainly not an endorsement of extremism, but it staked out another key intellectual pattern of the alt-right: the idea that the red-pilled minority was the only group willing and able to adequately grapple with previously unmentionable ideas. They were working, if you will, with a larger Overton Window.

Like a university classroom with a charismatic professor at its head, Unqualified Reservations created a small community, but one that soon began to project influence outside its own little sphere.

*　*　*

As the alt-right's public profile began to swell, reporters began to detect signs of Yarvin's ideas spreading to Silicon Valley and Washington. Peter Thiel, the PayPal founder and Trump advisor, picked up on neoreactionary ideas in his vision of oligarchic liberty.[49] "I no longer believe that freedom and democracy are compatible," he wrote.[50] In the early days of the Trump administration, Yarvin could reportedly count Steve Bannon among his fans[51]—although Yarvin himself claimed that he had never spoken to the White House chief strategist.[52]

Yarvin became one of a handful of key thinkers writing about neoreactionary ideas, or, as they later came to be known, the Dark Enlightenment. They also included the British philosopher Nick Land, who credits Yarvin as a key inspiration. "The single most provocative element in his thinking," Land told me, "is the fact that he breaks with the ideal of democratic government."[53]

Of all the intellectuals linked to the alt-right or cited by movement figures as an inspiration, Land is one of the most enigmatic. As a professor at Warwick University in the UK in the 1990s, he helped set up something called the Cybernetic Culture Research Unit (CCRU), an anarchic non-department department.[54] Land, who now lives in China, was a maverick inside Yarvin's Cathedral, described at various points as an "accelerationist," a "cyberpunk," a "speculative realist" and a "rabid nihilist." His more hard-core philosophic works were published mostly as shorter tracts in the 1990s. Accounts of the time concentrate on his personality and the unusual nature of the CCRU, which was more of a thought experiment than an official university project.

"What struck me upon meeting Nick Land at an event in Brighton's Zap Club in 1993 or 1994 was his presence," commented artist and writer Kodwo Eshun. "His manner was immediately open, egalitarian and absolutely unaffected by academic protocol and his style of speaking was extremely vivid." Mark Fisher, an accomplished academic and writer in his own right, although one with a very different political outlook, described a Land article like this: "I read it about ten times and still didn't completely get it ... often the concepts seeped in by osmosis, through repeated reading."[55]

But Land's later blog, "Outside In: Involvements with Reality" (www.xenosystems.net) was a more accessible take on his ideas, concentrating on the inexorable melding of humans and computers, our race towards a pure technological and technocratic future, and the superiority of city-state formulations of government, à la Hong Kong and Singapore. Land embraces the idea of the Cathedral, and devotes posts to railing against the media and government institutions. At one point he raged at Twitter, which temporarily shuttered his account for unknown reasons.[56]

On his blog, Land demonstrates sympathy with the anti-equality agenda, and posts about IQ differences across countries and ethnicities—a key theme of the alt-right.[57] He lauds technologically advanced city-states as "the most advanced models of neoreactionary social order on earth … combining resilient ethnic traditions with super-dynamic techonomic performance, to produce an open yet self-protective, civilized, socially-tranquil, high-growth enclave of outstanding broad-spectrum functionality."[58]

This he puts down to a highly selective immigration policy and an economy which draws in intelligent and productive people—an "IQ shredder." In fact, he shares with the alt-right a preoccupation with intelligence quotient. The Cathedral, he argues, doesn't want to hear it and quickly shuts down any mere mention of human biodiversity. This, he says, is where the stifling blanket of political correctness is at its most obvious.

"It's not just as if they have a political disagreement with you and it's not that they have an intellectual problem with what's being said," he told me. "Both of those things can of course be true, but the fundamental thing is that they have a sense of fundamental religious outrage, that certain core doctrines of the faith are being questioned."[59]

It is that sense of dogma that infuriates the neoreactionaries— although talking to the mild-mannered Land, you wouldn't think that he gets infuriated by very much. He patiently explained to me that neoreaction argues that notions of equality are derived from the spiritual equality of Christianity, and that shutting down talk of human biodiversity means "that you will misdiagnose social problems, you will try to solve things in a way that they are not soluble. You are just not dealing with reality at its true grain, and your solutions are not realistic."

It's this badgering insistence on an objective truth that is allegedly being censored or going entirely undiscussed which underpins alt-right thought. And yet for all of this laudatory talk and apparent alignment, Land, like others associated with the movement, found it necessary to reject the alt-right once it hit the mainstream. In fact, despite hitting on some of the movement's themes and decrying the current state of freedom of speech among progressives, on his blog Land was not afraid to call out the alt-right as fans of fascism in a passage that hints at some of the clefts in the movement that became glaringly obvious in the age of Trump.

"Neoreaction, as I understand it, predicted the emergence of the Alt-Right as an inevitable outcome of Cathedral over-reach, and didn't remotely like what it saw," he wrote, continuing:

> For the Alt-Right, generally speaking, fascism is (1) basically a great idea, and (2) a meaningless slur concocted by ((((Cultural Marxists))) to be laughed at. For NRx ([Xenosystems] version) fascism is a late-stage leftist aberration made peculiarly toxic by its comparative practicality. There's no real room for a meeting of minds on this point.

He concludes the post with something like a warning:

> None of this should be taken as a competition for recruits. The Alt-Right will get almost all of them—it's bound to be huge. From the NRx perspective, the Alt-Right is to be appreciated for helping to clean us up. They're most welcome to take whoever they can, especially if they shut the door on the way out.[60]

When I spoke to Land via studio link from Beijing early one morning in 2017, he told me that he considered the alt-right essentially a democratic populist movement. Neoreaction, he said, was essentially anti-democratic, and anti-populist. While the two strands of thought might unite in opposition to a common enemy, they could never really be bedfellows.

"The explosive emergence of the alt-right definitely took neoreaction by surprise," he said, "because the fundamental driver of the whole neoreaction thing was this basic sense of despair that you could ever have certain types of dramatic change under democratic auspices, that this democratic machinery was so well tuned and the Cathedral was humming along so smoothly that you should just abandon certain types of hope of radical disruption.

"It would definitely give a false impression if it suggested that there was some sort of hand-rubbing neoreactionaries seeing the alt-right appear and saying, oh, 'just as we planned.'"

It's telling that alt-righters looking to anchor their movement in a pool of academic thought latch on to someone like Land, who so starkly rejects their embrace. Post-Trump, there are not a whole lot of intellectuals who still have academic credibility and who would willingly associate themselves with the movement. The masthead of AlternativeRight.com and other alt-right websites include many who were kicked out of the Cathedral or who were never let through the church doors in the first place.

Of course, for many this is a badge of honor and a symptom of what they see as the stultifying and freedom-crushing chokehold that political correctness exerts on institutions of higher learning. But it's also been a problem for a movement that sees itself as essentially truth-seeking and intellectual, and throughout its early history mostly fought its battles online rather than through direct action or protests on the street.

* * *

Lacking a firm base from which to launch its assault on liberal multiculturalism, the alt-right might have remained an obscure preoccupation of far-out blogs, as outlandish and unpopular as some of its more extreme ideas—like Spencer's proposal to carve up the United States and march all the way to Istanbul.

The alt-right needed some big help to crack the mainstream: specific rallying points which would allow it to capitalize on populist anger, a Facebook-friendly new media empire, or a political candidate who channeled some of their ideas. And as unlikely as it seems, all those things came along, more or less at once.

2

The Racialists

Rachel Dolezal was nervous. In a tiny laid-back coffee shop in Spokane, doodly folk music playing on the stereo, she clasped her hands around a cup of tea as she recounted the instances of racial abuse that had been directed at her and her son. It was the spring of 2011, long before Dolezal had gained worldwide fame.

Extremists, she told me and BBC correspondent Jonny Dymond, had broken into, or attempted to break into, every home she'd had in the area.

"There were two nooses. There was a swastika affixed to the front door of my workplace," she said. "None of the cases have resulted in any suspects."

Dolezal told us that she was the daughter of a white mother and a black father, but that she identified, like Barack Obama, mostly with her black heritage. She had curly black hair, a copper complexion and the droll, slightly wandering voice of a Midwesterner who'd moved around the country. She taught art at local colleges in Spokane, a small city in eastern Washington state with an African-American population of just over 2 percent. The surrounding area, known as the Inland Empire, is more sparsely populated, and more white—and, as noted, has had a troubled history involving extremists.

"My son, who goes to high school, I actually bought him a pair of earphones, because on the school bus he hears the word 'nigger' every day," Dolezal said. "I do sometimes lay awake at night and wonder about living here. Mostly for my son's sake, if it's safe, really."

She began to cry.

"If something happens, I want them to know you stand strong and you stand up for what you believe in."

It was compelling stuff—but it was also mostly lies.

* * *

At the time, there were still active neo-Nazis and white nationalists in the area, but it later emerged that there was no solid evidence that Dolezal had been targeted in a concerted campaign. The reason no suspects had been arrested for the noose and swastika incidents is that they were likely made up, although police at the time told me they were taking Dolezal's complaints seriously.

More fundamentally, she was not by any stretch of the imagination black. She was born and raised by two white parents who described their ancestry as German, Czech, and part Native American.[1]

Dolezal's strange double life apparently began to unravel because of a dispute with her parents over alleged abuse, and a custody battle over one of her adopted brothers.[2] Her parents contacted the media, and she was interviewed by a local TV reporter in June 2015. The raw footage of the interview was posted on YouTube.[3] In it, the reporter, Jeff Humphrey from KXLY, slowly danced around the point before taking Dolezal to task on her family background. As his subject became more and more uncomfortable, the "gotcha" moment came when he showed Dolezal a printout from one of her social media profiles, of a black man she described as her father.

"Is that your dad?"

"Yes," Dolezal unconvincingly replied. "That's my dad."

"I was wondering whether your dad actually is an African-American man," Humphrey replied. After she trips over her response he followed up: "Are you African-American?"

Dolezal walked off.

The story spread fast, and the reaction was instant. Dolezal's name became a top trend on Twitter. When these facts came to light, African-American activists were outraged, and found her dressing-up party offensive, distasteful, or highly amusing.[4] Less noticed was the angry, sarcastic outcry from members of the nascent alt-right. "Rachel Dolezal, White self-hatred is sick!" shouted one supporter.[5] Another messaged me, after uncovering our original report: "Nooses in [Washington state]? In 2011? No offense, but that isn't remotely credible. Why such great desire to believe her?"

For a certain section of emerging white "identitarians" or "racialists," Rachel Dolezal was the ultimate embodied vindication of their beliefs. Here was a woman who was born white, who had tried to turn herself black. She had been married to a black man, with whom she had had a child. She was the leader of a local civil rights—or, in the pejorative term of the alt-right, "social justice"—organization. She was someone who had not only taken on a minority identity, but traded on that identity to become successful. She was proof, in their eyes, that racial justice had been twisted into a stick with which to bludgeon white people.

Alt-right jokers compared her to Caitlin Jenner—sarcastically arguing that if a person can change their gender, why can't they change their race? The implication was that liberal arguments about both human qualities are ridiculous. Phrases like "transracial" and "wrongskin" were soon trending on social media. "The dismissive attitudes and abuse that #RachelDolezal is facing proves that we #WrongSkin suffer more than naturally born black people," tweeted one troll who took the persona of an extreme "social justice warrior."[6]

It was beside the point that her fame and prestige were distinctly local and unremarkable. Outside of Spokane and northern Idaho, Dolezal was unknown. After her unmasking, I wrote about how I had been taken in by her story during our brief encounter.[7] Before the scandal, few journalists outside the area had ever found a reason to interview Rachel Dolezal. As activists went, she wasn't that influential; her local chapter of the NAACP didn't represent a huge community, and was not particularly powerful.

Ironically, her fame and influence were vastly greater after her racial unmasking than before. And because of the Twitter storm, it became a much bigger story than the incident that had brought me to Spokane in the first place.

Millions of people around the world are now familiar with the story of Rachel Dolezal, but how many have heard of Kevin William Harpham?

* * *

On January 17, 2011, Harpham, a former soldier, put a pipe bomb along the route of a Martin Luther King Jr. Day parade in downtown Spokane. The bomb was filled with fishing weights coated in rat poison, designed to both shred tissue and prevent blood from clotting. The shrapnel pieces were also coated with human feces, in order to cause infections.[8] Three workers who were cleaning the parade route found the bomb before it could explode. Otherwise, authorities said, dozens of people, including children, could have been killed and injured in horrific ways.

It was this terrorist bomb plot—rather than the alleged racial abuse suffered by a confused, troubled art professor—that initially drew me to Spokane.

It would be more than a stretch to call Harpham a member of the alt-right. At the time he was arrested, the movement hadn't received any mainstream media coverage, and Harpham's connections with long-running neo-Nazi organizations put him in a much more traditional extremist mold. He was more about old-school white supremacist message boards than Twitter or internet memes.

His ideas, however, were drawn from the same well that the alt-right drinks from, and his racial ideas drew a straight line between the cross-burners of old and today's millennial keyboard warriors.

The first clue was Harpham's connection to the Vanguard News Network (VNN). He posted on this white nationalist message board and donated money to it. His posts combine an obsession with race with a disdain for religion: "There is a need for a new party or group simply because there is not a single white org. that is Christian free and we need one that with [sic] a policy that excludes these nut ball hymn singers," he wrote. Like many alt-right activists, he was highly skeptical of organized religion.

On VNN, the very alt-rightish idea of "white genocide" is a near constant topic of conversation.[9] Those who use the phrase mean it seriously and literally; they believe there is a master plan dedicated to the total destruction of the white race. Usually (but not always) the supposed genocide isn't portrayed as an active one, carried out via gas chambers, nuclear bombs and Kalashnikovs, but a rather slower but no less radical demographic process of cultural integration and intermarriage, hurried along by low birth rates and legal abortion. The white genocide crowd has resurrected the "one drop" idea born in antebellum America, that any non-white ancestor fundamentally alters all lineal descendants forevermore. They argue that generational change is not a passive or desirable process, but is driven by forces engaged in an active conspiracy specifically targeting the white race. The alleged culprits vary—fingers are pointed at Jews, a shadowy cabal of elite globalists, other races, and liberals or "Cultural Marxists" who want not only white people destroyed but all vestiges of Western civilization eliminated forever. The "white genocide" idea was at the root of the chant "Jews will not replace us," heard at far-right demonstrations, perhaps most notably the August 2017 far-right rally and attack in Charlottesville, Virginia, which resulted in the death of a counterprotester and galvanized the country.

Wikipedia's entry on the subject is titled "White genocide conspiracy theory" and traces the idea to a Nazi pamphlet titled: "Are the White Nations Dying? The Future of the White and the

Coloured Nations in the Light of Biological Statistics."[10] Despite its less-than-stellar pedigree, "white genocide" is an idea that's absolutely central to the alt-right.

"I want my grandchildren to look like my grandparents," said Jared Taylor, demonstrating a profound confusion around the issue of hereditary traits and genetics. "I don't want them to look like Anwar Sadat or Foo Man Chu or Whoopi Goldberg."[11]

Beyond the genetic panic, the "white genocide" crowd targets academia and ethnic studies departments and encompasses the theory that while minority groups have been taught to be proud of their heritage, white people are discouraged from such feelings, instead being told that being white is shameful. One typical message: "There is nothing wrong with wanting to love and preserve your own race and heritage!"[12]

The bizarre idea that white people could be eliminated from the earth has enthralled extremists. In addition to Harpham, the threat of white extinction was a theme that popped up in the rambling manifestos of Dylann Roof, the white supremacist who shot eight people at a black church in Charleston, South Carolina,[13] and Norwegian terrorist Anders Breivik. Breivik's manifesto, *2083: A European Declaration of Independence*, is littered with alt-right ideas, including an obsession with "Cultural Marxism" and "multiculturalism," which at least in part explains why the intellectual wing of the movement was interested in studying it further.[14]

Putting aside for a moment the more violent end of the white genocide crowd, the idea of a politics based explicitly on racial identity appears to be one of the defining distinctions between the alt-right and the alt-light. Dedicated alt-righters don't question the usefulness of identity politics—indeed, they claim that it's a more or less inevitable worldwide tendency—and primarily argue that white people need their own political movement. Meanwhile, alt-lightish commentators criticize movements like Black Lives Matter as part of a wholesale rejection of identity politics. Some involved in the movement try to have it both ways and insist on either identity politics for all ethnic groups *or* for none.

The science-fiction writer Theodore Beale, who writes under the pen name Vox Day, is a big voice in the alt-right firmament. I asked him whether there was a clear contradiction in a movement including staunch opponents of identity politics—even in their most basic form, which for instance leads to the formation of an African-American interest group such as the NAACP—and people who embrace identity politics for white people.

He shot back: "The alt-right has never railed against identity politics. You are confusing us with conservatives, who abhor them. To a certain extent, the alt-right is what happens when the Right accepts the post-ideological reality of identity politics in multiracial and multicultural societies.

"History suggests there is no reason to believe that the European homelands would not be considerably better off in most aspects of society if left to their own devices," he continued, going on to make a strange claim: "Been to Paris lately? All that diversity is turning it into a dangerous, filthy place that no one even wants to visit."[15]

White genocide is a kooky theory with zero evidence to back it up, but that hasn't stopped it from filtering into the bedrock of the alt-right. And there's one place where it's taken as gospel, frequently cited as being beyond dispute: the "/pol/" message board on the website 4chan, which I will deal with at length later.

* * *

Harpham was something of an alt-right canary—he was exactly the sort of thuggish old-school supremacist that the intellectuals disdained, but at the same time a natural consequence of where their divisive ideology could lead when translated to the street.

As we'll see, the thought patterns which led to the Spokane bomb plot would be reflected in violence up to and including the mayhem and deadly attack in Charlottesville. At his court hearing, Harpham refused to take responsibility for his actions and told a judge that the bomb—despite the shrapnel covered with rat poison and shit—was only meant to break a window in a creative protest against "unity" and "multiculturalism."[16] He was sentenced to 32 years in prison.[17]

As for Rachel Dolezal, she was all over the news for a few days, but attention quickly moved on. There was a big political story brewing. Just a few days after Dolezal was outed, Donald Trump declared that he would run for president of the United States.

3

The Channers

Late on a Saturday night in June 2017, news broke of a terror attack on London Bridge. The attackers, three men inspired by radical Islam, were quickly shot dead by police after killing eight people. News flooded Twitter and other social networks. Along with eyewitness reports and authentic pictures from the scene, much of the information being passed around was wrong, misleading or inaccurate. There was nothing unusual about this—it's always the case after a terror attack or other disaster.[1]

Just minutes after the attack, however, one corner of the internet was buzzing with jokes, pranks, and general nastiness. For the uninitiated—and, let's be frank, for many of the initiated as well—4chan is a difficult read at normal times, but breaking news stories turn the discussion board from heated to frenzied to nuclear. At home that evening, in between monitoring breaking news alerts, I watched the alt-right propaganda machine gear up in real time.

"You voted for this," said one poster, just minutes after the news broke. Another commented: "That's what happens when you're too open with religions, nice job britons." Others praised the attacks (perhaps ironically), rooted for all-out race war, criticized the police, or got other political points in early: "REMINDER THAT THIS IS WHAT THE LIBTARDS WANT FOR AMERICA. MASSIVE MUSLIM IMMIGRATION AND FREQUENT RANDOM TERROR. GLOBALISM IS A CLEAR AND PRESENT DANGER."[2]

Among the messages and memes, one anonymous poster put up a message saying that one of the terrorists had been identified as "radical Islamist Samail al-Hayyid." The picture next to the message was a Photoshopped image of Sam Hyde, a comedian who at various times is described either as alt-right or as making fun of it (perhaps he's both, at the same time).[3]

Another posted a "picture of first confirmed victim." Within minutes, photos of the fake "suspect," the fake "victim" and dozens of other pictures of people who had supposedly been caught up in the attack were circulating on Twitter and other mainstream social networks. The alt-right trolls were coming out to play.

*   *   *

One of the hoaxes was started by a sort of spoof account. Its Twitter bio read: "Journalist for BLM [Black Lives Matter]. Always stayin woke," with the author claiming to be a "LGBTQ+ pansexual nonbinary POC transwoman." It was a poor satire of how a liberal "social justice warrior" might describe themselves. The person's actual tweets—which included the post showing one of the fake London Bridge terror victims—were a mix of alt-right memes, posts mocking black people, and jokes about sex and video games.

I shot the person behind the account a message. Most of the time, my attempts to engage with trolls are either ignored or met with a volley of abuse, but for some reason this person succinctly messaged back: "When I get back from church yes." If the situation hadn't been so troubling, I might have laughed. I already knew the bit about church was a joke.

The teenager behind the account briefly tried to insist that his persona and the terror victim he had made up were authentic, but he soon dropped the facade and said: "how much you paying me for this nigga." Then: "ill answer your dumb questions that was a jokw [sic]."

The hoaxer went on to identify himself as a 17-year-old "fascist" living in Pennsylvania. He said he had been expelled from high school and that he spent most of his time in front of a computer or working out. He said he was in the "altright tent of ideas" and defined his ideology as "a refutation of the world order established by the French in 17th century [sic] ... the toxic idea of 'equality.'"

Despite the apparently premature end of his formal schooling, my correspondent was clearly both erudite and pompous—so far, so alt-right. He said he invented the hoax victim as a joke, to get retweeted, and also to make a point—specifically, he wanted to provoke a reaction from "white liberals." It maybe worked a tiny bit. In the heat of the moment, many retweeted the fake pictures, although the hoaxers were soon sniffed out and called out by other Twitter users and by journalists.[4] There's no indication that any particular ethnic or political group was more guilty of spreading the message than any other. Still, the hoaxer was convinced that he had targeted and hit a specific cultural demographic. In his mind, he had struck a blow for freedom.

"They don't care about the victims as much as they care about making themselves feel good," he wrote, indignantly. "They dont care about people is my point."

Hmm, I thought. I typed: "So you care about people?"

"I am not a hypocrite. I see the worst in people, but do I care? Probably not. Everyone gets what they deserves."

He went on in that nihilistic vein: "Believe me there was a time I did [care about people]. A time I wanted to save everyone. But these 'people' [white liberals] welcome their own demise." It was a reference to the "white genocide" idea.

His hoax was a telling example of the disassociation that happens in front of a computer screen. Not only was this alt-right prankster not in the least bit remorseful about constructing a lie about the murder of innocent people at the moment those same people were lying dead or dying in the street, he claimed to be a hero: "that tweet was a public service ... If anything I should be lauded."

I suggested he might get out more.

"Why? The people arent worth the bother," came the response.

It was one of the dozens of conversations I've had with alt-right and alt-light types over the years, and I suppose in isolation it might seem bizarre and unsettling. But by then I had been inured to the darker personalities lurking around the fringes of the movement. Some seemed to have absorbed bits of the racialist utopian politics of the intellectual wing of the alt-right, but they were definitely much more into the internet than policy conferences and turgid blogs. Like many others, this hoaxer was deep into the culture of 4chan.

* * *

4chan is a large, freewheeling and often offensive message board, but that description is somewhat like calling Disney World a plot of land in Florida with a few rides on it. Technically the description is accurate but it doesn't come anywhere near close to capturing the nature of the beast.[5]

Founded in 2003, 4chan to this day retains the basic look of an early oo's webpage, with basic text, a blocky layout, and annoying banner ads. It's sometimes called an "image board" because it was based on Japanese discussion boards focusing on anime and manga, and users who originate 4chan threads have to post some sort of photo or meme. Responses can come in text, images, or both.

There are a few dozen subsections of 4chan devoted to all sorts of topics: video games, technology, weapons, business, LGBT issues, adult cartoons, toys. The alt-right HQ on the site is the board called "Politically Incorrect"—shortened in 4chan nomenclature to "/pol/."

4chan has a couple of characteristics which help create a hive mind of activity and which made it both a breeding ground and a destination for the alt-right. First of all, posters are anonymous and ordinary users without admin privileges can't create accounts or register with the site. Threads disappear after a few days or hours, so the overall risk in posting anything is low and the whole site has a feeling of constant experimentation and impermanence.[6]

4chan also takes, to put it mildly, a very libertarian view on free speech. Officially, on most of the site, moderators will remove "Trolls, flames, racism, off-topic replies," but 4chan is a site where "kill yourself" doesn't qualify as a flame and starting a "nigger hate thread" doesn't qualify as racism.[7] Moderators— called "janitors"—are an anonymous volunteer force and the reasons why a particular message is removed aren't always very clear, but it does seems as though 4chan is guided more or less by America's free speech laws. In practice that means specific threats against named individuals ("Kill Mr X," "Let's find out where Miss Y lives and post her address") tend to be deleted while general abuse or messages advocating group violence ("Black people are subhuman"; "It would be better if all Jews were dead") tend to stay. To wade into 4chan as a "normie"—someone who's "mainstream," the least bit conventional, or unfamiliar with the internet's dark underbelly—takes a strong stomach.

Part of the appeal of the website lies in its vintage design and its overall mood. It's sometimes hard to fathom how different the internet was in the 1990s and early 2000s, before Twitter and Facebook and today's general use, everybody-and-their-grandma web. In its first decade or so, the World Wide Web was populated by oddballs, obsessives, fanatics and fanboys who made up the rules as they went along and tested the limits of free speech without fear of reprisal. At the same time, they policed themselves according to the standards of their own select in-group. It was a place filled with alternative personalities, views well outside the mainstream and intentional online communities, a sharp contrast with mass social networks which are public, require real-name registration, and are designed to mirror real-life relationships.

4chan /pol/ is where the alt-right can go to test out memes, communicate with in-jokes, and plot raids against normies on other sites and networks. Over the years it has been in operation, 4chan has spawned all sorts of unserious pranks—it's where "rickrolling"[8] and LOLcats[9] originated—as well as more weighty political projects. It was, for instance, the key breeding ground for the hacker group Anonymous.

Anonymous was proof that something resembling a real political movement could emerge from the chaos of a name-free message board. It was, and to a degree still is, a movement which has taken direct political action, its first being an international "day of action" against the Church of Scientology in February 2008.[10] The political beliefs of Anonymous, while having a firm libertarian and anti-corruption streak, have veered across the political spectrum. Their aesthetic is directly inspired by the 1980s graphic novel *V for Vendetta*, which describes a fascist post-nuclear-war Britain, and, riffing on that book, activists come together annually on Guy Fawkes Day for protests in London and other major cities.

Anonymous has various factions and splinter groups, and these days activists are preoccupied with infighting and accusing each other of being CIA plants. But its emergence showed that some sort of at least temporarily cohesive movement could be built from the chaos. The movement which emerged from 4chan to have the most impact, however, was far from what the original Anonymous activists had imagined.

* * *

The first sign that 4chan was becoming a key hangout for the far right came in 2011, when the site's founder said that a board devoted to news items had degenerated into a version of the avowedly neo-Nazi website Stormfront—another site tied to the alt-right which I'll explore later.[11] In its place he created /pol/, which came with a few specific rules:

1. Debate and discussion related to politics and current events is welcome.

2. You are free to speak your mind, but do not attack other users. You may challenge one another, but keep it civil!
3. Posting pornography is not permitted. This is a politics board, not a porn board.[12]

The first and last rules are mostly followed, but, as with the 4chan-wide ban on racism, the concept of civility is so loosely defined as to be pretty much unrecognizable as a bar to contributing.

The attempt to detoxify the political discussion on the site by creating /pol/ backfired, as the alt-righters and associated trolls moved into the new space. A key moment came in 2014, when /pol/ became the main organizing platform for what became known as "Gamergate."[13] Gamergate, which I'll deal with at length in the next chapter, was an all-fronts battle against video-game journalists and feminist influence in the gaming world. It involved both above-board politicking through hashtag drives and the creation of propaganda videos, and more sordid campaigns including doxxing—revealing personal information—and threats of violence. Much of the activity, of all types, was coordinated on 4chan.

According to the academic Gabriella Coleman, an expert on 4chan and Anonymous, it was around this time that extremists started coming to /pol/ en masse, attracted to the free-speech ethos and the kinds of discussions which were happening around that particular controversy. "A lot of the /pol/ participants considered their form of racism and misogyny as ironic," Coleman told me. "Now I think it's difficult to really say 'oh well this is ironic' and 'this is not ironic', but let's just take their word for face value because what happened next I think really does matter."

White supremacists using other websites collected on /pol/, Coleman says, "to explicitly recruit [channers] and transform their kind of ironic racism to very earnest racism." As she points out, whether the extreme content that could be found on 4chan prior to Gamergate was really coming from a place of irony is a highly debatable question, and others have argued that the message board's far-right direction of travel was quite obvious from much earlier on. But Gamergate marked a turning point, in terms of the types who were attracted to /pol/, its importance among 4chan's many boards, and crucially the types of campaigns it was supporting and to what ends. Where Anonymous targets were made up primarily of institutions, corporations, governments and public officials, the new alt-right /pol/ contingent focused most of its fire on vaguely defined leftist groups, feminists and little-known social justice advocates—individuals who could be isolated and picked off not by hacks or demonstrations, but by online threats or angry hashtag campaigns.

Meanwhile, the way 4chan works, while baffling to newbies, had attracted an audience dedicated to creating memes, stories and images—a dizzying array of virtual *stuff*.

To begin with, there's the requirement that new threads begin with an image—novelty drives engagement as posters vie for attention with new pictures. One estimate found that 4chan users post a million new images about every two-and-a-half months, and that "the constant production of new content may be one of the reasons /pol/ is at the heart of the hate movement on the Internet."[14] The researchers found that about 12 percent of /pol/ posts contain some sort of hateful term, compared to just over 2 percent of other social media posts. For instance the word "nigger" appears in 2 percent of all /pol/ posts, and the amount of activity on the board means that that particular racial slur is used on average 120 times an hour.[15]

Throughout 2015 and 2016, as /pol/ was increasingly identified in news articles as an alt-right gathering point, the reports became, to a degree, self-fulfilling. The board is now firmly in the hands of the troll wing of the alt-right army, and anyone coming to the board with a different outlook is either undercover or just itching for a fight. On a random day in early 2017, the top posts included the following:

- PRESIDENT TRUMP GENERAL - BUSY MAN EDITION—a recurring thread which details the president's daily schedule, news reports on recent political developments, lists of pro-Trump songs and links to videos and other pro-Trump propaganda.
- A picture of conspiracy theorist Alex Jones along with the question "What's wrong with globalism /pol/"—Responses include: "Globalism isn't bad. The globalism that kikes try to push is fucked up," "Globalism is just another autistic form of Communism," and a stereotypical picture of a hook-nosed hand-rubbing Jewish person.
- "What will happen in the next 30 days"—Responses include "Kikes gassed; race war begins," "everyone will realize Hitler was right."

It goes on and on like this, hour after hour, day after day; and if 4chan isn't extreme enough for you, then there's 8chan, which mirrors the structure and style of 4chan but is even—if you can believe it—more clunky and less moderated.

The more "serious" channers discuss and build on theories based on the ideas of Spencer, Jared Taylor and the alt-right intellectuals, though usually without any small grain of finesse or, apparently, scientific background:

Lets try to rationalize why certain discrepancies exist /pol/ starting with blacks. Why do blacks have such low iq's compared to whites? I think it's because life isn't able to flourish in Africa, therefor the generations that stay will evolve into low intelligence people, why? because realizing your environment is shit for development is a sign of intelligence.[16]

The poster goes on to recount myths about race and the size of the male genitalia, making some bizarre deductions: "Asians have the highest iq, so the survival of their race isn't dependent on reproduction, so they never evolved sexually."[17] On

/pol/, the obsession with genetics is such that alt-righters post self-administered test results from DNA-analysis companies like 23andme. "Took it, was disappointed with the facts," reported one commenter who found that more than a quarter of their genetic heritage came from sub-Saharan Africa. Another anxiously asked: "Am I white?" when his results came back 99 percent European—but including 28 percent Ashkenazi—in other words, European Jew. "No you are not," read one response. Another user replied: "No. The rope is coming."[18]

Alt-right memes, pranks and slogans begin in the morass of 4chan and 8chan, and if they have any wider appeal they quickly migrate to more mainstream sites like Reddit and Twitter. On Reddit, the activity centers around the message board or subreddit r/The_Donald. In early 2017 the board had around 400,000 subscribers, which is a very large but by comparison not tremendous amount—the site's most popular subsections have millions, and The_Donald didn't break into the top 100 subreddits.

What it lacks in overwhelming popularity, however, it makes up for in passion—posters are hugely active. The_Donald is 4chan, albeit mostly without the extreme racial slurs or graphic violence or porn. Subscribers pump out stories about crimes committed by African-Americans and illegal immigrants, along with pro-Trump propaganda and attacks against liberals:

- Literally had a lib friend of mine tell me, "I don't care what facts you tell me, I will never think Trump is a good president." This is the unfortunate ideology of many leftists.[19]
- Hey FBI, I'm one of 60 million bots that Putin developed to sway the election in favor of Donald Trump. I'm such an advanced bot that I got in a car, drove it to the polling station, and cast a vote for Russia's Trump.... FUCK YOU COMEY, I'M AN AMERICAN, NOT A RUSSIAN BOT[20]

- BOMBSHELL REPORT DROPPED IN FRANCE! 33% OF YOUNG MUSLIMS THERE SUPPORT TERRORIST SCUM! FRENCH MEDIA FROZEN IN TERROR AS THEY REFUSE TO RELEASE FULL RESULTS OF SURVEY TILL AFTER ELECTION! SPREAD IT AROUND BOYS![21]

Although images aren't required on Reddit posts, they are easily attached to messages, and the site has an up/down voting system which allows posts to hang around longer than they do on 4chan, meaning that effective pictures or links to stories that really rile up a core group of users can reach a wider audience. It's not a domain that's exclusive to the alt-right—while The_Donald includes plenty of material on the movement's key obsessions, subscribers are also known to occasionally discuss things like job growth and tax policy.[22] But the board does serve as one crossover point for the movement into the mainstream—a bridge from 4chan and the hard-core alt-right to the wider world.

This is most acutely illustrated by the range of people whom moderators have managed to entice onto Reddit to hold "ask me anything" (AMA) sessions—sort of like open online press conferences. They include a mix of alt-right and alt-light leaders and figureheads (Twitter conspiracy theorist Mike Cernovich, and Chuck Johnson, the founder of several far-right websites), media personalities (talk-show hosts Tucker Carlson and Bill Mitchell), and other random Trump supporters (like Malik Obama, the former president's half-brother). Trump himself sat down to chat with members in a Q and A in July 2016.[23]

From The_Donald, the alt-right radiates out onto Twitter and other social networks, to Trump's own Twitter account, and from there to the mainstream press. This is the mechanism by which alt-right ideas, phrases and memes wormed their way into the public consciousness—starting with 4chan, gravitating into more popular social networks, and culminating in a tweet by a (possibly unwitting) Donald Trump and/or members of his inner circle. This pattern repeated itself time and again, through the election campaign and even after Trump was elected. The pipeline invented and spread rumors about the conspiracy theory dubbed "pizzagate"—more on that later—which ended in a shooting at a Washington, D.C. restaurant, created memes such as a video of Trump wrestling a man with the CNN logo superimposed on his head,[24] and consistently filtered news stories through a pro-Trump, white nationalist filter.[25]

In addition to the channers, there was another rich source of ideas and terminology feeding into the alt-right. The origin of the red/blue pill metaphor, among others, was the "manosphere." Like the movement as a whole, it was an inexact name for an amorphous hive of internet activity which actually concealed a broad diversity of thought on some central questions having to do with gender relationships. But this corner of the internet was populated almost exclusively by men brought together by one thing: their deep and visceral hatred of feminism.

4

The Meninists

Elliot Rodger was a grandiose, angry young man. Frustrated by his inability to get a girlfriend or a date, he channeled his anger into an autobiographical manifesto and murderous plan. "Women must be punished for their crimes of rejecting such a magnificent gentleman as myself," he wrote. "All of those popular boys must be punished for enjoying heavenly lives and having sex with all the girls while I had to suffer in lonely virginity."[1]

Rodger, the 22-year-old son of two film-industry workers, had reportedly been diagnosed with Asperger's syndrome as a young child.[2] He talked in his manifesto about being prescribed an antipsychotic medication which he refused to take. On May 23, 2014 he followed through with his threats and went on a gun, knife and car rampage in Isla Vista, California. Six people were killed, another 14 were injured, and at the end of it all, Rodger shot himself in the head.

In the aftermath of the mass murder, there were the usual conversations online about gun control and mental health. But many commentators also noticed Rodger's use of language common in the "pick-up artist" (PUA) community[3]—a group of gurus and followers who devote their lives to supposedly hidden tactics allegedly guaranteed to get attractive women to sleep with them.[4]

Rodger was a prolific poster on a site called PUAhate. com, where men who had tried and failed to use pick-up tactics congregated and blamed their romantic failures on the pick-artist coaches, but also on women, other men or specific ethnic groups.[5] One of his posts read:

Today I drove through the area near my college and saw some things that were extremely rage-inducing. I passed by this restaurant and I saw this black guy chilling with 4 hot white girls. He didn't even look good. Then later on in the day I was shopping at Trader Joe's and saw an Indian guy with 2 above average White Girls!!![6]

His manifesto was soaked with self-pity and grandiosity along with racial animosity, which he frequently twisted into a sharp hatred of females. At one point he recounts how an acquaintance, who was black, bragged to him about having sex with a white girl:

How could an inferior, ugly black boy be able to get a white girl and not me? I am beautiful, and I am half white myself. I am descended from British aristocracy. He is descended from slaves. I deserve it more ... if this ugly black filth was able to have sex with a blonde white girl at the age of thirteen while I've had to suffer virginity all my life, then this just proves how ridiculous the female gender is. They would give themselves to this filthy scum, but they reject ME? The injustice![7]

*   *   *

At first glance, pick-up artists seem like quaint scammers who attract a misfit group of men who have problems relating to females. They've been around so long that they were already a trope ripe for satire by the late 1990s. Tom Cruise's character in the film *Magnolia* struts around pushing a program called "Seduce and Destroy" and shouts "Respect the cock! Tame the cunt!" at a crowd of jeering losers.

But the movement grew, and by 2014 there was a thriving, mostly online-based, PUA industry. One "artist" who spoke to me after Rodger's killing spree described his interaction with a typical customer like this: "We teach him how to interact with women ... and give him the confidence and ability to date women."[8] Others were less straightforward, and claimed to have secret psychological tricks—available for a low, low price.

Obviously not all sexually frustrated young men turn into mass murderers, and attitudes towards women and racial minorities vary hugely among PUAs and their fans. But the Isla Vista shootings highlighted one notable corner of the larger "manosphere"—a collection of websites and social media accounts united in their opposition to feminism and their promotion of "men's rights." It was this corner of the internet that was about to become a fertile breeding ground for the alt-right.

* * *

The "men's internet" is just as amorphous as the alt-right, and politically even more diverse, running all the way from pro-feminist liberal professionals who fret about the right way to attachment-parent their sons,[9] to violent misogynists like Rodger and his online ilk.

It's a loose collection of blogs, Reddit topics, traditional web boards and social media accounts. Some are more or less self-help groups or concentrate on individual campaigns such as combating sexual abuse against boys or agitating for rights of fathers post-divorce. Some communities completely swear off sex and masturbation—while some (like the PUAs) are fixated on sleeping with as many women as possible. Some are obsessed with rape statistics and false rape claims. Some are simply devoted to cataloguing what they see as the evils of modern feminism.

The hubs of the manosphere tap into male anger and a general malaise, and many of the most popular sites and message boards use a few choice facts as jumping off points. Male life expectancy, for instance, is lower in most places than it is for women—the gap in the United States is around five years—and on that score men and women are moving in opposite directions.[10] More women than men attend university.[11] And today, women's issues of all sorts are better covered in the mainstream media than ever before. Even in the last few years, awareness of feminism has not just been raised but has more or less exploded, thanks to new online outlets and, of course, social media.

All of this has contributed to a countervailing rise in backlash chatter on the manosphere. For some men, gender issues outline a zero-sum game, one which Team XY is losing. As one man put it, in a comment featured on one of the most prominent manosphere sites, MGTOW ("Men Going Their Own Way," i.e. in a direction away from women):

> THANK F&^!#N God I found this site! So pissed off with the current state of the western world and how we men have been thumbed down into the lowest fucking class possible, yet are stil [sic] expected to pick the tab up for everything and be an empty nut sack gentleman.[12]

As you move to the more extreme end of the spectrum, the ideas of the manosphere start to dovetail quite neatly with those of the alt-right. The complicated language of pick-up artists and their "game" (a reference to a book that has become something of a bible for the PUA crowd) has popularized several terms that are now dictionary entries in the alt-right lexicon, chief among them the "red pill" concept. And one manufactured controversy, which emerged later in 2014 and was fueled by channers, not only galvanized that particular alliance but sharpened the rhetorical tactics that would later give rise to the mainstreaming of the alt-right. It came to be known by the pompous name "Gamergate."

* * *

If you discount the heavy political air, the facts of Gamergate seem petty, odd, niche, pretty sad and ultimately mundane. It began with the breakdown of an on-off relationship between a video-game developer named Zoe Quinn and her boyfriend

Eron Gjoni. Gjoni was angry, and he channeled his anger into a 9,000-word blog post.[13] It's ugly, emotional, gross and raw. It contains drama, chronicling a number of alleged infidelities, lies and the complicated emotions of two young people falling in and out of love. Gjoni concluded: "Seriously, you really don't want to trust Zoe Quinn."[14]

Gjoni's political sympathies seem to lie in a very different direction than the alt-right.[15] In his rant he mentions, unironically, that he's interested in social justice, and he has condemned the viciousness which happened as a result of his writing. But once his post was noticed by 4chan and the manosphere, his narrative became twisted, politicized and amplified. For instance, according to one popular but false claim, Quinn had traded sexual favors to boost positive coverage of her games.[16]

As a result of the blog post, a conspiracy theory developed, aimed at journalists covering the video-game industry and feminists working within it. On the surface, as it was played out on Twitter, Reddit, and the more popular blogs run by pick-up artists and manosphere heroes, the Gamergate hashtag was about "ethics in video-game journalism"—the idea that the substantial niche of media devoted to gaming and gamers was hopelessly corrupt.[17] The Gamergate crowd argued not only that games journalism had been influenced by feminist, politically correct ideas, but that the entire industry had been completely overrun to the point where games were receiving favorable reviews based not on their own merit but on how well their programmers conformed to progressive identity politics. Those who dared to go against such principles, the mob argued, were losing status, money and jobs.

Quinn was painted as the leading example of this phenomenon. But other feminist writers and academics who studied video games and were previously little-known outside their own small spheres were suddenly credited with wielding enormous sway over the industry. The Gamergate theory was an overarching, conspiratorial brand of logic that would form the pattern for other alt-right arguments in the future.

Had Gamergate really been about ethics, the agitators might have had a point. Anyone who's familiar with entertainment journalism might recognize that there is a legitimate debate to be had about the issue of undue influence. Freebies are doled out, relationships are often personal, there are a lot of unpaid and amateur writers on the scene, and journalists as a whole are paid less than the people they're covering. While ethical guidelines exist at many outlets, there are huge grey areas and massive potential for conflicts of interest. Of course, these issues are of much less concern than they would be for, say, journalists covering politics—the stakes are lower and the potential sources of information are much wider, and in the end it's pretty much just a matter of personal taste. If you're a gamer who doesn't like an article in, say, *The Guardian* about a narrative game with low-res graphics and feminist themes, there are hundreds of magazines and blogs out there reviewing something more to your taste—perhaps a first-person shooter featuring a soldier stuck behind the lines slaughtering alien terrorists in Iraq. In other words, while video gamer shouts about ethics might actually have had a point, it's a vanishingly small one.

In fact, credible reports of ethical transgressions in the business barely irritated gamers, unless they had a reactionary anti-feminist edge. Around the time of the outcry, one distributor offered free copies of a game based on *The Lord of the Rings*, but restricted the offer to YouTubers who agreed to review the title positively. Few Gamergaters seemed to care.[18]

Under the banner of ethics, truth, and free speech, Gamergate gave voice and political direction to the manosphere. Specifically, it amplified the lament that feminism had gone too far, that a normally male-dominated space was becoming feminized, and that "social justice warriors" were taking over.[19]

The arguments put forth by the alt-right Gamergaters did include some rational criticism of feminism which, no matter where you come down on them, were clearly within the bounds of rational discourse. Some, for instance, were critiques of feminist narratives about video games.[20] But a wave of threats and abuse soon drowned out any attempt at even-handed debate. Quinn was targeted, of course, but so were bloggers, journalists, and other female video-game developers. Female researchers looking at the games industry were sent death threats and doxxed—their addresses and phone numbers released online. Some were temporarily forced to leave their homes. One feminist critic was forced to cancel a lecture after a bomb threat, the seriousness of which was undetermined, but the text of which was a nice window into the fevered fantasies of the manosphere's dark side: "I have at my disposal a semi-automatic rifle, multiple pistols, and a collection of pipe bombs," the thread read. "I will write my manifesto in her spilled blood, and you will all bear witness to what feminist lies and poison have done to the men of America."[21]

Interestingly, the poisonous side of Gamergate became seen by activists not as a bug, but as a positive feature. Those involved in the campaign saw how effective trolling was in generating attention and silencing enemies, and it was soon adopted and celebrated as a tactic. The saga acted as a dress rehearsal for alt-right offensives during the Trump campaign.[22] Harassment and pranking was organized on 4chan—and later, when that board became inhospitable to the Gamergaters, 8chan—and made its way to Reddit boards, chief among them r/KotakuInAction.[23]

It's useful to think of r/KotakuInAction as a smaller and more niche precursor to r/The_Donald—a board filled with news links, anti-feminist propaganda, sarcastic jibes at the other side, mild disagreements on points of order described as fruitful intellectual engagements in a self-congratulatory manner, and snarky back-patting. But here again was a bridge between more extreme message boards and mainstream social networks.

And those networks—Twitter chief among them—provided the platform for spreading the message much more widely, drilling home the "ethics in journalism" message and catching the attention of journalists by pushing the #Gamergate hashtag to prominence. There's evidence to suggest that hashtag campaigns were organized by the chans and signal-boosted by sock puppets—accounts used specifically to push a particular message, usually working in collaboration with other such accounts. If you have a bit of technical savvy, a receptive audience and enough socks, Twitter's algorithm isn't too hard to game.[24]

Gamergate also helped develop the alt-right's rhetorical tactics. Gamergaters flipped the script on their opponents, portraying gamers rather than women as an oppressed group, and painted feminists as powerful censors rather than outsider critics. Supporters portrayed themselves as authentic crusaders and "real gamers" as opposed to their johnny-come-lately opponents— despite the fact that some of the loudest Gamergaters openly professed little interest in actually playing games.[25] These tactics would become standard operating practice on the alt-right for years to come.

One journalist in particular rode the controversy to prominence, and eventually to an almost unique position in the eyes of the alt-right. Milo Yiannopoulos wasn't too interested in gaming, and in fact was pretty scornful of gamers:

I understand why young people might get the odd thrill from beating up a bad guy, or catching a glimpse of a nipple or two. But there's something a bit tragic, isn't there, about men in their thirties hunched over a controller whacking a helmeted extraterrestrial? I'm in my late twenties, and even I find it sad. And yet there are so many of them—enough to support a multi-billion dollar video games industry. That's an awful lot of unemployed saddos living in their parents' basements.[26]

A year later, when Gamergate rolled around, Yiannopoulos was writing for Breitbart, the site run by Steve Bannon. His reporting had suddenly become very sympathetic to gamers, as he released leaked messages from a list for games journalists which he said proved a conspiracy to promote feminist and social justice issues:

> The emails proved that dozens of senior journalists from competing publications were colluding ... to push political and "social engineering" agendas in their coverage and blackball writers who tried to speak out about corruption in the press...
>
> Today, the release of a top-tier video game is accompanied by hand-wringing in the press about its "violent" and "sexist" content, despite the fact that the evidence about how games make people behave in real life is inconclusive at best. Ordinary gamers are left scratching their heads by all this.[27]

As will be covered in a later chapter, Breitbart would go on to become a focal point of the movement and the hottest media property associated with the alt-right. But already the catalyzing effect of Gamergate gave the manosphere mainstream prominence and boosted the reputation of some of its more extreme ideas and characters.

Among them was a pick-up artist named Daryush Valizadeh, who wrote under the alias "Roosh V." Valizadeh first gained prominence when he wrote a series of sex-themed travel guides. His site Return of Kings later operated under a code he called "neomasculinity," which seems to be a mixture of banalities ("Men and women are genetically different, both physically and mentally"), old-fashioned ideas dredged up to serve as outrage triggers ("A woman's value significantly depends on her fertility and beauty. A man's value significantly depends on his resources, intellect, and character"), and straight-up white-genocide-themed alt-right shout-outs ("Socialism, feminism, cultural Marxism, and social justice warriorism aim to destroy the family unit, decrease the fertility rate, and impoverish the state through large welfare entitlements").[28]

With headlines like "Why Men are Intellectually Superior to Women,"[29] "Women Should Not be Allowed to Vote,"[30] and "How to Turn a Feminist Into your Sex Slave,"[31] Valizadeh and his writers have constructed a world that's explicit and unapologetic. And yet, while celebrating more (if not necessarily better) sex, the site is also peppered with paeans to traditional gender roles ("Women belong at home, not at the office"[32]), biblical references, and critiques of libido-enhancing drugs for women[33] and feminist ideas on sexual liberation. Valizadeh has chronicled his sexual exploits around the world, but at the same time Return of Kings rails against women's sexual freedom and pushes a traditionalist, anti-birth-control line. In an article with the headline "4 ways that western women are ruining themselves," item number one is "promiscuity."[34]

In promoting sexual conquest while at the same time decrying female sexuality, Return of Kings is far from alone in the manosphere in displaying mind-bending levels of cognitive dissonance. Sometimes it seems as if pick-up artists and their fans never actually stop to think about what happens if all of their "game" efforts actually bear orgasmic fruit.

* * *

As with the channers, it's difficult to figure out exactly how seriously to take Return of Kings and many other manosphere websites. Valizadeh has been very good at manufacturing outrage to get attention and drive men desperate either for dates or an anti-feminist narrative to his website. One story with the headline "How to Stop Rape"[35] suggested making "rape legal if done on private property." It's an absurd suggestion that he appended with a note calling it a "satirical thought experiment"—but only after it generated a ton of clicks and outraged headlines.

On the other hand, the Return of Kings message boards, websites like A Voice for Men, and subreddits such as r/TheRedPill host post after post of conspiracy-minded content about women, feminists, custody battles, and, yes, rape. The latter category is usually the least edifying and most controversial. Sometimes those in the manosphere argue that rape doesn't actually exist—that all victims somehow want or will the sexual assaults upon them. A more common formulation is the baseless view that date or acquaintance rape never happens and is a fiction invented by feminists to try to get one over on men.[36]

"Have you guys ever tried 'raping' a girl without using force?" tweeted one-time PUA and alt-light squawkbox Mike Cernovich. "Try it. It's basically impossible. Date rape does not exist."[37] Cernovich, a Gamergate champion turned internet troll turned supporter of Donald Trump, parlayed the outrage he generated at each stage of his development into media attention to flog his manosphere-friendly self-help books. He also became a key proponent of conspiracy theories around Hillary Clinton's health[38] and the "pizzagate" conspiracy.

Strangely enough, the promise of male liberation and individual self-determination is never quite borne out in the manosphere. In the world of PUAs and meninists, gender roles aren't just prescribed for women, who are either submissive wives, fuck toys, or avoidable feminists, but also for men, who are either "alpha"—red-blooded, bedpost-notching hero-warriors—or "beta," i.e. weak, sexually frustrated losers. On the chans and alt-right Reddit, "beta" is thrown around almost as liberally as the insult "cuck." PUA boards are full of pleas for help from self-described betas—or worse, untouchable "omegas"—and tips on how to transform from an incel ("involuntarily celibate") beta into an "alpha." These sit alongside boasts from those higher-grade men recounting, sometimes in graphic detail, sexual encounters, often in a purely factual, clinical style, frequently devoid of any sign of joy.

Some men's rights gurus put forth the argument that the modern world is an ugly, alienating place, stripping men of agency and individuality, reducing whole groups to broad and stereotypical categories and atomizing what was once a rich and thriving male society. It's easy to see how, scrolling through the manosphere, you could actually come to the conclusion that they're right.

*　*　*

Through Gamergate, the meninists and channers found each other. The language and philosophy of the men's rights internet was lifted into alt-right discourse and thinking, and the factions united against modern feminism. (And sometimes pre-modern feminism. One post on 4chan read: "If you think women should be allowed to vote, you need to leave this board right fucking now and never return."[39])

Valizadeh is a prime example of the manosphere's shift towards politics. He stopped referring to himself as a pick-up artist and the content on Return of Kings increasingly started to encompass the larger racial and cultural obsessions of the alt-right. A post from March 2017 bears the headline "The White European Culture is Dead," and reads as if it could have been written by Richard Spencer:

Muslims are the new "barbarians." They will invade the West, adopt some of our technology and customs, and become the new civilized masses that have a higher birth rate than Westerners. And then the new barbarians, most likely Africans, who are even more fertile than Muslims, will repeat the cycle. Nature only cares about strength and fertility. We, as infertile and sterile beings, are the "error" in its eyes, and unless we wake up soon and re-focus on family and tradition, we will simply be replaced by those who do.[40]

It might seem odd to conclude that a niche group of alienated men and a manufactured controversy in the world of video games has a direct connection with an extreme political movement and the election of Donald Trump. But on the chans, where there's a lot of both authentic and tongue-in-cheek professed belief in "meme magic," that's exactly the conclusion that the alt-right reached. Take this grandiose and overblown—but, from the alt-right perspective, logically consistent—Gamergater account of recent history:

> A woman cheated on her boyfriend and fucked 5 guys, some of which were reviewing her shitty indie game...
> So a bunch of autists got together to see what other drama was there and uncovered a shitload of collusion and favor trading for shilling of each other's games and organizations....
> Then it kept growing and growing until it went mainstream. Celebrities chimed in, feminists went to the UN, federal investigations into harassment, etc. It got wildly out of control and redpilled a bunch of video game playing losers about how the media works to control narratives. How Jews and feminists and blacks use the same tactics to be victims that can only be helped through more shekels, etc.
> That redpilling led to a lot of new /pol/ members being born because people started seeing the same tactics in political media and started asking questions. It turned out shitposting about controlled narrative and happenings is more fun than video games because they all suck now.
> Then a bunch of stuff happened and Donald Trump is now the president.[41]

The manosphere was going all-in on the alt-right.

5

Language

The alt-right is essentially an online movement, and its political energy is concentrated on the internet. Sympathizers could be found at pro-Trump election rallies and increasingly appeared in clashes with anti-fascist ("antifa") groups after Trump took office, including the violent rallies in Charlottesville in August 2017. But the movement's lack of organizational structure meant that prior to Trump's win—outside of small conferences held by the National Policy Institute, the Mencken Society, and a few others—supporters didn't really gather for genetic science teach-ins or take to the streets to protest multi-ethnic democracy.

In common with other internet subcultures, alt-right followers have their own distinct language and, to an outsider, confusing style of argument. The confusion stems mainly from the layer of irony that's spread across the whole of the movement—a trait that stems from internet culture—and the effectiveness with which alt-righters have taken leftist arguing tactics and deployed them to their own ends. On the first point, it's difficult to underestimate just how deep the prankster itch goes, which often makes it impossible to tell just how seriously the activists take themselves or anything else. On the second, a key alt-right tactic is to play the victim. They like nothing more than to flip the script on their opponents, infuriating them with a different brand of identity politics.

Here's one example. Around the time of the release of *Star Wars: Rogue One*, the alt-right organized the hashtag campaign #DumpStarWars, encouraging a boycott of the film because of progressive and anti-white-supremacist messages pumped out by its writers. One alt-righter invented a story about the film being reshot to have a pop at Trump. Others decried the diversity of the cast.[1] A popular movie was somehow absorbed into the white-genocide conspiracy theory. "(((Star Wars))) Is Anti-White Social Engineering," wrote a poster on Reddit.[2]

There was no evidence that many people actually did "dump Star Wars"; Rogue One pulled in more than a billion dollars at the box office.[3] And, of course, organizing an actual boycott of a new Star Wars film was probably a pretty hard proposition in the first place. But there's also the distinct possibility that the campaign, like many manufactured alt-right outrage storms, was nothing more than an attention-getting exercise. At that, at least, it certainly succeeded, with coverage in hundreds of news outlets around the world.[4]

More to the point, the Star Wars controversy painted straight white men as a victimized group. When me and my colleague Emma Wilson reported on Clementine Ford, a controversial Australian female journalist who had been subjected to abusive language and threats online, but was also known to dish out nasty insults herself, an enraged bunch of men emerged to don the victim cloak.[5] "Her outbursts and radical ideals invite confrontation," read one email that landed in my inbox. Another complained about men being subjected to hateful online speech. They were among the legions of the alt-right devoted to pointing out hypocrisy on the left, tweeting out messages which amount to asking "who's the real racist?," "who's the real sexist?," "who's the real fascist?," and so on. They've amped up the jujitsu move that ideologues of all sorts have used for eons: if your opponent calls you a name, just shout it back at them.[6] The "feminazi" jibe, popularized by radio talk-show host Rush Limbaugh in the 1990s, is a good example.[7]

Often alt-right argument resembles a giant whingy shout: "But you do it too!"—a position they take up far more often than that of a principled stand in favor of free speech.

* * *

The alt-right's oft-noted internet-age "playfulness" has spawned everything from electronic dance music remixes of Trump speeches to memes of Jewish people Photoshopped into gas chambers.[8] Their sense of irony acts as a weapon and a shield. They may make jokes about Nazis, but if anyone accuses an activist of actually being a Nazi, they can turn around and mock the opponent for their lack of a sense of humor.

And so, having established that no political discourse is either out of bounds or should be taken seriously, the alt-right somehow hit the roof when, in December 2016, George Ciccariello, a professor at Drexel University, tweeted "All I want for Christmas is a white genocide." His university called the tweet "utterly reprehensible, deeply disturbing" (later the authorities said that the tweet was protected speech and didn't take action). Ciccariello, meanwhile, claimed he was joking.[9] Alt-righters might have been expected to respond to Ciccariello with understanding. But something altogether different happened.[10]

Richard Spencer—who, you may recall, presided over "Roman" salutes "clearly done in a spirit of irony and exuberance"—was compelled to try to rush to the scene, sending out a tweet begging someone to set him up with a speech at Drexel.[11] Breitbart harrumphed: "The professor's Twitter feed is filled with hateful, obnoxious messages, anti-Americanism, slams of President Donald Trump, attacks on Jews, as well as pro-Black Lives Matter and pro-communist sloganeering. He also tweeted a picture of a 'Make America Great Again' hat set on fire." And a prominent neo-Nazi blogger cheered the university's initial response and claimed the tide was turning—in *favor* of censorship of people like Ciccariello.[12]

While it might seem odd that the far right was positively encouraging less free speech, the pattern has been repeated time and again online. When it comes to anyone but themselves, alt-right activists seem to have a blind spot, a profound sense of humor failure.

* * *

So this is a good point at which to take a deeper dive into alt-right language code. The alt-right lexicon and tactical playbook has been cobbled together not only from intellectuals, bloggers, and pick-up artists, but also from video games, particularly MMORPGs (massive multiplayer online role-playing games), which increases in computing power and other technical developments have made possible in the last 15 years or so. There are battles against teams, large-scale coordination of tactics, "raids," and various specialized characters and units performing specific functions and drawn from the websites and alt-right slices I've outlined.

From the fundamentally experimental environment of the chans, Twitter, Reddit and blogs, a series of terms and phrases has emerged which help to define the alt-right worldview. Clearly, language shifts, and by the time this book goes to print some—maybe most?—of these terms will be hopelessly out of date or will have shifted in meaning. But here, at least for the moment, is a primer on some of the concepts embedded into words that might trip the uninitiated online.

1488/"14 words"
Literally: "We must secure the existence of our people and a future for white children"—a slogan coined by the neo-Nazi David Lane.[13] The "88" sometimes grafted on the end is grade-school code for the letters "HH" meaning "Heil Hitler." The frequent use of these tropes by alt-righters, particularly on the chans, would seem to nail the case that they are pretty obviously fascists. But constant Hitler and Nazi references are marginally more complicated than that. Sometimes the alt-righters hide behind

their "just joking" excuse while harder-core elements accuse such jokers of not taking fascism sufficiently seriously.[14]

There's also a significant faction which thinks or claims to think that jokes about the Holocaust are effective, taboo-busting, anti-PC humor. They don't really care about the offense their memes and words might cause.

A 16-point list of alt-right principles written by Theodore Beale, the alt-right sci-fi novelist who goes by the pseudonym Vox Day, included the 14 words. Beale certainly wasn't joking when explained to me that: "The 14 words serve to keep out the one cohort we don't want anything to do with, the moderate surrender monkeys who will do anything to avoid being called racist. The Swastika Panties, as I tend to think of them, are harmless, irrelevant, and can even serve as useful media flak jackets ... Furthermore, what sort of monster could possibly oppose the 14 words? Who seriously wishes for the extinction of the white race or believes it should be denied self-determination?"[15]

Anudda Shoah

An exaggerated faux-Yiddish reference to the Holocaust. Like the other neo-Nazi tropes in this glossary, some alt-righters fess up to authentic anti-Semitism when they use these words, or take them on as a taboo-busting mantle of free expression. But as this term is usually directed at actual Jewish people and/or is used in reference to the actual Holocaust, it can be hard to see where the actual joke is.[16]

"Anti-racist is code for anti-white"

Another phrase plucked from old-school white nationalism. This one was invented by Robert Whittaker, a key proponent of the "white genocide" conspiracy theory.[17] Whittaker's killer line came at the end of a short blog post called "The Mantra,"[18] a short online far-right rant about the perceived lack of diversity in non-Western countries. "ASIA FOR THE ASIANS, AFRICA FOR THE AFRICANS, WHITE COUNTRIES FOR EVERYBODY!"

Whitaker blasted. He carried on with both the sweeping generalizations and the all-caps shouting: "Everybody says the final solution to this RACE problem is for EVERY white country and ONLY white countries to 'assimilate', i.e., intermarry, with all those non-whites."

Sometimes The Mantra is formulated as "Diversity is code word for white genocide." Anti-racists have taken down the idea, pointing out its logical inconsistencies, bad statistics (based on the "one drop" racial theory), and false assumptions.[19] But the real secret of The Mantra is in its execution of the alt-right disinformation strategy of painting the enemy as the opposite of what they are. According to the Anti-Defamation League:

> "The Mantra" attempts to rebut accusations of racism by claiming that people who profess to be anti-racist are actually trying to destroy the white race and that the term "anti-racist" is equivalent to "anti-white." Whitaker's followers have convinced themselves that if they simply repeat The Mantra, or the slogan derived from it, that they can somehow capture or reframe debates about racism.[20]

The Mantra belongs to the more extreme alt-righters, and is another direct link to the more old-fashioned style of white nationalism. It's a favorite choice, for instance, for Ku Klux Klan activists who have money to spare to spend on billboard displays.[21]

Although it's often repeated on rank-and-file alt-right forums and social media accounts, not everyone is on board with the style of the message, even if they sympathize with the sentiments behind it. "It's bad rhetoric," said one commenter on Vox Day's blog. "How do we know this? Because it's not working."[22]

Autist
An autistic person. Can be used either pejoratively for someone who displays obsessive habits, or to attack someone of a different

political persuasion when they lash out in response to online abuse; or positively[23] in the case of people who doggedly Google until they find, for instance, the home phone numbers of feminists or anti-fascist activists which they then post on 4chan and 8chan. Like many scientific concepts the alt-right picks out, they can play fast and loose with studies in order to boost their cause, conflating young male obsessions with computers and role-playing games with autism, or even, in the case of one blogger, twisting brain research on autism, which disproportionately affects males, into an argument which denies the existence of discrimination in the workplace.[24]

Channers who like to sling around the word have also invented terms like "autistic screeching," which, like "virtue signaling" (see below), can mean anything from digital tantruming to the simple fact of stating a belief in public. Unusually for a movement with a professed devotion to free speech, the alt-right hates that sort of thing.[25]

Centipedes
A supporter of Donald Trump. This term is derived from a YouTube mash-up of Republican primary debate footage of Trump and audio from a nature film of a centipede killing a tarantula. Subscribers to the Reddit forum r/The_Donald are called "centipedes" or "pedes," and one of their favorite slogans is "Can't Stump the Trump."[26]

Chimpout
Any sort of notable act by a black person or group of black people—anything from a peaceful protest to a violent crime. Or as one definition had it: "An event that occurs when there's a nigger."[27]

The term shows up on neo-Nazi websites and can function as something of a litmus test. The hard-core straight-up fascist wing that wants to claim the whole of the alt-right as their own—typified by sites like the neo-Nazi Daily Stormer—regularly use the term alongside pictures of monkeys or deliberately offensive caricatures of black people.[28]

Alt-lighters skip the gratuitous racism and just deploy the phrase as a dog whistle, describing, for instance, protests by journalists or leftists in general, in a wan attempt to dilute the clear racist roots of the term. And they also use the ironic alt-right rhetorical trick—i.e., claim it's just a joke.

Crybully
A person who simultaneously complains and uses his or her victim status to try to boss people around. The alt-right uses this one exclusively against the left, and fails to see how it might apply to a group of people who claim victimhood when their absolute freedom of speech is being impinged upon, and send death threats to nasty evil SJWs[29] (see below).

Cuckservative/Cuck
Cuck is one of the most popular alt-right insults and one which has crossed into the mainstream. But it also has a very telling and little-mentioned etymology.

The word is most often directed at mainstream conservatives, sometimes at "virtue signaling" liberals, often white men who are standing up for some minority person or group.

In literal terms, "cuckold" is a medieval insult, meaning a man whose wife has had sex with another man. Alt-righters tend to be more familiar with porn than Chaucer though, and they're referencing a specific pornographic genre that usually has a racial element. Dana Schwartz, writing for *GQ*, put it both delicately and accurately:

> The cultural importance of the cuckold in America is rooted in racism: in pornography, the wife of the cuckolded (almost exclusively white) husband is most commonly sleeping with African-American men, meant to provide an additional layer of humiliation if the white husband sees that man as "inferior."

In the world of pornography meant to elicit humiliation as an erotic sentiment, cuckold porn takes advantage of its viewers' racist perceptions.[30]

When a channer calls someone a "cuck," they're saying that person is an inferior man who lets his partner sleep with men from an inferior race. In the transfer from the world of the chans to Reddit/Twitter to the mainstream media, the origins of the word—while not hidden—have not exactly been made, shall we say, *explicit* in most casual uses. And this is how it ends up being used on cable news programs without context.[31]

Cultural Marxism
Pretty much anything from the left of the political spectrum is at risk of being tarred by this particular brush: feminism, gay rights, birth control, socialism, atheism, relativism, environmentalism, immigration, multiculturalism. In the eyes of the movement, it's an all-encompassing conspiracy being driven by an uncertain cabal—depending on which branch of the alt-right is speaking, the plot is a subversive one pushed by bankers, Jews, leftist intellectuals, the establishment, the deep state, or any number or combination of groups or sub-groups that come under the vast umbrella of the Cathedral.

As you can imagine, a conspiracy theory this vast, with so many sources, variations and end products, is almost infinitely malleable. It can be deployed by hard-core neo-Nazis writing stories with titles like "The Jews Behind Pro-Globalist Super Bowl Advertisements,"[32] or by mainstream conservatives such as the editor of the British *Daily Mail*.[33] Scholars have traced it back to the Frankfurt School of philosophy and to the "cultural Bolshevism" (*Kulturbolschewismus*) criticized by the Nazis.[34]

Of course, most channers aren't thinking deeply about the philosophy of Walter Benjamin when they trot out this argument. Instead they are simply saying they dislike stuff that liberals embrace, and implying some sort of shifty motive behind often earnestly held beliefs. The phrase itself took off in the 1990s, and shouts of "cultural Marxism" show the alt-right at its most blinkered: arguing that an obscure group of philosophers or assistant professors in sociology departments have been the driving political force of modern times, rather than Silicon Valley entrepreneurs, banking CEOs, diplomats or neoconservatives.[35]

Degenerate

Someone who keeps the company of races other than their own, or a homosexual, or someone with a perceived sexual perversion. Another all-purpose insult, this one applies to morality, and is another point of division in the movement. Traditionalists and overt racists use it to slam others as "alt-light" opportunists, while gay alt-righters and those who would rather put the emphasis on libertarian and freedom of speech issues sometimes proudly take it on as a mark of separation from the far right.

In one typical use dating from 2014, Richard Spencer wrote: "Martin Luther King Jr., a fraud and degenerate in his life, has become the symbol and cynosure of White Dispossession and the deconstruction of Occidental civilization. We must overcome!"[36]

Dindu nuffin/"Dindu"

"Didn't do nothing," transliterated into a cod African-American ergot. It's usually used as a noun describing a black criminal. There's a rough equivalent to describe Muslims: "alahu snackbar," but, perhaps tellingly, no real alt-right analogue for white people.

(((echo)))

This method of pointing out a Jewish person's heritage began as an audio effect on alt-right podcast The Daily Shoah (a sideways reference to "Anudda Shoah," see above). When mentioning a Jewish or Jewish-sounding surname, the podcast producers would layer on an echo effect. The alt-right blog The Right Stuff, which puts out the podcast, rather cryptically describes it like this: "All Jewish surnames echo throughout history. The echoes repeat the sad tale as they communicate the emotional lessons of our great white sins, imploring us to Never Forget the 6 GoRillion."[37]

During the summer of 2016, Jewish journalists began noticing that alt-righters were typing their names in parenthesis—(((like this)))—in a written simulation of the sound effect.[38] Some tagged with such punctuation got an extra helping of anti-Semitism in the form of death threats and Photoshopped pictures of themselves in concentration camps.

The point of all this, was of course the conspiratorial allegation that Jews wield conspiratorial influence and power over the world. An editor of the The Right Stuff explained:

> The inner parenthesis represent the Jews' subversion of the home [and] destruction of the family through mass-media degeneracy. The next [parenthesis] represents the destruction of the nation through mass immigration, and the outer [parenthesis] represents international Jewry and world Zionism.[39]

Fag

Everyone is a "fag" of some description to the alt-right, and again this flexible term can be used to denote gay people, or not, and can be used in a positive sense or a negative one. Avowed race warriors are "Stormfags"[40]—after the neo-Nazi website Stormfront. "Live action role-players"—and more broadly, people who are unserious about political activism—are LARPfags.[41]

It's a term that comes from chan culture, and the suffix -fag can be tacked on to pretty much any adjective to produce an instant alt-right denotation device.[42]

Fake nerd

Or "fake geek," or, in many cases "fake geek girl." A favorite of Gamergate fans who criticize the allegedly put-on gaming enthusiasm of women. Pointing out double standards or sexism, however, tends to trigger (see below) alt-right-leaning male gamers.[43]

Fashy

Short for "fascist"—usually in reference to clothing, hair (a fashy haircut is short on the sides, long on top, popular in 1930s Germany and 2010s hipster neighborhoods) or some other fashion or cultural signifier.[44]

Fashy style serves two different purposes—distinguishing the alt-right from thuggish white nationalists in hoods or biker jackets or covered with tattoos, and mainstreaming the bearers of otherwise toxic ideas. A number of serious news outlets have remarked, with some surprise, about how Richard Spencer and other alt-righters are dapper and well-dressed compared to old-school white race warriors.[45]

The fashy haircut in particular also demonstrates the alt-right's shrewd co-option of popular trends. As the movement has very little cultural production outside of internet memes, it borrows pop culture with a wink, knowing that trying to repaint (to take a few examples) the "OK" hand symbol, Taylor Swift, and even milk drinking as an "alt-right thing" will cause certain sections of the media to freak out. And once a few stories appear online, the co-opt technique might for a minute sow doubt in liberal enclaves: is that guy with the haircut a hipster, or an alt-right type? Sneaky.

God Emperor

A jokey reference to Donald Trump and a jumping-off point for hundreds of memes: Trump in a full suit of golden armor, Trump as a Roman centurion, Trump as an American founding father, Trump as Jesus.[46] The Trump hero worship is over-the-top, often intentionally hilarious, but at the same time demonstrates just how strongly the movement has yoked its fortunes to one particular politician.

Human biodiversity (HBD)/Race realism
As mentioned earlier, a cornerstone of alt-right thought. In the normie world (see below), it goes by the name "scientific racism." "Race realists" assign broad intelligence averages across groups to whole populations. Environmental effects and epigenetics are ignored. Racial interbreeding with "lower" groups is seen as automatically reducing intelligence—feeding into the hysteria over cuckolds.

Some alt-righters insist that "both sides" of the debate over race and intelligence should be reflected, arguing for false equivalence in the same way that conspiracy theorists demand that scientists and journalists give credence to their fringe arguments.[47]

Others just swallow and regurgitate the arguments, and pretty much everyone playing the HBD game shows a profound ignorance of the significance of IQ tests.[48] In the alternative-fact world of race realism, such tests are held up as an entirely objective measure of inherent qualities, as completely unaffected by external circumstances, and as near-perfect indicators of economic success on both an individual and societal level.

When it comes to IQ in particular, the alt-right imagines a specific, rigid, scientifically unsound racial hierarchy which goes something like this: Asians and Ashkenazi Jews are at the top, non-Jewish whites just slightly below them, Arabs way below, and blacks at the bottom.

Or, as one channer less-than-eloquently put it (sharply undermining his own argument?!), alongside a picture of pseudoscientific race-based charts: "It's not necessarily race it's iq and niggers are really dumb and 90% need to die over 5 generations for blacks to be like whites."[49]

huWyte
A celebratory transcription of the way alt-right intellectual hero Jared Taylor pronounces the word "white." Taylor has an unusual accent, most likely the product of early life in Japan and (perhaps

oddly for someone who's a hero of "anti-globalists") a life spent in a number of different countries and cities around the world.[50]

Taylor founded *American Renaissance*, a magazine that predates the alt-right by a couple of decades, to serve as a vehicle to promote the interests of white people under the banner of "race realism" (see below). In recent times it has been comprised mostly of wholesale copy-and-paste jobs from mainstream media sites, often with an added tagline for some extra racial spin.[51]

There are also far-right commentaries from a range of crusty paleoconservatives. After Hurricane Katrina, Taylor wrote: "Blacks and whites are different. When blacks are left entirely to their own devices, Western civilization—any kind of civilization—disappears." The extract is typical of the kind of stuff which can be found on American Renaissance.[52]

Taylor also serves as a spokesperson for the Council of Conservative Citizens, a pro-segregation group that inspired Dylann Roof, who murdered nine African-American worshippers in a church in Charleston, South Carolina in June 2015. Roof's manifesto mentions the group, and in a statement, the council said the slaughter was an example of "the danger of denying the extent of black-on-white crime." "We utterly condemn Roof's despicable killings, but they do not detract in the slightest from the legitimacy of some of the positions he has expressed."[53]

Kek

A noise of mirth, laughter and triumph, and also, a shifty god-like figure. The word originally came from the online game World of Warcraft—when one group of players typed "lol," the game's software would spit out "kek." It was a not-very-political part of internet culture for years before it was appropriated, like a clutch of other geeky things, by the alt-right. "Kek" might be the best example of the alt-right's playful, unserious, childish side, something that sharply distinguishes it from previous generations of white nationalists. Kek was an ancient Egyptian god of darkness,[54] sometimes depicted as a frog—coincidences that are catnip for pattern-seeking alt-righter pranksters and which have been teased out into a tongue-in-cheek "cult of Kek" and a campaign to get "Kekistani"[55] listed as an ethnic group in the British census.

The kek fandom sniffed out other cultural references—for instance, there's a popular Turkish cake with the brand name "Topkek"—and endlessly remixed and reworked them into YouTube videos and Photoshopped memes. You can imagine the quiver of excitement when the first alt-righter discovered that an unheralded Italian disco band from the 1980s had once released a song called "P.E.P.E." and that the vinyl single even had a picture of a frog on it. The band's name, Shadilay,[56] became a sort of greeting or Amen amongst the cult of Kek, and joking proof of "meme magic" (see below).

Libtard/shitlib

Clunky insults meant to apply to less-intelligent liberals,[57] these words are generally chucked at anyone from the left and anyone who dares to express political views out of step with the alt-righters. These are terms which function suspiciously like "racist" or "sexist" on the other side—meant to shut down debate and put the original speaker into a box from which they cannot escape. Also in common with their rivals on the opposite side of the political spectrum, alt-righters have a tendency to focus on the most extreme, egregious and unreflexive arguments made by the other side when slinging the "lib" labels.

Meme magic

The idea that thousands of YouTube videos, GIFs and pictures with witty captions can swing an election and affect the course of history, and even have an effect on things like the weather. Again this is a concept that is taken with highly varying levels of seriousness by the alt-right itself. And those who dare to accuse an alt-righter of actually thinking that memes can cause thunderstorms are setting themselves up to be laughed at with maximum kek.

In terms of the impact on the 2016 election, three of the most experienced academic researchers on trolling mostly dismissed the notion of meme magic:

> It is certainly true that the alt-right's pro-Trump "shitposting"— the act of flooding social media with memes and commentary designed to bolster their "God Emperor" Trump—raised the public visibility of the alt-right and its memetic handiwork. And it is also true that this uptick in public visibility forced people to focus on Trump more than they would have otherwise...
>
> But that activity didn't happen in a vacuum, and wasn't self-propelling. "Trolls" and the alt-right may have played a prominent role in the 2016 election, but that fact is dependent upon and cannot be untangled from journalistic coverage that amplified their messaging—shitpost memes very much included.[58]

On the other hand, you're reading this book. Indeed, any real power derived from meme magic seems to be strictly perceptual—in other words, it's entirely plausible that the alt-right only has any influence at all when reports suggest that they might. This could explain why attempts to export the "Great Meme War" to elections in Europe have largely fallen flat—while countries throughout Europe have substantial alt-right cohorts and sympathizers, they've often failed to coalesce or to get quite the same amount of attention as their American counterparts.[59]

The raw statistics of the 2016 election tell a confusing narrative. If the efforts of the channers and all the other alt-right factions were effective, you might have expected Trump to increase his share of the white vote, the youth vote, the college-educated vote and the male vote. The biggest preliminary exit poll showed that his share of the white vote barely budged compared to that of Republican Mitt Romney in 2012 (Trump made much bigger percentage gains among Asians, Hispanics and blacks). Under-30s shifted towards the Republican, and so did men, but increasing education level corresponded to increased support for Hillary Clinton.[60]

Meme magic, it seems, is not only difficult to measure, but probably doesn't exist at all.

Misandry

According to the anti-feminists, this is the most serious gender issue in Western society today. The evidence they point to for this theory is varied, sometimes comes from scientific or social attitude polls, and is often developed from a grain of truth: for instance the statistics which show that more women graduate from university than men.[61] The meninist crowd also love to point to surveys which, for instance, indicate that men are the targets of a disproportionate amount of online abuse, while at the same time glossing over much of the fine detail about the nature and extent of harassment.[62]

Alt-righters point to these often flimsy examples as proof of structural bias against men, mirroring feminist arguments about things like the male–female pay gap. Interestingly, while quantifying and explaining the gender pay gap is an extremely complicated thing, alt-righters are often again happy to dispense with nuance and dismiss it as exaggerated, non-existent, or a conspiracy theory.[63]

Other alleged cases of man-hate are less rooted in hard numbers or reality. Men's rights activists argue that men are discriminated against in hiring or that fake rape claims are rife— more generally that feminism "has gone too far."[64] And they particularly love finding women who agree with them.[65]

For the misandry brigade,[66] feminists are to blame for the second-class status of men. But unlike their counterparts on the left, they are rarely compelled to do anything about it.

Occasionally I seriously suggest to men's rights activists that they could help their cause by, say, supporting a local Boy Scout group, getting involved in grassroots mentoring organizations, volunteering at a sports club, or getting off Twitter and spending some time with a young male relative or friend. The reaction is rarely positive.

Normie

A normal person, someone who doesn't "get" internet culture or the alt-right, or who might slightly blanch upon viewing 4chan. Normies haven't yet taken the "red pill." "Normie" has a slightly larger meaning in the broader internet universe as a bland vanilla person with mainstream tastes, and people who congregate on all sorts of message boards and Reddit forums, from the chans to obscure music websites, snicker at those who aren't part of their subculture.[67]

A normie might, for instance, be an unironic Taylor Swift fan rather than getting into the singer because, as one alt-right meme goes, she's secretly a white nationalist (just to be 100 percent clear, there's no truth to this particular joke[68]). Male normies are sometimes called "Chads," another term of derision borrowed from the pick-up-artist community.[69] Chad is portrayed as a strapping, straight-arrow, unthinking all-American dude—complete with a counterpart girlfriend dubbed "Stacy"—who's blissfully unaware of red pills, meninist politics or PUA tactics.

The alt-right's entry into electoral politics via Donald Trump presented them with a quandary when it came to normies—they realized that for their ideas to have real impact, they need to start converting on a massive scale people who are ignorant of 4chan, and they began devising schemes to gradually convert Chads to the alt-right. "Say '65 million migrants since 1965,' and then point out which COUNTRIES/REGIONS those migrants have come from," wrote one Reddit user. "Do not say what race or what IQ they are. That is too much for the Normie mind."[70]

Overton Window

As mentioned earlier, this refers to the relatively narrow range of public policy ideas that are considered politically acceptable. The concept was invented by Joseph Overton, who worked at a little-known free-market think-tank in Michigan. The right latched onto the idea and particularly Overton's notion that the window can be adjusted or moved over time, simply by talking about prescriptions outside normal discourse.

The Overton Window has a certain common-sense appeal, and, taking the long view, it's easy to see how certain once-radical ideas became mainstream. In the 1990s you could for instance pick up the radical anti-consumerist magazine *Adbusters* and read about the crazy idea that cigarettes should only be sold in plain unbranded packages, to remove the cool cachet of smoking. That once far-out idea is now law in Britain and other countries.[71] From the right, Brexit is another good example of a large shift in public thinking.[72]

And so, through Curtis Yarvin's Unqualified Reservations and other channels, the Overton Window idea gained currency on the right—Glenn Beck wrote a best-selling novel by the same name.

The idea is also trotted out to explain to some degree why the anti-establishment alt-right fell in love with a billionaire businessman named Trump. By calling for a Muslim ban and a huge border wall, he was seen as smashing the politically correct elite consensus and yanking the window towards their end of the spectrum (at the same time, a parallel movement was happening on the left in the US and the UK, with the insurgent campaigns of Bernie Sanders and Jeremy Corbyn).

By 2016 the idea of the Overton Window was common not only on alt-right-friendly blogs and places like Breitbart, but was a favorite of commentators across the political spectrum, even though others were pointing out its flawed assumptions about the nature of the center of political discourse.[73] For instance, it's far from clear whether there's much evidence that, particularly in the short term, radical proposals really do shift public policy one way or the other, rather than just appealing to citizens at one end of the political spectrum or a rump of people who feel they've been shut out from the mainstream.[74]

In *New Republic*, Laura Marsh wrote:

> While Trump has certainly lowered the standard of debate on the right, he didn't have to move the consensus rightward; he played to a bloc of voters who already found his proposals desirable. Sanders, too, connected with bottom-up movements such as the Fight for $15 and Occupy Wall Street. To chalk up their successes to shock tactics is to ignore the long-simmering populism that swept both right and left in the presidential primaries. It is impossible to understand what drives these movements without engaging with the economic and cultural circumstances that underpin them.[75]

In fact the Overton Window is an example of pop political science. It's barely mentioned in the academic literature,[76] is most often cited in commentary and, despite its common-sense appeal, is less a real theory than a sort of—in the words of one political scientist blogger—"vague assertion."[77] While there are many academics who point out the limits to acceptable discourse and examine how such limits can be shifted, the Overton Window is an oversimplified conjecture taken to ridiculous and unscientific extremes to bolster the alt-right worldview. It's just not a fact, as some 4channers would argue, that a Trump tweet or an internet comment thread can move the needle of political debate in any discernible way.

Like the "red pill/blue pill" concept, the Overton Window seems to describe the patterns of thinking of a group of individuals rather than a general theory of political change.

Pepe

The cartoon frog that became the mascot of the alt-right. Pepe has a kek-like backstory—originally a non-political bit of internet culture, he was adopted by the alt-right and, as they began to get mainstream attention during the Trump campaign, became almost exclusively tied to the movement (at least in the minds of normies), to the extent that the Anti-Defamation League called the amphibian a hate symbol.[78]

Pepe is so ancient in internet terms that he began life on the coolest social network *circa* 2005: MySpace. An American comic artist, Matt Furie, first drew him as part of an online zine called "Boy's Club." Pepe was sort of an archetypal stoner or slacker, and had a catchphrase: "feels good man." There was really not a whole lot more to it than that, but he developed something of a cult following on early 4chan. The connection between the alt-right and the frog was solidified in October 2015 when Trump tweeted out a meme of himself as Pepe, like some sort of ghoulish green David Ickeian nightmare.[79]

It's unclear whether Trump's campaign knew much about the frog or its origins. Since then, however, there have been countless alt-right Pepe permutations—showing the frog as a caricature of a Jew, a black person, a Nazi concentration camp guard, a Ku Klux Klan member, and many other characters beside.[80]

Channers mocked the Pepe moral panic—how could a sad green frog be a white nationalist symbol? Even after Trump's election, alt-righters would continue to mock journalists and experts who pointed out Pepe's use by the far right.[81] To be sure, most deployments of Pepe are a joke—the meme can be seen as just one massive playful bit of internet culture. But that doesn't stop troll armies from sending cartoon frogs dressed in German military uniforms to Jewish journalists.

No matter the amount of coordination or directed purpose behind it, Pepe has become political. Is he a complicated little green blob? Yes. Is he sometimes joking? Yes. Is he alt-right? Now, definitely.[82]

Shitposting

A sort of heavy-duty brand of trolling—posting extreme content (or extreme amounts of it) in an attempt to derail a discussion or make a message board unusable. Despite the scatology, it's not seen as necessarily a bad thing—as part of their rejection of norms and their self-perception as rebels, the alt-right sees shitposting as a useful tactic in political discourse. The movement takes trolling so seriously that rumors even swirled of a pro-Trump group with a high-profile Silicon Valley backer dedicated to proving "that shitposting is powerful and meme magic is real"—although there's not much evidence the group actually did anything.

On the face of it, shitposting is just another annoying alt-righter tactic and probably a rhetorical dead end—always annoying, rarely clever—although some observers see something more nefarious developing. "Shitposting, whether from the left or right, is perilously close to delivering an online metastasis of Orwell's Two-minute Hate," said one,[83] while another lamented: "Maybe the 2020 election would be all shitposting."[84]

Snowflake

A precious, emotionally vulnerable person, usually a millennial and usually a social justice warrior (see below). If you're offended or call for a "trigger warning," you might be a snowflake.[85]

In the novel *Fight Club*, Chuck Palahniuk put the following words into his protagonist's mouth: "You are not special. You are not a beautiful and unique snowflake." The film, with its aggressive violence, heavy questioning of reality and normie life, and fuck-you to the establishment in the form of the climactic destructive scene, rivals *The Matrix* as an alt-right cultural touchstone.

Alt-righters put some of the blame for the climate of political correctness on teachers who have mollycoddled their students, refraining from criticism and making their young charges unable to deal with speech that threatens their worldview. But the insult has also been generalized, becoming an all-purpose sticker for people who claim to be offended or, more broadly, push for a liberal agenda or express some sort of emotion in defense of their political views.

Social Justice Warrior/"SJW"

Simply, someone who pushes for equality in some arena of human endeavor. "Social justice warrior" is the go-to alt-right slur for anyone on the left.[86] Like "politically correct," it's a phrase that on the face of it doesn't necessarily sound particularly pejorative, but is almost always used in a negative way.

The etymology of the term is interesting. There were a few scattered mentions of the phrase in printed citations dating from the 1990s, and those were mostly positive. "Social justice warrior dies" read a headline on an obituary of a Houston minister in 1992.[87] But well before it went into common use on the alt-right during Gamergate, the connotation of "social justice warrior" had completely flipped.[88]

"SJW" is the ultimate "you-do-it-too" alt-right insult—the stereotypical social justice warrior is obsessed with identity, easily triggered, politically voracious, and willing to engage in all sorts of nasty tactics to push their point online. One libertarian pointed out the similarities between the two groups:

The Alt-Right is an ill-tempered movement of people that feel victimized, ignored, abused, and are fighting for attention. Their tactics include shaming, bullying, and ruthlessness that they justify with a sense of moral righteousness.

Social Justice Warriors are an ill-tempered movement of people that feel victimized, ignored, abused, and are fighting for attention. Their tactics include shaming, bullying, and ruthlessness that they justify with a sense of moral righteousness.[89]

Another blogger with a mainstream conservative site put it more succinctly in a headline: "The only difference between SJWs and alt-righters is which identities they hate."[90] While this is overstating the case—it's hard to identify a simple parallel of radicalization which links "SJWs" to regular violent extremism—it does sharply point out the obsession with identity politics that consumes both of these amorphous internet subcultures.

Trigger

Simply: to upset. The idea of a "trigger warning" began as an authentic and widespread idea from the campus left, with the acknowledgement that some discussions may be distressing to people who have had traumatic experiences or suffer from post-traumatic stress disorder.

Trigger warnings come in all shapes and sizes, and are really nothing new. Media companies, for instance, routinely warn viewers if content is distressing or contains flashing lights of a kind that could cause a seizure in those with photosensitive epilepsy. Most countries classify films according to their content and whether they should be seen by children. But those aren't really the trigger warnings that the alt-right is concerned with. Instead they focus on a censorious movement that seeks to slap a label on anything from Ovid's *Metamorphoses* (which contains scenes of rape and oppression) to Chinua Achebe (for depictions of racial violence).

Amongst the academic left there's far from a unified view on trigger warnings. In 2015, the liberal academics Greg Lukianoff and Jonathan Haidt published a much-discussed article in *The Atlantic* titled "The Coddling of the American Mind," describing some outlandish examples and arguing that warnings actually hurt students: "Rather than trying to protect students from words and ideas that they will inevitably encounter, colleges should do all they can to equip students to thrive in a world full of words and ideas that they cannot control."[91] The article prompted reaction, some of it outraged, from other online portals and individuals on the left. But most alt-righters ignore any subtleties in such debate and insist on a universal—and universally evil—leftist juggernaut slapping trigger warnings on anything they dislike. To the "absolute free speech" crowd, any insinuation that speech needs a warning is an affront.

As a reaction, the more trollish elements actually see triggering—provoking a strong reaction from social justice warriors—as a goal. In March 2016, alt-righter Lauren Southern began a campaign with a tweet: "Can we start a day called 'The Triggering' where everyone just posts "offensive" things on their social media in defense of free speech?"[92] Southern's fans responded with messages like "There's no 'gender pay gap'—but there should be" and "Niggers always resort to violence," along with other, more reasonable, tweets ("I believe in free speech, freedom of expression and diversity of opinions (even yours)") and reactions from alt-right opponents.[93]

Even though it was mostly indistinguishable from any normal day of alt-right output on social media, the hashtag #TheTriggering did manage to briefly reach Twitter's top trends list, and prompted a number of similar campaigns.

Tumblrina
A sensitive, easily triggered social justice warrior who has an account on the social blogging network Tumblr. In her analysis of the symbiotic relationship between 4chan and Tumblr, Angela Nagle identifies Tumblr as one of the key nodes of "call-out culture" and campus-based identity politics—"in which everything from eating noodles to reading Shakespeare was declared 'problematic', and even the most mundane acts 'misogynist' and 'white supremacist'."

The "deplorables", from the Trumpian trolls to the alt-right, view the Hillary loyalists—the entrenched identity politics of Tumblr and the intersectional anti-free speech campus left— as evidence of their equally bleak view of a rapidly declining

Western civilization, as both sides have become increasingly unmoored to any cultural mainstream.[94]

The main agent of call-out culture and the object of alt-right hatred is the Tumblrina—a person usually portrayed as female, feminist, ugly, and fat. Reddit hosts a number of groups with thousands of members who trawl hashtags looking for outraged Tumblrinas who they in turn can get outraged by. One such subreddit, TumblrInAction, doles out "Special Snowflake" points for top posts and explains its purpose in cod SJW-speak:

> Seen a horribly oppressed transethnic otherkin blog their plight? Wept at how terrible it is for the suffering of multiple systems to go unheard every day? Been unable to even live with the thought of the identities of someone's headmates being cisdenied?
> Then you've come to the right place![95]

Rapefugee

A refugee who has committed a sexual assault—or, more generally, just a refugee. This mouthful of a term quickly found its way into public discourse on conservative websites[96] and a Twitter hashtag, particularly after the rash of sexual assaults in German cities on New Year's Eve 2015.[97] In the aftermath of those attacks and other reports of sexual assaults by migrants who had recently arrived in Europe, memes began circulating amongst the alt-right warning of a huge tide of crime and lawlessness brought along with the refugees.[98]

Rape by a strange brown foreigner is a basic trigger for the alt-right, feeding directly into the previously discussed fear of cuckoldry, but the Cologne incident also presented something of a quandary for the movement, with an anti-immigrant story coming up against a tale of violence against women.[99] Would the manosphere's obsession with false rape claims trump the political capital to be made by blaming the attacks on Islam?

One prominent men's rights blog ran a post with the headline "Questioning the Rape Narrative in Cologne, Germany":

Last weekend we were treated to "news" on social media that a thousand Muslim men had descended upon Cologne Germany and, while shooting fireworks in their faces to disfigure them, raped 100 women. The tale was somewhat confirmed by Breitbart and other sources, but amazingly, many of the reports of even "sexual assault" turn out to be unconfirmed and in many cases to have been attempts at harassment and intimidation, but are certainly not rape or severe sexual assault.[100]

But while a few alt-righters came out to question the narrative and suggest that maybe Germany's women were in the grip of a mass delusion, the loudest voices blamed feminists and the mainstream media for failing to denounce the attacks in strong enough terms. Many, pointing to delayed reactions by the police and the German media, argued that there had been an establishment cover-up. Feminism had shown its true colors, they said, as a conspiracy solely targeted against white men.[101] The rapefugee was born, and from Cologne onwards the alt-right would jump upon any reports of crime, particularly sexual crime, allegedly committed by migrants to Europe. It was a theme that worked its way into the Trump White House, notably in February 2017, when the president made a garbled reference to reports of crime and terror: "We've got to keep our country safe. You look at what's happening in Germany, you look at what's happening last night in Sweden."[102]

Regressive left
Someone who has become so liberal or into identity politics that they have turned their back on freedom of thought and speech. The term appears to have been coined by Maajid Nawaz, a former radical Islamist who turned his back on extremism and criticized

"an inherent hesitation to challenge some of the bigotry that can occur within minority communities ... for the sake of political correctness, for the sake of tolerating what they believe is other cultures and respecting different lifestyles."[103]

The term was mainly used by liberal free speech advocates and journalists until late 2015, when it was picked up and memefied by the alt-right. At the same time it lost its specific meaning regarding liberals and Islam and became more of a general anti-SJW rant, applicable to anything from Bernie Sanders to calls for more trigger warnings.

Buzzfeed reporter Joseph Bernstein observed: "It's become a catchall for any element of the dominant new media culture that the anti-SJW internet doesn't like."[104]

Virtue signal

Initially this was a conspicuous message sent by someone with the specific intent to curry favor with social justice warriors, but has since come to mean any message deemed to be somehow pandering to people who may hold progressive values—like, say, a Super Bowl car commercial that raised the issue of the gender pay gap.[105] The term originally came from a branch of evolutionary biology as a way of explaining why people might express unselfish views—to establish their place in a group with a moral purpose, is the short answer.[106]

The alt-right usage most often implies both hypocrisy and keyboard-warriorism of the worst sort, which is interesting considering the movement it springs from ("Is calling out a virtue signal itself a virtue signal?" is a question that leads you down the rabbit hole).

More generally, the phrase capitalizes on the eye-rolling frustration that millions of us feel when we see people pump out social media inanities about huge, world-level events like wars, populist revolutions or terrorist rampages.[107] The posturing of social media personalities has been enough to give the term a level of currency among a larger audience. You don't have to be alt-right to get annoyed at people "showing off to [their] friends how right-on [they] are."[108]

And yet the sinfulness of virtue signaling has been inflated to a degree where the phrase is both approaching meaninglessness and demonstrating the poor logical follow-through of alt-righters online. David Shariatmadari spelled it out in *The Guardian*: "Anyone who makes an argument that casts them in a good light can be accused of 'virtue-signaling'":

In many cases, the thinking goes like this (with the left a frequent target):

1. Bill is saying something right-on
2. Virtue-signaling is when you say something right-on just to sound good
3. Therefore Bill is virtue-signaling

But 3. is not justified by 1. and 2. You can argue for something that happens to make you look virtuous because you genuinely think it is the best solution. ...

What started off as a clever way to win arguments has become a lazy put down. It's too often used to cast aspersions on opponents as an alternative to rebutting their arguments. In fact, it's becoming indistinguishable from the thing it was designed to call out: smug posturing from a position of self-appointed authority.[109]

* * *

Even as I write, the language of the alt-right is shifting, expanding and sometimes creeping into mainstream discourse. It was unremarkable during the last stages of the 2016 presidential election to hear the word "cuck" thrown around on cable news discussion shows, albeit usually with a halting explanation or a stab at context. The words activists use are reflective of their preoccupations and subtle attempts to shift mainstream political discourse. And although they hate the mainstream media, they crave attention and validation—especially the repetition of their in-language on popular platforms.[110]

But behind the craving for publicity, the freewheeling playfulness and the angry verbosity, there may be more going on here than just an internet subculture developing some tough-to-decipher lingo and trying to surreptitiously slip it into the mainstream. Cognitive linguist George Lakoff sees dark parallels with another race-conscious movement.[111] Whether in jest or not, the alt-right doesn't even shy away from the Nazi connotations, even plucking phrases like "degenerate" from Germany's dark past.

"The strategy is to control discourse," Lakoff told the *Washington Post*. "One way you do that is preemptive name calling … based on a moral hierarchy. … God above man, man above nature, men above women. The strong above the weak. Christians above gays." An alt-righter might put it like this: men above feminists. The red pilled above the blue pilled. Nationalists above virtue-signaling social justice warriors. The *Post* story continued:

> Lakoff emphasized that this is different from the Democrats' labeling some conservatives racist, sexist or homophobic— which they do—if only because that usage is not as "canny" or strategic.
>
> "Take Donald Trump's repeated characterization of Hillary Clinton as 'Crooked Hillary,'" Lakoff said. Say it often enough in public, and people start to believe it, and before you know it people such as Clinton are discredited. "The whole idea is not to be civil," Lakoff says. "The idea is to win."[112]

And that is the point of the alt-right's lexicon. The focus on winning, and the language and tactics which were developed in the pre-Trump years, brought them out of dusty think-tank offices and fringe academia and into mainstream prominence.

Framing politics as a life-or-death battle, and formulating an entire language within which their core concepts were embedded, attracted video gamers, alienated men and prank-loving channers.

And the alt-right's rise came just as a few people figured out a complimentary effective strategy for building a media brand in the social networking age—pick a highly engaged subgroup, feed it loads of red meat, and prioritize winning at all costs.

6
Media

The video is—unintentionally—hilarious. It starts with 20 seconds of a producer mumbling unintelligibly in the background while the two men in vision—Sean Spicer, who at the time was the White House press secretary, and a reporter from Breitbart—fidget awkwardly. Suddenly the producer says "Oh, nope—we're live now," and the reporter moves his mouth for a bit before finally springing into action. He stumbles through an introduction before launching a softball question at Spicer about a court ruling which struck down President Trump's ban on visitors from predominately Muslim countries.[1]

"What can you tell us about this?" the reporter asks. Spicer recites some boilerplate while the screen randomly flicks through awkward close-ups of each of the men in turn. The audio sounds as if it has been recorded in a swimming pool, and halfway through the video, the cameraperson walks shakily towards the subjects. After a few more jarring cutaways and Spicer's mild insistence that "we did what was in the best interest of this country," the video finally ends, after an excruciating two and a half minutes.

The *Washington Post* called it "the most awkward thing ever"[2] and it became a roundly mocked mini-sensation online, with half a million views on Facebook. One journalist put it like this: "In just two minutes, it captures so much about what's weird about the media today: the populist-white-nationalist paranoia, the sycophantic bids for access to power, the skin-crawling awkwardness with which journalists are approaching new technologies and platforms, the bizarre spectacle of Sean Spicer himself."[3]

Even in the mind-melting era of Trump, this particular incident was a standout example of how the world—or at least the media world—has changed. Never mind the execution of it, the fact that Breitbart was given an exclusive with Spicer demonstrated how this formerly obscure conservative news site had become a major player in the media landscape.

Breitbart was getting access to the White House that other, much bigger media outlets were routinely denied because its former executive editor was serving as President Trump's top advisor. During the summer of 2016, Stephen Bannon bragged to a reporter from the left-wing magazine *Mother Jones* that his site had become "the platform for the alt-right." At the same time, however, he seemed a bit hazy about the movement's core values:

> "Look, are there some people that are white nationalists that are attracted to some of the philosophies of the alt-right? Maybe," he says. "Are there some people that are anti-Semitic that are attracted? Maybe. Right? Maybe some people are attracted to the alt-right that are homophobes, right? But that's just like, there are certain elements of the progressive left and the hard left that attract certain elements."[4]

Despite Bannon's words, Breitbart would later kick back at descriptions that it was an "alt-right" website, lodging complaints with several major news organizations that used the label when defining the site.[5]

So what exactly is Breitbart, and how did it become "the platform for the alt-right"—and in fact a key node in the web of new alt-right and alt-lightish conservative media, around which the movement flowered?

* * *

The site began life in 2005 as an eponymous outlet for Andrew Breitbart. Breitbart the man was a conservative, but also a hired gun—he'd been involved in the Drudge Report and the launch of the Huffington Post. In its early days his website collected links, but it later morphed into a "news network" after launching sections devoted to "Big Government," "Big Hollywood," "Big Journalism" and opening bureaus in California, Texas, London, and Jerusalem.[6]

It built a reputation off the back of Andrew Breitbart's frequent appearances on cable news shows, his gleeful Twitter insult-slinging, and the posting of videos targeting liberal groups and politicians. One of its targets, the Association of Community Organizations for Reform Now, closed down[7] after a series of heavily edited undercover videos appeared to show employees condoning human trafficking.[8] Another story, also involving a heavily edited video, resulted in the resignation of a minor Obama administration official.[9] The site scored a major scoop in 2011,[10] when it exposed former Democratic congressman Anthony Wiener's sexting scandal.

Most of the time, however, the "Big" sites were rather staid lists of stories by mainstream conservatives along with a few oddballs and outliers. By Breitbart's current standards, the content was tame: inside-the-Beltway commentary, arranged in a straight-forward layout, with headlines using lower case letters rather than ALL CAPS. Liberals were attacked, sure, but there was also plenty of pointy-headed analysis and attempts at thoughtful cultural criticism.

At the same time, Andrew Breitbart's Twitter feed[11] was a stream of invective directed at Democrats and journalists, and he had a particular fondness for retweeting nastiness directed at himself. But despite the social media battles, Breitbart eschewed some of the wackier fringes of the conservative movement. For instance, at times his sites vehemently denounced the "birtherism"[12] of Donald Trump, who alleged that President Obama had not been born in the United States and thus was ineligible for America's highest elected office.[13]

Breitbart.com and its related sites were on a path to becoming the right-wing equivalent of the Huffington Post—a nimble new media start-up unencumbered by legacy costs or institutions, drawing a steady stream of traffic and poking at the establishment. Then, in 2012, Andrew Breitbart died of heart failure. Bannon became executive chairman. There were reports of infighting as the site backed Mitt Romney's failed—and rather conventional—campaign. A particularly bitchy Buzzfeed article outlined staffers' annoyance at Bannon and the new editor-in-chief, Joel Pollak:

> The staff reserves blame for Pollak and Bannon, who are viewed by some internally as opportunists parleying their position into personal prestige in Republican circles.
>
> Complained one staffer: "It has nothing to do with what Andrew stood for. I don't think he would even read the site or like it. I think he would detest what it's become."
>
> "Andrew wasn't a flack. He wanted to take them all on," said a former Breitbart employee, complaining that the site is now run by "partisan hacks."[14]

By 2012, the site was already something of a phenomenon on the right. Buzzfeed pointed out that with 3 million page views a month, Breitbart was more popular than conservative websites like The Daily Caller and the Weekly Standard, although its traffic stood at about a tenth of the Huffington Post. It was still very much a niche player, a role it continued to play as it developed a more aggressive style.[15]

Then came Trump, and the alt-right. Breitbart took off.

* * *

In the autumn of 2016, after Bannon was appointed Trump's campaign chief and navigated the teetering organization to a surprising victory, journalists from a number of news organizations threw together collections of Breitbart's most offensive headlines. A few appeared in nearly all of the lists, for example:

BIRTH CONTROL MAKES WOMEN UNATTRACTIVE AND CRAZY

BILL KRISTOL: REPUBLICAN SPOILER, RENEGADE JEW

WOULD YOU RATHER YOUR CHILD HAD FEMINISM OR CANCER?

HOIST IT HIGH AND PROUD: THE CONFEDERATE FLAG PROCLAIMS A GLORIOUS HERITAGE[16]

To be sure, obnoxious stories produced by people trying to be deliberately offensive was one strain of Breitbart content. "WOULD YOU RATHER YOUR CHILD HAD FEMINISM OR CANCER?"[17] is a short video of two students wandering around the University of Michigan campus posing the headlined question to baffled young people in a roundabout promotion of a debate between then-Breitbart editor Milo Yiannopoulos and the feminist Julie Bindel. In terms of production values it's a notch or so better than the Sean Spicer interview. "BIRTH CONTROL MAKES WOMEN UNATTRACTIVE AND CRAZY"[18] was written by Yiannopoulos—it's a sort of satirical story citing a bunch of scientific studies which supposedly support the headline's odd conclusion.[19]

The average reader, living outside the alt-right media bubble and who resists clicking on the links to these sensationalist splashes, might get the impression that Breitbart is a clickbaity opinion website written by trolls with a broken caps lock key who run around proclaiming with their Confederate flags, and think it makes perfect sense to compare political ideas to deadly diseases. But while it's tempting to draw that dismissive conclusion, it both obscures the site's real influence while serving up a caricature of a bully for a few satisfying whacks. During the Trump campaign Breitbart actually offered a mix of content including:

- straight news ripped from the wires (usually with a dollop or spin in a Breitbart-written headline)
- cherry-picked reporting designed to whack liberals, Muslims, or conservatives deemed not sufficiently conservative
- Scurrilous conservative opinion (including, but not limited to, pieces friendly to alt-right ideas)
- Satire or other half-serious, half-jokey attempts at humor along the lines of the BIRTH CONTROL article
- (Self-)congratulatory stories praising the site, Donald Trump, or conservatives who fit its brand of orthodoxy
- A lightly moderated user comment section that attracts all sorts of comments including content that wouldn't look out of place on r/The_Donald or 4chan. The comment section might well be what Bannon was referring to when he said his site was the "platform of the alt-right."[20]

To parse these categories, you have to do something that very few people ever do—go to the site itself, start clicking at the top, and work your way down. No Breitbart articles are labeled "news," "opinion," "satire" or otherwise. They're all mashed into one jumbled mass, given shouty headlines, and spat out on social media (where the site has been tremendously effective).

Although Breitbart's attitude towards individual politicians wavers over time—at one point it was producing stories in favor of Ted Cruz —its political leanings are more or less consistent. It's against immigration from the developing world to the West, and especially opposed to incomers from Muslim countries. It's anti-political correctness. It's skeptical of women's equality— albeit more in word than deed (several of its higher-profile reporters are female). It has a similar approach to elitism, and regularly rails against "globalists," which can include anyone from pro-free-trade Republicans to anarchists marching on European streets. At the same time, many of its highest-profile reporters are drawn from the same affluent pool that the rest of the media drinks from.

Breitbart clearly isn't a staid traditional news source shooting for objectivity or balance. On the other hand neither is it part of the "fake news" phenomenon—it doesn't pump out completely made-up stories designed purely to drive traffic. Breitbart journalists often deploy facts, but nearly always for specific political purposes. Its reporters claim they are simply doing what mainstream media outlets have always done, only being conscious, overt, and right-wing about it. They are up front about their biases, which resonate with and whip up their core audience. It's a messy, shouty tabloid mainlining hashtag steroids.

Patrick Howley, a former Breitbart reporter whose beat was the Hillary Clinton campaign, told me that the "the ethic of objectivity as it's traditionally formulated is not practiced there."[21] Howley resigned from Breitbart on the night of the US election. We spoke by phone a few days later, and he cheerfully explained that he left the organization because Breitbart had grown substantially in the time he was a reporter there, and he was interested in doing other things.[22] He told me that there was no written code of ethics or guidelines at the time he worked there.

He defended the spin by saying Breitbart reporters were at least up-front about their pro-Trump biases—unlike many mainstream media reporters who were rooting for Clinton but didn't or couldn't say so. "We are honest about it," he told me. "If you suspend objectivity you can build great sources and develop an audience and the information is all the same. ... I never made any pretense about the fact that I did not want Hillary Clinton to be president."[23]

But is all of the information really "all the same"? I looked at several Breitbart stories in some depth to try to understand how it operates. One in particular concerned a yogurt plant in Idaho. At first glance the subject appeared rather obscure for a politics-focused site: "TB SPIKED 500 PERCENT IN TWIN FALLS DURING 2012, AS CHOBANI YOGURT OPENED PLANT."[24] Tracing the origins of this story gives a bit of clarity about the Breitbart approach. Let's start with the company. Chobani is a trendy and phenomenally successful Greek-style yogurt brand invented by a Turkish immigrant to the United States by the name of Hamdi Ulukaya. Ulukaya bought a defunct dairy plant in upstate New York and grew it into a multi-billion-dollar business by perfecting and adapting an old family recipe.[25]

It's not unknown for conservative news outlets to heap praise on bootstrapping entrepreneurs who make vast fortunes and pledge to donate money to good causes.[26] But Ulukaya triggered Breitbart in the opposite direction, as his was the wrong kind of success story. He pledged to donate $2 million to help refugees and spoke at the World Economic Forum in Davos and at a Clinton Global Initiative event.[27] Perhaps worst of all, Ulukaya hired hundreds of refugees to work in his yogurt plants.[28]

In mid-2016, Breitbart sent a reporter from Texas to Idaho to write stories about Chobani. They had headlines like "TURKISH CHOBANI OWNER HAS DEEP TIES TO CLINTON GLOBAL INITIATIVE AND CLINTON CAMPAIGN." Breitbart stories about two cases of alleged sexual assault in the town attempted to link the Chobani case with three boys accused of the crime, who were reported to be refugees.[29] The boys had no apparent link to Chobani. Breitbart also attempted to link Chobani and refugees to disease. Thus: "TB SPIKED 500 PERCENT." But the story below that shocker didn't really back up the punchy headline:

> One case of active TB was diagnosed in the South Central Public Health District that includes Twin Falls in 2011, and six active TB cases were diagnosed there in 2012, the year Chobani opened the world's largest yogurt factory in the small southern Idaho city with the help of $54 million in federal, state, and local financial assistance.

There was one other problem with Breitbart's take on the terrifying tuberculosis outbreak that affected half a dozen people. The reporter left out a key fact: the Chobani yogurt plant didn't actually open until the very end of 2012.[30]

An employee of the Idaho Department of Health and Welfare told me in an email that all tuberculosis cases in the area were diagnosed prior to the plant opening, and since 2012, TB cases in the area had actually decreased. Tom Shanahan added that it's unlikely that the cases occurred in the refugee population, because refugees are subject to rigorous screening before arriving in the United States. "The numbers used by Breitbart came from us and are accurate, but their analysis of the numbers is weak. From a statistical standpoint, the rate did not 'spike dramatically' and labeling it as such was misleading," Shanahan said.

The Breitbart story was a political slur built on a trumped-up charge based on one itsy-bitsy statistical fact. But it and the rest of Breitbart's reporting was picked up by social media, other blogs and alt-righters who slung abuse at Ulukaya[31]—a string of events that culminated in a story on the conspiracy website Infowars headlined "Idaho Yogurt Maker Caught Importing Migrant Rapists."

Chobani sued. Infowars founder and dedicated conspiracy theorist Alex Jones—about whom, much more later—was forced to do something he hated: apologize.

* * *

The Idaho saga was just one example of how Breitbart operated once it settled on an enemy or a line of attack.[32] The site's selective approach applies not only to small towns and immigrant businessmen but also to big breaking news stories. Take for instance the murder of British Member of Parliament Jo Cox. It was a shocking outburst of political violence just days before the UK's referendum on EU membership. News outlets initially reported that the attacker had shouted out "Britain

First" as he stabbed and shot Cox to death—a slogan that was widely interpreted as either a reference to a fringe British far-right political party, or a general anti-foreign, perhaps anti-EU sentiment (Cox herself was a Labour Party MP and an advocate for remaining in the European Union—in the wake of her murder, more than a few alt-righters refused to express sympathy over the death of a "globalist").

Breitbart joined the fray. It ran a live blog[33] in the hours after the murder in an attempt to disassociate the killer, a man named Thomas Mair, from the far right—and indeed, from politics at all.

Cox had intervened in an argument between strangers, Breitbart reported: "If true, the report may suggest the attack was not necessarily targeted."[34] Other updates declared that a "Widely quoted local admits he didn't hear 'Britain First," highlighted the killer's history of mental illness, and quoted a local resident who said that Mair had no strong political views.

The site's attempts to keep Mair at arm's length from the far-right exceeded even Britain's most fervent anti-EU tabloids, some of which played down or cautiously reported details pertaining to the killer's potential motivations.[35] But soon the truth became unavoidable, and even Breitbart could not maintain the fiction of an apolitical, mentally ill man randomly attacking an MP. It swiftly came out that Mair had been in touch with extremist groups in South Africa and the United States. When he appeared in court, instead of identifying himself by name, he said: "death to traitors, freedom for Britain."

Breitbart pumped out stories— more than 30 in all in the week after Cox's murder[36]—several of which accused the pro-EU "Remain" campaign of using the killing for political ends:

REMAIN CAMPAIGNERS RUSH TO BLAME BREXIT FOR MP ATTACK[37]

JO COX FRIEND AND EYEWITNESS: "IMMORAL" FOR HER TO BE USED AS REFERENDUM TOKEN[38]

OFFICIAL REMAIN CAMPAIGN TELLS SUPPORTERS:
USE JO COX DEATH TO ATTACK BREXIT[39]

Meanwhile Breitbart's comments section spun into ever-greater levels of alt-right flavored conspiracy mongering (all *sic*):

"Do you think the attack is legit, or done as a false flag attack to demonize the group?"

"false flag has to be. When was the last time a MP was stabbed or shot."

"Who shouts ['Britain First']? A plant"

"Or made up by one of [the UK's] nefarious tabloids."

"It was made up by a muslim shopkeeper. What a surprise."

Given the intense effort devoted to covering Cox's murder, it might have been expected that Mair's subsequent trial would be of big interest to the Breitbart audience. And yet the site was largely done with the story. Unlike most of the rest of the British media, Breitbart gave only cursory coverage to the case, running two wire stories during the trial.[40] The concluding story made no mention of Mair's "Britain first" shout.

After the verdict, Breitbart London's executive editor James Delingpole weighed in. He acknowledged Mair's Nazi sympathies, but continued to cast doubts on his motivations, calling him a "random loon." "According to several reports at the time of the death—subsequently disputed—he is said to have shouted as he stabbed and shot Jo Cox 'Britain First, this is for Britain.'" Delingpole wrote.[41] The court was less equivocal. In fact, Mair had shouted:

"Britain first, this is for Britain.
"Britain will always come first.
"We are British independence.
"Make Britain independent."[42]

When a yogurt entrepreneur disagreed with Breitbart's worldview, he was attacked with dubious stories. When an assassination didn't fit into their frame, the solution for Breitbart appeared to be: seed doubt, try to ignore it, then heap on some doubt again.

* * *

Picking out a couple of examples of Breitbart's anti-immigrant, far-right-sympathetic agenda is like picking out a few of Donald Trump's tweets: there's a huge variety to choose from and you're going to run into some massive internal contradictions along the way. Although it's certainly not the case that all Breitbart writers and readers are aligned with the alt-right or even very friendly towards it, throughout the 2016 election campaign and beyond, the site's main preoccupations and agenda lined up neatly with the white genocide crowd on 4chan. And there was one person who solidified Breitbart's role in the emergence of the alt-right.

When I met Milo Yiannopoulos, he was clutching a Louis Vuitton handbag and looking slightly frantic. He was in high demand. He'd just been live on an edition of the BBC Radio 4 series *The Moral Maze*, talking about worldwide populist revolts, and I was now dragging him to another radio recording, this one specifically focusing on the alt-right. Although he always denied being a member of the movement, he had become one of its key apologists.

I ushered him into a lift and asked him how the first show had gone. The segment was a few minutes long, he shrugged: "Not nearly long enough to get into trouble." I pointed to his hat: a bright red baseball cap, on which was printed, not "MAKE AMERICA GREAT AGAIN," but the eagle, gun and flag motif of the National Rifle Association. "NRA LIFETIME MEMBER" it said. "Are you one?" I asked. He looked at me as if I had pointed out that he had exactly two eyes and one mouth. "Of course," he said. "I think everyone should be one."

* * *

Yiannopoulos was at the time Breitbart's senior technology editor, but he didn't—as that job title might imply—spend a lot of time investigating Google or reviewing new iPhones. A Catholic who is also part Jewish, half-Greek and flamboyantly—to put it very mildly—gay, he's a one-man industry, with a constant series of in-your-face lecture tours, a podcast, books, large followings on major social media platforms with the exception of Twitter— he was banned—and an extensive line of merchandise. He was one of the few activist-journalists connected to the alt-right who not only had a substantial platform and an online following, but who enthusiastically participated in trolling campaigns and willingly attached his own name to everything he participated in.

Yiannopoulos had obtained a very modern type of internet fame (his byline on Breitbart omitted his surname; like some sort of enigmatic rock star, he's known to fans only as "Milo"). He spent a few years in the early 2010s writing for tech websites that had sprung up in London. Friends at the time remember him as an only slightly more subdued version of his current personality—argumentative, headstrong, but not yet thoroughly marinated in the politics of the right.

At one point in 2011 he figured he could do better than a gigging freelance career and struck out along with some partners, creating a website called The Kernel. The business was a failure.[43] Around this time, his writing took a turn—he was, it seems, a megaphone looking for a movement.

At Breitbart he rose to prominence by bashing feminists during Gamergate and writing satirical pieces like the one about birth control. His relationship with channers and alt-right bloggers meant he was sent tips about liberal activists and feminists. For instance he cast doubt on the ethnic background of a Black Lives Matter activist, Shaun King, by citing a blogger who had dug up King's birth certificate. He had an instinct about what would rile his audience, which tidbits of news would really push their buttons, and compared the case of King to that of Rachel Dolezal.[44]

In another story dating from 2015, he uncovered the alleged pedophilic and white nationalist sympathies of a little-known critic of Gamergate.[45] Yiannopoulos, incidentally, would later be caught up in his own scandal over pedophilia comments.

The anti-feminism of Gamergate boosted Yiannopoulos's status and made him a hero among some gamers. Many alt-righters picked up his rhetoric and style. Here was someone who, despite his establishment roots, seemed part of their own imagined counterculture. He was gay, and thus his hatred of feminism and some women didn't spring from the same well as the pick-up-artist wing of the manosphere. He was a point of difference from stuffy Tories and Republicans with their outdated values and distaste of the more vulgar aspects of internet culture. And both personally and through his stories, he fed the "we are the real victims" narrative.

"Yiannopoulos's act is the political equivalent of an N.B.A. guard flopping in the hope of drawing a foul," wrote Jelani Cobb in *The New Yorker*, "a rendition of victimhood so aptly executed as to pass for the real thing."[46]

* * *

Back in the Radio 4 studio in the summer of 2016, Yiannopoulos was appearing on an episode of *The Briefing Room*, in the studio with me and presenter David Aaronovitch. It didn't take long for the conversation to get shouty. "Black Lives Matter is far worse (than the KKK)" Yiannopoulos said. He had successfully yanked the chain of thought away from racially charged memes by attacking his enemies. "They go after their own people. They leave black cities in flames because they're so self-destructive...."

He was gesticulating wildly. The conversation moved back to alt-righter pranksters: "What they're resisting is this constant hatred of the apocryphal straight white male of liberal journalism," he said.

> What they're saying is that you're constantly telling us white people are the source of all evil and that white people have all this stuff to apologize for. Well you know what, we're not that bad. We did some pretty good stuff. We did Mozart and Rembrandt and Descartes and Beethoven and Wagner, and we went to the stars, we explored the oceans, we built Western Civilization, we're not that bad.

Aaronovitch drolly observed: "Your 'we' shifted from being 'white males' to being 'western civilization'. Now that's an interesting conflation."[47]

* * *

If Gamergate agitation and alt-light sympathies had been all he brought to the party, we probably wouldn't have invited Yiannopoulos into that radio studio. But there was more to it than that. His key contribution to the movement was a galvanizing story he co-authored in March 2016 with Breitbart colleague Allum Bokhari.[48] The headline was "AN ESTABLISH-MENT CONSERVATIVE'S GUIDE TO THE ALT-RIGHT," and it was illustrated with a depiction of Pepe the Frog hovering over a scared elephant and a tombstone with an inscription reading "GOP 2016."[49] The story would become perhaps the most widely cited article about the movement—a first reference for journalists attempting to get their head around the alt-right, and a foundational document for channer activists.

Bokhari and Yiannopoulos wrote:

> A specter is haunting the dinner parties, fundraisers and think-tanks of the Establishment: the specter of the "alternative right." Young, creative and eager to commit secular heresies,

they have become public enemy number one to beltway conservatives—more hated, even, than Democrats or loopy progressives.

It went on to read in part like a sound and reasonable explanation of a movement. It accurately traced the intellectual roots of the alt-right and identified the key players. At 5,000 words, it followed the alt-right rule of never using one word when a few hundred will do just as well. The piece was coherent and even, at times, well argued. It consistently portrayed alt-righters as young, creative and countercultural, although the evidence for that claim is scant—the "creative" description is only stood up by a few memes. More to the point it was an apology for the movement, an argument in favor of its supposed countercultural values, and a near-total dismissal of all of its varied and nasty extremist elements.

It was, in the Breitbart fashion, facts layered with spin deployed for a political purpose:

The alternative right, more commonly known as the alt-right, is an amorphous movement. Some—mostly Establishment types—insist it's little more than a vehicle for the worst dregs of human society: anti-Semites, white supremacists, and other members of the Stormfront set. They're wrong.[50]

The authors contrasted the movement with its far-right antecedents: "The alternative right are a much smarter group of people—which perhaps suggests why the Left hates them so much. They're dangerously bright."[51] The pair namechecked the major movement leaders and websites, but curiously, as the conservative writer Cathy Young pointed out to me, Yiannopoulos and Bokhari didn't actually link to any of the sites they mentioned. It's an odd omission for an explainer story—surely the audience would like to easily click and check out such sites for themselves?

Interestingly, they pointed to social psychologist Jonathan Haidt as a key identifier of supposedly innate alt-right values among huge swathes of the population. Haidt is the liberal academic who wrote the *Atlantic* article decrying trigger warnings, and the authors boiled down Haidt's book *The Righteous Mind*—a fascinating volume about the various evolutionary and social influences on conceptions of morality—into a structure of two camps of people, outlier natural liberals "who instinctively enjoy diversity and are happy with radical social change—so long as it's in an egalitarian direction," and sensible natural conservatives who "have other concerns: the preservation of their own tribe and its culture."

This is a clear oversimplification of the moral values matrix that Haidt has sketched out, drawing on the tribalism of ancient man and analyzing the influence of genetics, which is one of many factors that plays into our political beliefs. But in the story, just as Yiannopoulos tried to do in the BBC radio recording, the authors made a deft switch in order to defend the alt-right's pro-segregation stance:

> The alt-right's intellectuals would also argue that culture is inseparable from race. The alt-right believe that some degree of separation between peoples is necessary for a culture to be preserved. A Mosque next to an English street full of houses bearing the flag of St. George, according to alt-righters, is neither an English street nor a Muslim street—separation is necessary for distinctiveness.
>
> Some alt-righters make a more subtle argument. They say that when different groups are brought together, the common culture starts to appeal to the lowest common denominator. Instead of mosques or English houses, you get atheism and stucco.[52]

It's not immediately clear why this would be so—somehow the alt-righters the writers spoke to aren't familiar with, say,

American cuisine or the Brazilian national football team.[53] But again it's hard for an outsider to evaluate this or any other argument in the piece in full. There are few links to blog posts; no quotes from 4chan.

The authors did mention that they had interviewed enough activists to make definitive determinations about the composition and demographics of the alt-right, and furthermore, established to their own satisfaction that they're not really racists after all— or at least, that if they are racists, the left is worse. Their focus soon shifted to the meme creators. Because despite Dylann Roof, police shootings, demonstrable economic equalities, and a variety of other evidence, racism (according to Yiannopoulos and Bokhari) does not really exist in twenty-first-century Western society:

> Racism, for [young people], is a monster under the bed, a story told by their parents to frighten them into being good little children.
>
> As with Father Christmas, Millennials have trouble believing it's actually real. They've never actually seen it for themselves—and they don't believe that the memes they post on /pol/ are actually racist....
>
> Another, more palatable, interpretation of these memes is that they are clearly racist, but that there is very little sincerity behind them....
>
> Everyone on the anonymous board hurls the most vicious slurs and stereotypes [at] each other, but like jocks busting each other's balls at the college bar, it's obvious that there's little real hatred present.[54]

This might be true some of the time on /pol/. But it's also clearly untrue a lot—perhaps even most—of the time, as anyone who has spent any significant amount looking at 4chan can easily tell. Day after day, thread after thread, /pol/ users post streams of invective towards black people, women, gays, liberals, and any other perceived enemy. If they were all joking, the humor would have gotten old years ago. If they were just doing it for laughs they wouldn't include wonkish charts and serious-looking graphics. There's really only so many times someone can call for genocide and brush off criticism by saying they were just joking. To claim that you can't glean any serious intent or determine a community's overall worldview just because it's made up of anonymous people on the internet is disingenuous.

The authors drew a direct line from the "new left" movement of the 1960s to the alt-right, claiming that "young rebels" aren't drawn to the movement because of innate conservativism but because it provides transgressive fun. But nowhere did the story quote these young mischief-makers or ask why this supposed new and revolutionary countercultural influence hasn't produced any original cultural artefacts of note beyond a few frog memes.

In any case, Yiannopoulos and Bokhari then moved on to their main mission: minimizing the influence of hard-core fascists on the movement:

> Anything associated as closely with racism and bigotry as the alternative right will inevitably attract real racists and bigots.
>
> These are the people that the alt-right's opponents wish constituted the entire movement. They're less concerned with the welfare of their own tribe than their fantasies of destroying others....
>
> But if you want to use the 1488ers to tarnish the entire alt-right, you need to do the same with Islamist killers and Islam and third-wave feminist wackos with the entire history and purpose of feminism....
>
> Every ideology has them. Humorless ideologues who have no lives beyond their political crusade, and live for the destruction of the great. They can be found on Stormfront and other sites, not just joking about the race war, but eagerly planning it. They are known as "Stormfags" by the rest of the internet.[55]

To back up their argument, the Breitbart writers deployed—for the first and only time in their piece—quotes from the keyboard of a rank-and-file alt-right tweeter: "'I have no interest in the 1488 crowd,' tweeted Paul Ray Ramsey. 'A toxic mix of kooks and ex-cons turned informants. LARPing the Third Reich.'"

Ramsey later wrote that although a series of his tweets was reproduced in the article, neither author contacted him for an interview. He does however qualify as one of the more "moderate" alt-right mouthpieces, and tiptoes a fine line. While he calls himself an American nationalist and pines for a homeland based on whiteness, Christianity, and the English language, at the same time he calls white nationalism a "cult." He sketched out his philosophy in a YouTube video:

> What does it mean to be an American? Is it just a proposition nation that anyone can be an American? No. It's a heritage. It's basically a white heritage, Christian, English-speaking. But it's not 100 percent purity, it never has been. So what in practical terms we Americans would like is our own homeland again. And I don't know whether that would be obtained through secession or through some other means ... if you prefer diversity, you can live in your diversity country.[56]

Ramsey, like Richard Spencer, has pined for the breakup of the United States. At the 2013 American Renaissance conference, he stated: "We need to Balkanize and create our own homeland. We have a right to exist."[57] These views weren't reflected in the Breitbart article.

In later writing, Yiannopoulos described hard-core neo-Nazis as "5 percent" of the alt-right,[58] but it's unclear where he gets that figure from—he cites no research or study. The anonymous and amorphous nature of the alt-right makes a statistical analysis impossible, so the figure could be right, but so could a figure of 15 percent, 50 percent, or whatever.

Taken in the strictest literal terms, neo-Nazis—people who deeply believe in the ideology of the German Nazi Party of 1920–45—are certainly a minority in the movement. But that's a distinction lacking a hugely significant difference. Alt-righters are advocating a style of politics based on racial groupings, and use pseudoscientific concepts at the same time as making constant references to Nazi themes. It's easy to see—for anyone but the alt-right defenders desperate to push a more "moderate" image of the movement—how all of this might be interpreted as a serious appeal to extremist ideas. Because it pretty clearly is.

*   *   *

I've spent a lot of time dissecting this one story—one of many that sprung up about the alt-right around this time—because in the midst of the feverish 2016 election campaign, it was definitely the most comprehensive one coming from the biggest media outlet friendly to the alt-right. And in fact it became a touchstone and galvanizing document for the movement—established truth for the defenders of alt-light and alt-rightish positions. Far-right identitarians latched onto this idea of themselves as harmless pranksters, racist only in jest, mildly corrupted by a small minority of actual bigots, a real youthful freewheeling counter-culture. YouTubers and blogs cited the story,[59] and it was bolstered by some old-school hard-core neo-Nazis who denounced it and claimed that authentic racism and anti-Semitism were the point of the alt-right, which of course was taken as even more evidence that there were only a few such marginal types.

But it was clear to any observer of 4chan, Twitter and Reddit throughout 2016—and later as street violence ramped in the following year—that mocking "stormfags" wasn't anywhere near a main thrust of alt-right conversation. Nor, in fact, was "culture," "counter" or otherwise. In large areas which were essential to the oppositional coolness of subcultures from the 1950s Beats onwards, the alt-right really isn't in the game. There are documentaries about red pilling, sure, and more talky YouTube videos than anyone could watch in 20 lifetimes, but precious little else that might get a wider cohort enthused enough to think twice about ethno-nationalism. Tracks on alt-right music playlists tend to be either mediocre obscure tunes that inadvertently reference alt-right terms, or attempts to co-opt songs from people who would rather not have anything to do with the movement, thank you very much.[60]

Instead of channeling creative energy into the kind of cultural output that defines and expands a movement, many more alt-righters were posting Pepe Stormtrooper memes and sending pictures of gas chambers to Jewish journalists. And as we'll see, there's a strong possibility that the demographic makeup of the movement is not as youthful as the alt-right propagandists might hope.

The Breitbart article concludes with a plea for a renewed emphasis on genetics and tribalism and a dismissal of some of the most important issues in American politics:[61]

The Establishment need to read their Haidt and realize that this group isn't going away. There will be no "progress" that erases the natural affinities of conservatives. We can no longer pretend that divides over free trade and the minutiae of healthcare reform really represent both sides of the political spectrum in America. The alt-right is here, and here to stay.

I asked Haidt about the story via email. He said he was "mortified" that Breitbart used his photo, and declared that he has nothing to do with the alt-right. It is indeed the case that political groupings are related to heritable traits, he said, and that compared to progressives, conservatives are "more tribal, more susceptible to a sense of 'us vs. them' and of having pride in 'us.'" But he went on to write, in response to my questions in June 2017, that there's nothing inevitable about the development of a political tribe based on race or a genetic or ethnic interpretation of "Western civilization":[62]

> My research is on the foundations of morality—what is innate that makes some kinds of ideas more learnable than others. So IF we have a society that emphasizes racial and ethnic identities, and that has a great deal of racial identity politics, THEN I would agree that this way of thinking is likely to spread to white people and strengthen a white conservative identity movement. I do believe that the excesses of the left have motivated and nurtured excesses of the right.
>
> BUT, in the kind of society that I favor—the "melting pot" approach to ethnic identity that was so successful for America in the early and mid 20th century—then I think it is not inevitable that there would be a white identity group that spread beyond the fringes of society. This is why I am such a fan of the Western liberal tradition, and why I am so fearful of the illiberalism that I see brewing on the far left (on campus) and the far right (the alt-right).

He ended his message with a prescient observation:

> I am very afraid that America has now reached a state of mutual assured outrage in which the actions of each side, amplified and distorted via social media, goads the other side into another round of escalation. In 2017, for the first time since the 1970s, political violence seems to be spreading.

*   *   *

Breitbart burnt the trail for a host of alt-right and alt-light copycat media agitators and politicized imitators, as the ability of social media and the internet to pound home a pro-Trump message and give a megaphone to persistent online warriors became blindingly obvious to anyone with a smartphone.

Among them were Mike Cernovich, the author of a PUA-flavored self-help tract and guides on juice diets, and prime pusher of the "pizzagate" conspiracy theory; Cassandra Fairbanks, a writer of popular tweets and much less popular opinion pieces for the Kremlin-funded website Sputnik News; and Jack Posobiec, who once plotted to plant a "Rape Melania" sign at an anti-Trump rally in an attempt to discredit the protesters.[63] These largely self-taught reporters, while occasionally scoring an occasional scoop due to their new mutual friendliness with the White House, were primarily engaged in erasing the line between journalism and activism. Cernovich told *The New Yorker*: "I use trolling tactics to build my brand."[64] Later he told me via email: "My job has always been to share the truth as I see it. That's something most people miss. I share my truth, which finds the audience as none of us are particularly unique."[65]

Posobiec takes a similar line, saying: "I also do what I call 4-D journalism, meaning that I'm willing to break the fourth wall. I'm willing to walk into an anti-Trump march and start chanting anti-Clinton stuff—to make something happen, and then cover what happens. So, activism tactics mixed with traditional journalism tactics."[66] If that sounds something like mixing together ammonia and bleach, you get an idea of the nihilistic thrill that spurs on some alt-light media personalities.

Twitter, of course, allows this new breed of journalist-agitators to do their work and build their brands with amazing speed.

In the course of an on-the-record but private (direct message) conversation with Posobiec about his role in spreading emails leaked from French President Emmanuel Macron's campaign, he took a screenshot of one small part of our conversation and posted it on his public Twitter feed.[67] Before we had even finished speaking, aggressive tweets and emails were flowing in my direction. Of course, Posobiec didn't tell people to fire off messages, he simply posted a question I'd asked about bots repeating his #MacronLeaks hashtag, and implied that one big BBC Twitter account was followed by a lot of bots. After seeing his goading post, his followers did the rest. It was "activism tactics" mixed with "traditional journalism" tactics.

* * *

The post-election rift between the alt-right intellectuals and the alt-light media would continue to grow, with many of the latter steadfastly distancing themselves from the movement. But what about the neo-Nazis, who even the alt-right's defenders admitted made up at least some part of the movement? What exactly was their role in influencing and spreading the identitarian message?

7

Neo-Nazis

In response to that key Breitbart story, an article appeared on the neo-Nazi website Daily Stormer. Its headline, "Breitbart's Alt-Right Analysis is the Product of a Degenerate Homosexual and an Ethnic Mongrel," was actually a line plucked from the Breitbart piece itself—Yiannopoulos and Bokhari's projection of what hardcore racists might think about the Breitbart writers. The neo-Nazi behind the Daily Stormer, while irritated at the overall analysis of the alt-right, agreed with that one particular assessment. Andrew Anglin wrote:

> Upon finishing the [Breitbart] article, one is left with two pressing questions:
> 1) How is it possible that this article does not mention The Daily Stormer? and
> 2) Why does this article not talk about Jews?[1]

What follows on the page are pictures of Hitler, slurs against Jews and black people, amid lots of general vileness, all deployed in denial that the alt-right is anything but deadly earnest in its fascism. The neo-Nazis, Anglin declares, are not messing around, and the alt-right are neo-Nazis: "Maybe it was true in 2005 that we made racist jokes about Jews and hajis for the lulz, but then things got real ... No, seriously: we sincerely are racists."[2]

Anglin later published his own analysis of the movement: "A Normie's Guide to the Alt-Right," aping the Breitbart story but putting the 1488ers squarely at the center of the movement, and making what he saw as his primary life goal quite clear: "We are now an exploding movement. Not just this site, of course—I didn't mean to imply above that we're the only site that matters. We just happen to be the biggest. But there are many, many others involved who care about the real issue: stopping these Jews."[3]

* * *

The Daily Stormer is at the extremist end of the hardcore wing of the alt-right. Although Yiannopoulos's "5%" neo-Nazi figure is of dubious provenance, it's probably safe to say that many alt-righters wish this particular website would go away. Some I've spoken to don't mind the Stormer, either arguing that there "are no enemies to the right" or insisting on clinging to the logical contortion that Anglin doesn't really mean what he says even when he is adamant that he means what he says. The Stormer shows how extremists have latched onto the alt-right and how effective they've been in aping—and sometimes shaping—the movement's internet tropes and argumentative techniques.

Let's be clear: when it comes to race hate, the Daily Stormer isn't messing around. The site's name is an homage to *Der Stürmer* (The Stormer), a newspaper published by the Nazi Julius Streicher, who was executed for crimes against humanity in 1946.[4] It's clearly aimed at a younger demographic than Stormfront, once the most-visited neo-Nazi site on the internet. Where Stormfront mostly takes the form of a traditional, rather boring-looking message board, the Daily Stormer is decorated with Pepe memes, flashing GIFs and provocative headlines. Anglin, a one-time vegan, punk and world traveler, grew up in Ohio and ran a few fascist-themed websites before hitting on his current iteration.[5]

He has claimed that his is the most popular neo-Nazi website, and while the evidence for that assertion is mixed,[6] Anglin has managed to insert himself into the alt-right movement by deploying and sharpening a particular brand of attention-seeking extremist trolling—the natural outgrowth of the alt-right's fast-developing online tactics.

In the Daily Stormer lies the dark heart of the extremist wing of the alt-right, incontrovertible proof that the serious unironic hardcore racists and anti-Semites exist—the only questions being how many of them there are and how influential they are. They swim firmly in the tradition of small groups of extremist white nationalists who piggyback onto and co-op larger movements to exaggerate their own impact. Sometimes these efforts border on the try-hard ridiculous. In the wake of the British EU referendum, for instance, the Stormer was adorned with celebratory Brexit banners and a vision of a placid Jerusalem, as if the vote was some sort of fascist triumph.[7] The bandwagon jumping got even more ridiculous when it endorsed the British Labour Party leader Jeremy Corbyn.

But despite all the blustery self-puffery, the site does have one domain of real and to some degree measurable influence. Its small but fanatical user base has coordinated a number of attack campaigns against its enemies—mostly prominent Jews. It has created and boosted campaigns of abuse for political ends, a classic alt-right tactic. Among the site's targets was British Member of Parliament Luciana Berger. She was sent Photoshopped pictures of herself with a yellow star on her head and the hashtag "#Hitlerwasright."

In October 2014, a member of the small neo-Nazi British organization National Action—a group that later became the first white nationalist organization proscribed as a terrorist entity in the UK[8]—was sentenced[9] to a prison term for sending offensive messages to Berger. News reports painted the 21-year-old troll, named Garron Helm, as a sad case. He was described by the *Daily Mail* as an "immature loner who found friends online in extremist groups." After his father died and his mother suffered a mental breakdown, Helm was expelled from school and fell under the influence of the far right. It was another scrap of evidence pointing to the fact that the alt-right's self-image of themselves as a force made up of ranks of hipsterish, erudite, well-educated men is misleading.

For the Daily Stormer, however, this small, sad case became a platform on which to build a mini extremist cause célèbre, a campaign which demonstrated the depravity of the neo-Nazi mindset. "I declare a new operation against the filthy communist Jewess, which will be known as Operation: Filthy Jew Bitch," Anglin wrote. He laid out basic instructions for a Twitter campaign against Berger and urged his readers to:

> Call her a Jew, call her a Jew communist, call her a terrorist, call her a filthy Jew bitch. Call her a hook-nosed yid and a ratfaced kike. Tell her we do not want her in the UK, we do not want her or any other Jew anywhere in Europe. Tell her to go to Israel and call for her deportation to said Jew state.
> Do it over, and over, and over and over again.
> Tell her that "#HitlerWasRight," and then tell her that six million more times.[10]

As a result of this charming missive, thousands of vile messages and memes flowed Berger's way—the issue was even raised in Parliament, where Speaker John Bercow called the abuse "despicable and beneath contempt."[11]

But even as politicians and the mainstream media took notice, the origin of the campaign was mostly ignored, or, more likely, poorly understood. The parliamentary and public discussion around the online abuse focused not on the Daily Stormer or neo-Nazi organizations, but on the role of Twitter and the social network's responsibility for policing hate speech.[12] It had all the hallmarks of the alt-right: a campaign of abuse devised on a shadowy message board, spread by anonymous or pseudonymous accounts, leaking out onto the major social networks and gaining mainstream attention while the real force behind it remained obscure.

Anglin knows the law, and is very careful to step up to certain lines without crossing them and overtly encouraging violence. Even in his frothing Berger post he wrote:

Do Not:

Call for violence, threaten the Jew bitch in any way. Seriously, don't do that.

Just to be crystal: Andrew Anglin nor The Daily Stormer support or endorse any form of violence against the sickening Jew Luciana Berger. We believe she should be either legally tried and imprisoned for purposefully undermining the British people and nation, or simply deported to Israel.[13] (Italics in original.)

Not all of his moronic minions stuck to the script, and so of course Berger received death threats.[14] One man was sentenced to two years in prison for racially abusive blog posts inspired by the campaign. Joshua Bonehill-Paine Photoshopped a Star of David on Berger's face and copied the Stormer's suggestion that the politician be informed that "Hitler was right." That phrase, by the way, is common among alt-right trolls, many of whom call it "ironic," but when Bonehill-Paine's lawyer argued that his client's posts were "satire" and "pathetic puerile rubbish," the jury remained unconvinced.[15]

Over the next two years, Berger became a Daily Stormer obsession—the site posted more than 40 articles about her, and at least one other man went to jail for spitting out online threats. Anglin continued to encourage his followers to send Berger nasty tweets.[16]

The MP was one of the site's first big targets, and the campaigns of hate continued. The Stormer went on to coordinate campaigns against an Australian Muslim activist,[17] a Nintendo employee with outspoken feminist views,[18] and Julia Ioffe, a journalist who wrote a piece about Melania Trump.[19] Ioffe got a phone call from someone who played Hitler speech. In one meme, a picture of her face was superimposed on a scene from Auschwitz. Ioffe was quoted as saying that the abuse reminded her of the type of anti-Semitic abuse her family had endured before emigrating to the US from Russia.

Through Anglin's careful disclaimers and his hidden location—he asks that donations for the site be sent to his father's office in Ohio, but Anglin himself lives outside the United States[20]—the mastermind of the Daily Stormer had managed to keep out of legal trouble even as his followers have landed in prison. But as his troll army stepped up their campaigns and the site got a blast of publicity from its co-option of the alt-right and the Donald Trump campaign, Anglin soon found that his days of flying under the radar were over.

*　*　*

This particular story takes us back to Richard Spencer's hometown of Whitefish, Montana. In the wake of Spencer's Hitler/Roman-salute notoriety, there was increased local resistance to the alt-right leader's presence in the town. Spencer's mother, Sherry Spencer, owned commercial property in the town, and was contacted by a local real estate agent, Tanya Gersh. Gersh says she sympathized with the fact that Sherry Spencer was being targeted by protesters because of the actions of her son, and offered help in selling the property. But later, Sherry Spencer wrote a blog post accusing Gersh of putting pressure on her to sell and threatening her with the prospect of demonstrations outside her door.[21]

Whatever the facts of the discussions between the elder Spencer and Gersh, Anglin smelled blood, and jumped to rally his troll army to the cause. He posted Gersh's address, phone number and other personal details online—including her 12-year-old son's photo and Twitter handle. "Again—as always—don't make any threats of violence and certainly don't do anything violent," he wrote, although later in the post he walked right up to that legal line and even put a toe or two on it: "Please call her and tell her what you think. And hey—if you're in the area, maybe you should stop by and tell her in person what you think of her actions."[22]

There's no indication that the Spencers had anything to do with the harassment. After the Daily Stormer campaign kicked, off, Sherry Spencer added to her original blog post the following: "I strongly urge that everyone stays within the bounds of respectful, civilized discussion of this matter by refraining from abusive comments or targeted harassment of any of the parties involved, or their families."[23]

But it was too late. The Stormer campaign had already kicked off the usual waves of obnoxious memes and messages. Gersh quit her job, suffered panic attacks and entered therapy as a result, and her family nearly moved from their home in the middle of the night.[24]

Anglin continued to step up the intimidation. He tried to organize an armed march through the town, which he cannily scheduled for Martin Luther King Jr. Day in 2017,[25] but the plans fell through when he failed to comply with the most basic requirements for a parade permit.[26]

Gersh then took an unprecedented step. With the help of the Southern Poverty Law Center, she sued Anglin in a Montana court. As of writing, Anglin had just been served with the suit via a Columbus, Ohio newspaper, and the case had not yet gone to trial.[27] "In the old days, they would have burned a cross on Tanya's front lawn," said the SPLC's Richard Cohen. "Now, in the digital age, they launch a troll storm."[28]

*   *   *

The cleavage between the identifiable neo-Nazis and the people who are simply obsessed with race and eschew outright white supremacy is one of the key splits in the alt-right. Andrew Anglin opportunistically put himself and his website at the center of the tussle between avowed racists, hardcore white supremacists and anti-Semites, and the rest of the movement. Posters on Stormfront, the older white nationalist site, regularly accuse him of being a plant, a government or leftist operative, and a criminal.[29]

At the same time, some alt-righters look at Anglin and the Daily Stormer with a mixture of horror and exasperation.[30] The site carries some of the extremist rhetoric that can be seen on 4chan and 8chan to its logical conclusion—targeted hate campaigns presented in a freewheeling style with plenty of memes. Understandably, some alt-lighters are turned off by the Stormer, even if they may have some sympathy for its views or the manner in which they are expressed. Sometimes it's that the Stormer "goes too far"—even for the free speech absolutists—and other times it's the fact that some alt-righters would prefer that the uglier parts of their worldview not be laid bare in such an open forum. The more self-aware activists know that overt trolling in the name of neo-Nazism, even if they have some sympathy with such views, is just not a good look. And like the old-school neo-Nazis on Stormfront, some harbor paranoia, believing that Anglin is being secretly funded by shadowy anti-fascist forces to discredit their own side.

Jared Taylor, of American Renaissance, rather diplomatically commented: "They have an extremely harsh, dismissive and insulting tone towards blacks. I think that kind of rhetoric is extremely unhelpful."[31] Paul Ramsey tried to distance the rest of the movement from the Stormer fanatics:

I found the Alt Right movement to be exciting in that it provides White people with a possibility of identity without the Hollywood Nazism baggage ... Most normal White people are ready for identity politics...

The Daily Stormer quickly moved to associate Nazism with the Alt Right. Previously, they were opposed to the "Alt Kike." But once they saw it gain popularity they knew they had to co-opt the movement.[32]

Ramsey, like the Stormfront brigade, accused the Daily Stormer of being a front—only this time for the Anti-Defamation League—dreaming up the preposterous theory that a liberal anti-racist group would secretly fund hate campaigns against prominent Jews in order to provoke a backlash. The more prosaic explanation is that the Daily Stormer was much more central to the alt-right than many alt-righters were comfortable with. It had more ideas in common with the rest of the movement than activists were willing to admit, and it made them all look like pretty terrible human beings.

The network of connections centered on the Daily Stormer gives a clearer sense of the contours of the far reaches of the alt-right and its connections with extremists, violence and terror. One of the most prominent contributors to the site is Andrew Aurenheimer, a hacker who goes by the name "weev." In 2012, Aurenheimer was sentenced to 41 months in prison after he exposed an AT&T security flaw. His conviction was later set aside,[33] but while in prison he had become a neo-Nazi.[34]

He began contributing to the Daily Stormer—in one piece, he blamed Jewish and black people for his legal troubles[35]—and in one notable prank, blasted out anti-Semitic flyers to thousands of unsecured printers in universities across the United States.[36] He was also a full-throated supporter of Gamergate and other alt-right causes, again using the strategy of piggybacking on mass movements to try to gain legitimacy for ultra-extremist causes.[37] In 2017, Aurenheimer was apparently hanging out in eastern Ukraine,[38] and demanding more than a thousand dollars per hour for an interview.[39]

Violent criminals and terrorists were also attracted to the Daily Stormer. The Charleston shooter, Dylann Roof, likely commented on the site using the pseudonym AryanBlood1488, according to a textual analysis by the Southern Poverty Law Center.[40] Roof appeared to swallow the site's extremist messages.[41] And although the Charleston killer was initially condemned by the Daily Stormer,[42] Anglin later concocted a bizarre, wholly unsupported conspiracy theory—so bizarre, in fact, that it could possibly be a "joke": "Dylann Roof ... clearly acted in self-defense after a black mob attacked him in a church, apparently trying to steal his wallet and cellphone. However, the politically correct establishment is persecuting him because he is white."[43]

Joshua Goldberg, who would go on to face terror charges in the United States (much more about him later), published articles on the site using the pseudonym "Michael Slay." Anglin called him "clearly intelligent and a skilled writer," but when his subterfuge was found out, lashed out at his actions and his ethnicity: "The Daily Stormer was subjected to an attempted infiltration by the insane Jewish terrorist Joshua Goldberg."[44]

While the site is mostly careful to keep on the right site of incitement laws, it is not afraid to celebrate violence when it occurs in apparent furtherance of its goals. When the German politician and immigration supporter Henriette Reker was stabbed, the site gleefully reported the attack, calling Reker a "feminist hag."[45] After the murder of Jo Cox, the Stormer Photoshopped a logo of a pornographic website onto her picture and claimed the world was a better place without her. "Jo Cox was evil and she deserved to die. Her death was not a tragedy, it was justice," Anglin wrote.[46] One British teenage reader of that particular story was later convicted of constructing a bomb.[47]

* * *

Hardcore white supremacists aren't joking when they express their thirst for racial confrontation. But the Daily Stormer's online blitzkriegs gave the alt-right a blueprint for trolling projects that would go beyond anti-Semitic hate campaigns.

The game plan goes like this: first a prominent alt-righter pinpoints a specific target. They could be a politician, a journalist, or a feminist activist, like those who had bull's-eyes painted on them by the Gamergate crowd. Next, the ringleaders include some version of plausible deniability. The Daily Stormer, as it dances so close to the law, is forced to routinely make its anti-violence pose explicit. Alt-righters with big Twitter followings don't have to wade anywhere near the line of violence; simply drumming out a few rude messages will rally the troll army. For people on the receiving end of the storm, the experience ranges from unpleasant to downright frightening.[48] And, as we've seen, in some cases and in some jurisdictions the trolls clash with the law.

But courting trouble—whether it's with the law or more often with mainstream social networks, usually in the form of account suspensions—is not just an unfortunate externality of the trolling business. In fact, for the alt-right, it's at least half the point. Falling afoul of the rules prompts another backlash, against Twitter or UK speech laws or whatever institution is allegedly promoting political correctness and curtailing freedom of speech. If they're banned by social networks, the alt-right instigators can then claim they are being treated unfairly, flip the script and embrace what Breitbart once called "sweet victimhood action"—ostensibly a tactic employed by dissembling leftists.

The troll tactics developed during Gamergate were perfected by the neo-Nazi wing of the movement and adopted widely across the various factions of the alt-right. Perhaps the classic example, from July 2016, involved Milo Yiannopoulos, who directed a series of tweets at the black female American comedian Leslie Jones. Yiannopoulos apparently didn't like the remake of *Ghostbusters*, a film Jones starred in and which became something of an alt-right rallying point due to its diverse, female-led cast.

As far alt-right trolling campaigns go, Yiannopoulos's twitter storm was initially rather mild. "If at first you don't succeed (because your work is terrible), play the victim," he tweeted at Jones. He soon ramped things up: "EVERYONE GETS HATE MAIL FFS [for fuck's sake]." He called Jones a "black dude" and the *Ghostbusters* cast "Fat and ugly, ugly, ugly, fat" and "teenage boys with tits," and circulated fake Jones tweets that included anti-Semitic and anti-gay slurs and so on and so on.[49]

He didn't explicitly call on his more than 300,000 Twitter followers to start a concerted campaign against the actress, but then again, he didn't have to. They got the message and the much nastier messages started flowing Jones's way.[50] Yiannopoulos, who had sparred with Twitter before, got a permanent ban from the social network shortly thereafter.[51] And that's when the script was flipped: "With the cowardly suspension of my account, Twitter has confirmed itself as a safe space for Muslim terrorists and Black Lives Matter extremists, but a no-go zone for conservatives," Yiannopoulos complained. "Twitter is holding me responsible for the actions of fans and trolls using the special pretzel logic of the left. Where are the Twitter police when Justin Bieber's fans cut themselves on his behalf?"[52]

Yiannopoulos was cannily referencing a 2013 prank where 4channers tried to trick young people into slashing themselves out of devotion to the singer.[53] But the analogy doesn't really make sense. Justin Bieber doesn't sing songs or write tweets about how nasty and fat teenage flesh is and how ugly it looks.

*　*　*

After years of hate, Anglin and the Stormer hit a serious roadblock after the events in Charlottesville in August 2017. Anglin began to make excuses for James Fields, the 20-year-old who drove into a crowd of counter-protesters, and insulted the woman who was killed, calling her a "drain on society" because she was unmarried and childless. The material wasn't markedly different from what he had posted before, but this time his writing caused a media furor. For his web-hosting company, it was finally a step too far, and the Daily Stormer was forced to relocate to the unregulated but less publicly accessible dark web.[54] Its future, at time of writing, remains uncertain, but it appears that its days as the loudest, most obnoxious public neo-Nazi portal may be over.

The troll army game plan was effective and the tactics not only worked, but maximized media attention on the movement. But there was a further consequence. The campaigns of the Stormer and those that resembled them blurred the lines between the relatively moderate alt-light and the relatively extreme alt-right factions. Like the ironic stance, the use of Daily Stormer-type tactics painted the alt-right as an obnoxious horde (not that they care very much, as long as the horde looks as large and as loud as possible). Where do most alt-righters really fall on the political spectrum? It's almost impossible to tell. What's the difference between an alt-right troll tactic and a neo-Nazi troll tactic? It's almost impossible to say.

But while there are no opinion surveys or detailed demographic surveys to speak of, I decided to try to add to my collection of years of random encounters with the trolls and the extremists. Maybe there was some point in trying to talk further to the rank and file, the "ordinary" alt-righters.

8

Ordinary Guys

I'd been interacting with the alt-righters for a few years, ever since I started working on BBC Trending in 2014. Along the way I'd written stories directly about the movement, or about other online trends which alt-righters were interested in. Through these stories, I'd chatted with alt-righters, sparred with a few on Twitter, observed them on the chans, and even, in an internet sort of way, got friendly with a couple of self-identified identitarians.

Still, while compiling the research for this book, I felt the need to speak to members of the movement and question them directly about their background and motivations. The conventional wisdom, established by the Breitbart story and largely unquestioned by other media within and outside of the alt-right, was that the people within the movement were by and large young pranksters who didn't take things, including themselves, too seriously. They had been painted as a counter-culture, railing against a politically correct establishment, with spiritual—if not political—links to groups such as punks and hippies. I had already suspected that narrative was slightly off, but I wanted to hear from more people who identified themselves as alt-right.

In addition to a lot of time spent on 4chan and r/The_Donald, I and my colleagues sought out alternative alt-right meeting spaces, chat apps, internet relay chats and other places where alt-righters tended to congregate. In these places, alt-righters talk more openly and less ironically than they might on Reddit or Twitter. For instance, I went to Gab, a message board set up by entrepreneurs who wanted to build a social network free of what they saw as the undue restrictions placed on free speech by Twitter and Facebook.[1]

The Gab founders didn't describe themselves as part of the alt-right, but as conservatives bucking against Silicon Valley political correctness. The site's logo was a drawing of a frog. Although it doesn't look particularly Pepe-ish, anyone familiar with the far right and with the internet in 2016 would get the hint. Founder Andrew Torba insisted that his mascot was a biblical reference to the plague of frogs mentioned in the book of Exodus.

"The frog to us serves as a metaphor," Torba told my BBC Trending colleague Will Yates. "It's releasing the frogs on Silicon Valley to expose their corruption, their censorship and the information monopoly that they have on the web."[2] The site first gained attention after a cluster of alt-right accounts were banned from Twitter. Some of those chucked off the much bigger social network huddled together on Gab.[3]

Driven by those exiles and the publicity that came with them, Gab's right-wing—if not exclusively alt-right—tendencies then became sort of a self-fulfilling narrative about the direction of the network. In reporting on the site, we pointed out that the founders claimed they had attracted all sorts of users: Catholic stoics, Hindu philosophers, Canadian rap artists. But conservative political ideas were the overwhelming topics of conversation. The biggest hashtags on the network in late 2016 and beyond were #MAGA and #Pizzagate, the latter a conspiracy theory inflamed by alt-right activists which resulted in bullets being fired.

I had set up a Gab account, and the reporting me and my colleagues had done on the network had put us in touch with a cluster of Gab users, so I pinged out a short copied-and-pasted message to my small group (60 or so) of followers, asking if they'd like to talk to a journalist about the alt-right. The Gab river brought forth frogs abundantly (as the Book of Exodus put it[4]):

how about you write about #rotherham and the hundreds of thousands of white British school children who have been raped over the last decade by Muslim pedophile gangs you weaselly spineless faggot. ... piss off, wanker.

There are people of ALL TYPES ON GAB. You need to go apologize to all the people you spammed, you pre-judging piece of shit. Until you do, go fuck yourself, and if you won't: Fucking kill yourself.

stop being such a try hard dick sucking faggot.

Within hours, my posts on the site had been down voted more than 1,000 times, an impressive number on a network with only a couple of hundred thousand accounts. Paranoid allegations were thrown at me and my employer. Still, some Gab users braved the wrath of others and agreed to answer a few of my questions.

There was Richard, a man in his late 30s who said he was a disabled military veteran. He described himself as an "objectivist" and said he was motivated by a libertarian notion of fairness:

My first red pill moment came when I got my first paycheck. I was dating a girl whose single mother was on welfare ... I got my first job and worked incredibly hard to earn enough money to live on my own. When I got my first paycheck and saw how much taxes were taken, then thought back to my girlfriend's mom buying vices and never looking for work, it made a real impression on me.[5]

Another correspondent called himself a meme warrior. He was in his 60s and said he was an "aspie" (someone with Asperger's Syndrome) and that the alt-right was "quite different than anything we've seen before, possibly unique in the history of mankind." He told me he had developed a grand theory of memes and disavowed the white supremacist wing of the movement: "Politically, I don't fit into convenient ideological boxes. The closest approximation you might understand would be libertarian anarchist, Jeffersonian anti-federalist, or even classical liberal."

There was a 30-year-old fascist Midwestern fast-food worker, and a 51-year-old man from Chicago who told me he had grown up in Chicago working in kitchens: "Moved all over the country and worked in a lot of different environments (hotels, resorts, guest ranches, hospitals, jail, etc)." He described the alt-right as "Race realism + nationalism."

A 50-something Canadian economist described his agenda like so: "Secure borders, intelligent immigration (properly vetted, skilled immigrants who want a better life and will contribute), small government, country and citizens first, less war, a hand up not a handout, anti-racist, support free speech and in the US the 2nd amendment."

None of the dozen or so who responded were college age or younger. If anything was common to all of them, it was the Trumpian "America in decline" theme. As one wrote:

Our "representatives" are paid liars masquerading as "public servants," taking money from lobbyists, amassing millon$ on a $200K salary, importing jihadists and paying them welfare for their 20 kids and 5 wives, getting involved in endless and pointless wars in moslem hell holes, draining our blood and treasure in the sand ostensibly fighting terrorism but actually wasting time and money on 7th century savages who want us dead.

Meanwhile the libtard "teachers" are teaching our children to be politically correct, and not much else, Johnny can't spel, we've slipped to 12th in the world rankings for student academic outcomes, don't salute the flag, gangs running rampant, and yet the constant refrain is "more money for education."

Most respondents seemed in earnest, but there was in many of the responses an undercurrent of suspicion or mischievous troll-like behavior. I wasn't sure, for example, whether to take all of the responses at face value. Some were clearly joking:

> My main "redpill" moment was in elementary school. I was heavily disliked because the other children viewed me as more intelligent than them, thus that made me a target. One day I managed to grab one of those red bouncy balls so I could play with it by myself, and the teacher made me hand it over to other students because, and I quote, "that's democracy." I long knew these people around me were mentally delusional inferiors, that event set me off into looking at non-liberal democratic, anti-modernist literature.

The sample size was small and certainly not scientific. But my encounters with Gab, and many other exchanges I had had online, didn't exactly fit with the established conventional wisdom that had grown up around the alt-right. Largely as a result of the Breitbart story and the alt-right's own propaganda, the movement had built an image of itself as a cool posse of young intelligent kids. The people who talked to me were older—in some cases old—and skewed working class. It could be that the younger people were more hostile to the media than older alt-righters who may have come to the movement through more mainstream conservativism. And it must be said that some who have interviewed the rank-and-file have indeed found a movement made up mostly of young college kids.[6] When the British organization Hope Not Hate recruited a young Swedish man to infiltrate the alt-right, he found a mix of older leaders, fringe types who have long been involved in extremist politics, and young acolytes.[7]

That said, there just haven't been a whole lot of journalists who have spent much time with "ordinary" alt-righters—they are, as mentioned, rather prickly when it comes to the media, and the stuff chucked at me on Gab (if you can believe it) is a rather low-key example of the kind of thing that activists routinely hurl at reporters, sometimes even without being sent triggering interview requests.[8]

But over the years I've engaged with a number of alt-righters and alt-lighters on Twitter, and many just don't fit the mold laid out by Breitbart and others. They might skew male, and they might be internet-savvy, but they're not particularly young, or countercultural. Mostly they seem to just harbor lingering resentments against political correctness, and their actions tumble forth from there.

There was, for instance, the 40-something American who trolled as a sort of game, signing up for Twitter accounts and abandoning them when he got bored, or when holidays and family gatherings took up more of his time. When I prodded him about his beliefs, he compared his "red pilling" with religious conversion.

> I was raised Catholic but I've always held a suspicion of religion. It was more like when a person hears a certain band or a songwriter for the first time. "These songs are how I feel!" That kind of thing. It wasn't a conversion because I had always felt this way even if I didn't completely realize it.

He was inspired by the alt-right to, among other things, make up prankish fake news about terror attacks, like the London Bridge channers from Chapter 3. He stopped tweeting from the account I had contacted him on soon after our exchange.

Another correspondent was happy to chat despite his low opinion of my profession: "the BBC and other mainstream media outlets are all garbage." He considered all the principal known characters of the alt-right to be too soft, too alt-light for his tastes. The extremists were the real movement, he told me. "The alt-right [leaders] the BBC reports on have no issues with sodomites or race mixing," he declared. His primary activity online? "Shitposting." "Shitposting makes our movement fun and anti-establishment, which is why so many are young adults or teenagers," he said, giving his age as somewhere in his 20s.

Some of the alt-right kids may find a visceral thrill in annoying people online—but does that translate into a real enthusiasm for politics? When my BBC colleague Alex Dackevych visited a Helsinki art gallery that was hosting a piece of performance art by Hollywood star Shia LaBeouf, he spoke to some of the alt-righters who had descended on the scene (LaBeouf's anti-Trump art had made him and his performances a prime channer target). Young Finnish males pranced around the gallery waving "Make America Great Again" hats. They were pranksters and 4chan fans, for sure, but they were only there for the lolz, to trigger and troll LaBeouf, and seemed supremely uninterested in discussing ethno-states, nationalist politics, or anything of much seriousness at all.[9]

Other, sometimes secretive, alt-right hangouts show little sign of the movement's touted sense of humorous irony. I lurked for a while in an alt-right group on the chat app Kik. The messages posting give a flavor of what alt-righters are like when they think no one's looking. "There is literally an Islamic centre 10 minutes from my house," commented one poster. Another responded: "You know what to do;))))). Dylan Roof [sic] it." And another: "If you could kidnap 100 muslims and murder them, guaranteed not to get caught, would you?" The chat about hypothetical mass murder continued for a while before turning to Jewish stereotypes and the alleged perils of race-mixing. There was no hint of irony in sight.

Other evidence suggests the prankster teens are somewhat less than committed to the cause. When my colleagues Megha Mohan, Anisa Subedar, and Hélène Daouphars gained access to alt-right groups on the chat app Discord as part of their reporting on the 2017 French presidential elections, they saw that groups that had been slavishly devoted to Donald Trump had gone dormant after the US election, only to flare up in an ill-fated attempt to support Marine Le Pen. After Le Pen lost, the groups went quiet again. It raised the prospect of alt-righters simply getting bored and moving on to the next exciting thing—not exactly the recipe for a world-changing movement.

One oft-repeated demographic observation about the alt-right does appear to be based in some truth—its ranks are mostly made up of men. Men have been the overwhelming presence at the handful of protest rallies and the movement's few high-profile women appear to be the exceptions that prove the rule. Richard Spencer says he expects to see alt-right marriages and babies very soon,[10] but also estimates that only about a fifth of the movement is female.[11] The video of his infamous Nazi/Roman salute shows a crowd made up almost entirely of men.[12]

Taken together, all of this raises the distinct possibility that the conventional wisdom about the alt-right might need some serious adjusting. It's doubtful that the real force of the movement consists of young trendy college students kicking against political correctness on their snowflake-covered campuses. There are several possible interpretations that can be drawn from this. One is that the movement actually has wider demographic appeal than at first appears—and indeed, its leading-edge concerns about the insecurity of once-dominant groups have wide resonance in normie society. But another distinct possibility is that the hardcore ethno-nationalists aren't tapping into some youthful surge. Maybe they're just drinking in some of the energy of older white nationalist movements, capitalizing on the general Western anti-establishment feeling, drawing in social outcasts and the bitterly disappointed, and—perhaps—catching a few alienated digital natives in the process.

* * *

"Don't you want British wine?" I jokingly suggested. "Or at least Australian?"

I was standing in an upmarket supermarket in a suburb about 30 miles outside of London, along with a self-described "shitposter" who had agreed to meet me IRL—in real life. I first interviewed Iain Davis in the summer before the US election, and he lucidly described an ethnocentric nationalism softened at the edges by European socialist tendencies and the welfare state. He also mentioned he didn't have a huge problem with fascism.

We peered at the wine rack and he plucked out a bottle of Chardonnay. "As long as it's *white*," he said, winking at me, "It's fine."

Iain was 48 years old, and before we met in person I expected a bigger man, if only because his various Twitter aliases ("big snout," "bigly snout," and other variations) were porcine-themed. Instead he was a slim guy wearing a large blue T-shirt and black Converse trainers. He was clean shaven, had a full head of salt-and-pepper hair and teeth stained by years of roll-up cigarettes.

Before our supermarket visit, we spent a few hours chatting in a pub garden near where he lived with his father in a detached house on a quiet street with a carefully maintained hedge in the front. It was the summer of 2017, a time when the movement's splintering process was well underway, so I asked him whether he still identified as "alt-right."

"I'd go a little bit further and say I quite like national socialism—or I cannot dismiss it out of hand," he said, between sips of Amstel Light. "Definitely alt-right though."

He went on to say that he "quite likes" the Daily Stormer, but poured scorn on Stormfront and what he called the stupid end of white nationalism. Davis's ideal version of Britain would be one in which a law was passed to keep non-white minorities at a level less than 20 percent of the population.

I asked whether the people around him knew about his political beliefs.

"My family know everything. My friends—yeah, I've been quite open with them about it. It's not that hard because I have a small group of close friends who will listen and hear the depths of my depravity, which isn't all that deep." He laughed. "I used to be a massive lefty." He described to me a misspent youth hanging out at art colleges, festivals, and raves. "And for all that time, I was a depressive wreck, I took far too many drugs and drank far too much. For all the time I was a lefty I had a terrible life. I thought I was happy, I thought I was having a great time, but it was a horrible depressing life," he said.

I asked him how he got into the movement. Iain was a gamer, and involved in online atheist groups, and he blames social justice warriors for ruining the fun of one of his favorite games, Mafia Wars. "Probably for me it was 2011, I started noticing the change in leftist rhetoric," he said. "You'd find yourself getting chucked out of groups, getting called out by the 'call out culture' which was very annoying."

He traced his red pill moment to Gamergate, and specifically his feeling that that particular movement should have been more explicitly political from the start:

I was thinking, this Gamergate thing is not going far enough. Especially when we got to the stage where we were not talking about the political ramifications, people were saying, "It's just about ethics in games journalism, you can't let it be about anything else, otherwise it's too racist, it's too sexist." I thought, No, actually we are directly talking about these wider issues, we're talking about ethics in games journalism because that's the tool that the mainstream media will understand.

But eventually, he said, gaming became a "less important battlefield." At the time we met in that pub garden, Iain was spending most days shitposting and "signal-boosting"—repeating messages and memes and crafting his own. Unemployed, he collected disability benefits and spent a couple of mornings a week volunteering in a local charity shop, testing electrical goods. It was a lifestyle that gave him ample time to spend on the internet.

"I look at YouTube, news groups and news sites all day long, and post the stuff that fits our narratives and what fits my news beat, what's topical and what my audience likes," he said. He reckoned 4chan was a bit "cucked"—using the term to mean corrupted and less pure in its outlook—as a result of the sale of the site by its founder in 2015,[13] and by a wave of opponents of the alt-right flooding onto the site as they realized it was an organizing ground for the movement. But told me he still watched the /pol/ board and 8chan "religiously."

I put it to him that, unlike the people he hung out with in his youth, the alt-right had failed to produce books, music, and film in any significant numbers. Without such production, I said, it would be difficult to sustain the argument that the alt-right is a real countercultural force. He agreed, and lamented the fact that his leftist enemies were "so good" at creating things. Perhaps, he thought, as his movement grew up, it would become similarly interested in soft power.

I was about to ask him why he and some of the other alt-righters I knew hadn't started families. For a group obsessed with the promulgation of a race, many activists seemed supremely dis-interested in actually breeding. But then, as our food arrived—I ordered a steak sandwich, Iain had a starter portion of kebabs—he casually mentioned a teenage son. "His mother's very much a feminist lefty," he said.

He started to explain that many activists might appear childless because they don't talk much about their families. But then he tried to tot up the people he knows in the movement who have children. He didn't get very far: "My god there are a lot of us who are singletons," he admitted. "Yeah, there are a lot of us who haven't procreated."

Iain could reel off the 14 words, and he had little time for watered-down versions of the alt-right philosophy. "We don't disavow the alt-light, but we do think their ideas won't work. We think they're cucked. Our worry is always people taking this [movement] off for their own reasons, off for their own ends, and not concentrating on the 14 words." He continued:

> There's a vast group of people who've attached themselves onto the alt-right ... who are weakening the movement more than they are bringing people into it. They are presentable people who can sell their ideas, and their ideas are weak versions of ours in all the areas that matter. They are not going to pay any attention to the "Jewish question." They might talk about globalism, but they don't see it in the Republican Party. We don't consider them to be careful enough, we don't consider them to be committed enough.

On the other hand Davis was not an ethnic purist, and his belief system allowed for racial homelands for everyone and even immigrant communities in the West—perhaps making him a bit alt-lightish himself. "I don't want to see a white planet. It would be awful. Everyone on the alt-right is less worried about what we're going to do when we win than just being wiped out, and being forced into the recesses and margins of society, till eventually we don't exist—a slow genocide," he lamented.

Although he said he'd been arrested a couple of times for assault and affray during his heavy-drinking leftist days, he was adamant he had no interest in political violence, or even in offending anyone he encountered in real life. "I take great pride in making sure that nobody I meet or interact with from any race or that sort of thing is affected by my beliefs in any physical way," he said. As for the radicals on his own side: "If people get nasty and violent, I won't talk to them at all."

He listed a few radical groups including the banned National Action, but said there's little talk of organized violence online—and in fact a paranoid tendency in alt-right forums to label anyone suggesting violence as a government agent. "There's no big chunk of people who wish to use political violence, but you'll get every so often this one nutter, usually with a history of a bunch of other things, and he'll do it," he told me.

Before we leave the pub he gave me a pin—a British flag in the shape of a heart, the symbol of the charity which runs the shop where he volunteers.

"I thought it looked vaguely nationalist," he told me. "If any antifa comes up to you and says, 'Are you some kind of nationalist?,' just say no, it's just heart research."

* * *

Iain Davis may have objected to violence and disdained the nuttier fringes of the alt-right movement. For him, like for many in the movement, politics is almost strictly an online endeavor. But beyond the slightly more respectable-looking facade of the alt-right and the clusters of alt-light celebrities, there is a large group of people who are willing to take more extreme measures to advance their goals. Alongside the formation of the alt-right a fevered industry developed, devoted to spreading conspiracy theories and capitalizing on fear and paranoia, sometimes with shocking consequences.

9

Conspiracy Theorists

Edgar Maddison Welch wasn't a well-educated hipster. He was 28 years old and lived in a small town in the middle of North Carolina. His Facebook profile photo showed him gurning while riding a roller coaster, and police records showed he had a number of arrests, for drug possession and drink driving.[1] He'd been listed in the credits of a number of obscure films—he was production assistant in a low-budget horror flick called *The Mill*, set in an abandoned textile factory.[2] His Facebook profile indicated he was a fan of typical dude-bro pop culture—video games, *Fight Club*, the TV series *Breaking Bad*—sprinkled with interests in both Christianity and conspiracy theories. He had two children. He could handle a gun.

On a Sunday morning in early December 2016—about a month after the US election—Welch, dressed in a blue T-shirt, blue jeans and work boots, left his children in the care of his girlfriend, got in his silver Toyota Prius, and began to drive north towards Washington, D.C. Along the way he recorded a video on his phone, telling family members that he loved them. He said he hoped he had "showed it" and that he would be able to "tell [them] again." "And if not," he said on the video, "don't ever forget it."[3]

If traffic's not bad, the drive from Salisbury to Washington D.C. takes about six hours. Welch arrived in the city mid-afternoon, and parked his car near Comet Ping Pong, a pizza restaurant. He took an AR-15 assault rifle and a .38 calibre handgun out of his car and entered the restaurant. One witness said he looked like a security guard, and although diners began to panic, he didn't trouble them but headed quickly towards the back of the building.[4]

Once inside, Welch began "investigating." He was looking for hidden rooms or tunnels. At one point, he later told police, he encountered a locked door. When he couldn't open it with a knife, he fired several shots at the lock. It still didn't open.[5] An employee, who'd been out back fetching pizza dough from a freezer, heard the shots and went inside, only to see the gunman and hear panicked customers fleeing. Welch turned in the direction of the employee, who high-tailed it back outside and ran to alert police.

The cops were familiar with the place—they had recently responded to other incidents at Comet Ping Pong, although none as serious as this one. Within half an hour they had the building surrounded. Welch left his guns in the restaurant, which had completely emptied out, and gave himself up. An officer handcuffed him, and asked him why he'd fired a weapon inside a crowded family friendly pizza joint.[6] He said he'd read online that Comet Ping Pong was harboring child sex slaves, and he wanted to see for himself whether they were there, and perhaps rescue them. He was taken to jail.[7]

* * *

The incident at Comet Ping Pong was the climax of a conspiracy theory that had been planted, fed and watered by the alt-right. It was conceived in the frantic atmosphere of the final days of the presidential election campaign, advanced by a mix of delusional white nationalist trolls and internet pranksters, and became real in the minds of many because of a confluence of paranoia, rumor, fake news, and violence.

The full story of "pizzagate" begins with an incident which was big news during the presidential campaign. Hillary Clinton's campaign chairman, John Podesta, had had his emails hacked and leaked. Podesta had been tricked by one of those alarming spammy emails warning that there's something wrong with one of your accounts and containing a link to a fake website. Podesta and his aides were fooled, and he clicked on it.[8] As hacking tactics go, it was crude, but in this case, effective.

Security experts traced the hack to a Russian group called Fancy Bear, and Podesta's emails surfaced on Wikileaks. The emails contained some genuinely juicy details, including details of Clinton's speeches to Wall Street bankers and messages revealing that she had been given some primary season debate questions in advance.[9] Wikileaks drip-fed the emails to the public in batches starting in early October and continuing through to the election.

On November 3, just five days before the vote, a user on 4chan /pol/ posted a message citing the latest batch of leaked emails.[10] The author of the post weaved a complicated tale of innuendo and speculation, starting with flight logs allegedly from an airplane owned by a sex offender who was a close associate of Bill Clinton, a photo featuring two American reporters who were captured in North Korea, and the Podesta emails. The link between all these, according to the anonymous channer, was the word "pizza."

"Sleuthing around for Pizza related things led us to this email," the channer wrote, linking to a Podesta email chain that included a message from a man named James Alefantis. The poster explained: "The owner of Comet Ping Pong, JAMES ALEFANTIS was the gay lover of David Brock for a while. He stars in a number of creepy ads for the pizza place. The Pizza place also has hidden doors to rooms according to their webpage."

It was the start of a fake conspiracy theory which eventually led to Welch's raid. The 4chan post played on rumors and fake news stories about the Clintons that had been circulating for some time.[11] It seemed to prove the adage that you can find evidence for anything as long as you look hard enough. And because it seemed to ground the false allegations in "facts" in the form of the leaked emails, alt-righters and others took the links and ran. Self-described investigators began digging through the emails. One posted a made-up key of "doublespeak" words— common foodstuffs which apparently held sinister references to child pornography. According to the code, "hotdog" meant "boy," "cheese" meant "little girl," "walnut" meant "person of color." As with everything on 4chan, it's hard to tell how seriously the post was meant to be taken, but soon alt-right activists were eagerly spreading the code and scouring Podesta's emails for the key words.[12]

The following day, November 4, the alt-right Twitter personality "Pizza Party Ben" made a dramatic announcement to his tens of thousands of followers. The real person behind the Twitter account was unknown,[13] but at one point contributed a nasty story to Breitbart, slamming a conservative critic of the alt-right, Ben Shapiro.[14] Pizza Party Ben, whoever he is, tweeted: "Alright you guys ready for this comet pizza thing? I'm bout to drop everything I know on it, go investigate for yourself after." The tweet was later deleted. When I sent him a direct message as the conspiracy theory gained steam, he jokingly wrote back: "Nope no idea what a pizzagate even is."

For something arising from a movement supposedly obsessed with facts and the truth, the "pizzagate" phenomenon was desperately thin on both. Most cover-up theories that take off have at their heart an astonishing but real event—the assassi-nation of John F. Kennedy, the moon landing, 9/11. "Pizzagate" had no victims, no physical evidence, and was initially based on a few references to one of the world's most common dishes. And yet the story quickly took on a political bent, and became a weaponized conspiracy theory.

The rumors spread via the usual alt-right pipeline. From 4chan, the conspiracy spread to subreddits, to Facebook and Twitter, and to dozens of YouTube videos. Activists plucked photos from Alefantis's Instagram feed and concocted wild theories about pedophile sex-trafficking rings that weren't just hiding in plain sight, but supposedly broadcasting coded signals via social media.

Although the rumors had begun before the election, the chatter really took off in mid-November. It was around this time that president-elect Trump dropped a campaign pledge to investigate and prosecute Hillary Clinton.[15] After the juicy prospect of putting their arch nemesis in prison seemed to evaporate, alt-righters grasped at another potential scalp-claiming scandal.

The "investigators" pointed fingers not only at Podesta and Alefantis but dozens of their associates, employees, neighbors, and relations. They posted pictures of what they called "degenerate" artwork on the restaurant's walls. They archly speculated about why Comet Ping Pong hosted "all ages" music shows—in total ignorance of the fact that the term refers to alcohol-free events which allow youngsters under the legal drinking age of 21 to attend.[16]

To take just one much-discussed piece of "evidence," a picture taken from Alefantis's Instagram feed showed a young girl smiling as she looked into the camera. Her wrists were taped to the table. When confronted by conspiracy theorists, the restaurant owner explained that the picture was of his goddaughter, who'd been playing with another child: "It's two kids playing together."[17] The sinister interpretations lived not in the pic but in the minds of the conspiracy theorists.

Alefantis initially tried to engage with the conspiracy theorists, but after a while realized what he was up against. Just days before Welch stormed his restaurant, the owner told me of his exasperation with the delusional "pizzagate" hoards. "They ignore basic truths," he said. For instance, the trafficking operation was supposedly run out of the restaurant's basement. One small problem: "We don't even have a basement."

But nothing Alefantis could do would stop the alt-right-inspired campaign. While thousands of self-appointed investigators frantically gathered "evidence," others just tweeted out sinister drumbeats. The chief influencers spreading the conspiracy theory online were Mike Cernovich and Brittany Pettibone, a Trump-supporting sci-fi author who hosted a podcast called "Virtue of the West." Their crusade was not just an internet quest. From the start, the activists talked about turning their "investigation" from online chatter into real-world action. Someone using Chuck Johnson's alt-right crowdfunding "bounty" website Wesearcher raised $2,625 from people in an attempt "to establish the presence of tunnels underneath or very close to being underneath Comet Ping Pong Pizza."[18]

Cernovich himself tweeted about "pizzagate" around 60 times before Welch went into Comet Ping Pong with his guns. He did not restrain himself to talking about the restaurant, instead spewing rumors and engaging in some classic script-flipping. If people dared to question his narrative, they were "in" on the conspiracy:

> Lots of people in "entertainment industry" attacking me tonight. Gee I wonder why. #Pizzagate[19]

> Media claims to be worried about rumors leading to harm, yet they will not report on violence against Trump supporters. Why? #PizzaGate[20]

> Paul Ryan and Ben Sasse are also part of #pizzagate.[21]

> Parents: What do you see in this video? #Pizzagate[22]

This last tweet was posted along with a short video clip from C-SPAN showing Vice President Joe Biden meeting a family at the White House and placing his hands on a young girl's shoulders.

"Pizzagate" showed how an outlandish web of speculation and innuendo could rally thousands online, and draw in people who would appear to have little common cause with the alt-right. Researchers have linked belief in conspiracies to fear and lack of control.[23] Other scientists have found that low self-esteem, distrust of authority, and low agreeableness are common traits of conspiracy believers.[24]

Those characteristics might be particularly common in the extreme right, but they certainly aren't the preserve of any one political camp. And so "pizzagate" broke out of 4chan and alt-right Reddit and drew in people from the left, or formerly from the left, some of whom were at one point Bernie Sanders supporters. They included David Seaman, a former Huffington Post writer who started to post creepy videos to his YouTube account, and Cassandra Fairbanks, the alt-lightish reporter who wrote for the Russian state-funded news outlet Sputnik. Fairbanks, moonlighting for a blog, wrote:

> Whether this is a case of confirmation bias, or something more sinister—one thing is certain: People really do not trust Hillary Clinton—to the point where thousands of people are actually having serious discussions about whether or not she is involved in a child sex ring. Perhaps the Democrats should consider bringing Bernie Sanders back now.[25]

After I spoke to Alefantis and wrote a story for the BBC Trending blog,[26] my email inbox was flooded with messages from both alt-righters and others of various political persuasions. I had been prepared for the reaction, but the backlash from the hardcore conspiracy theorists was quite different to anything I had seen before. They included professionals, business owners, a nurse in California, an artist in Brooklyn. And they were angry.

> Conspiracy or not ALL allegations should be treated seriously and investigated swiftly with competency.

> You're soul is sold or your eyes are closed [sic]

> I don't support Trump or Clinton. I am politically independent. However, you don't appear to have a shred of objectivity.

Among the conspiracy theorists, there was a particular and perhaps unusual crossover with people who were interested in the Dakota Access Pipeline (DAPL) project—a tussle between Native Americans supported by liberal activists and oil companies that wanted to build a pipeline through Native land in North Dakota. The common link in these seemingly widely disparate stories was a profound distrust of the mainstream media.

Welch himself was aware of the DAPL protests. Three days before he drove to Washington he'd been chatting with a friend about his plans. The friend texted him: "Tell me we r going to save the Indians from the pipeline." Welch responded: "Way more important, much higher stakes … Pizzagate."[27] DAPL featured on several alt-right blogs and YouTube videos.[28] Fairbanks, the Sputnik reporter, wrote several articles on the protests,[29] and several of the people who contacted me had tweeted about DAPL as well as Comet Ping Pong.

The "pizzagate" story appealed to people, linking some on the far left and the alt-right, and even gained traction amid conspiracy lovers outside the United States. Turkish fans of Turkish President Recep Tayyip Erdoğan spread the rumor with the help of pro-government activists. The made-up scandal came at a particularly fortuitous time for Erdoğan's supporters, just as he had shut down the country's biggest child-welfare charity and was trying to push through a controversial draft bill that would have given amnesty to child abusers if they marry their victims.[30]

The incident showed the potential of the alt-right social media machine to scoop up the conspiracy-minded, those attracted to fringe movements or who hate the establishment media and politicians, to whip up an international frenzy, and to motivate one activist to "self-investigate" with a carful of loaded guns.

*   *   *

Welch's misadventure gave the "pizzagate" rumor a publicity boost, but it also gave it a measure of hot-headed reality that it had previous lacked. Some conspiracy theorists, as conspiracy theorists do, quickly tried to fold Welch into their overarching narrative.

"CONFIRMED," tweeted alt-right activist Jack Posobiec, leader of a group called Citizens4Trump. "Comet Pizza Gunman Edgar Maddison Welch is an ACTOR." Posobiec had perfected the trademark alt-right blend of fact, fiction, and hype. Welch had acted in the past, so in the strict sense the message was true, but the implication of pointing out that particular fact in ALL CAPS was clear—and clearly wrong.[31] Welch had appeared in movies—but wasn't acting when he marched into Comet Ping Pong. As evidence, it also didn't make much sense. The conspiracy theorists who imagined that the world's most powerful people had covered up a huge child sex and trafficking ring couldn't quite explain how such alleged criminal masterminds were unable to cover their tracks on the crowd-sourced Internet Movie Database.[32]

Other prominent "pizzagate" exponents peeled away from the campaign, realizing that association with it was suddenly not a great look. Cassandra Fairbanks complained on Twitter: "People are accusing me of starting #Pizzagate," adding a link to her original article. "Doesnt mention comet ping pong," she protested.[33] And yet Fairbanks later wore a Comet Ping Pong badge to the Delploraball,[34] an alt-right gathering to celebrate Trump's inauguration. She told me via email that someone at the ball had a bag of the pins and that she put one on her dress: "I just left it there because I thought it was a weird/funny thing for someone to bring." She also clarified her views on the whole affair: "I don't think people are being held in the basement of a pizza parlor if that is what you mean. I don't doubt that there are pedophile rings that exist, though, in general." But from the start, pizzagate was never a general anti-pedophile campaign. Alleging that children were being held in the basement of a pizza parlor was the whole point. And painting political enemies in the worst possible light was the aim.

After the shooting Mike Cernovich also dodged responsibility. On his website he posted an article with the script-flipping headline: "Mike Cernovich Responds to Fake News Media Conspiracy Theories About #Pizzagate." "There is an active pedophile ring in Washington, D.C. This pedophile ring included Dennis Hastert (who was called a 'serial child predator' by the judge who sentenced him to prison), among others," he wrote.[35]

Hastert, a former high-ranking Republican, was sentenced to 15 months prison in 2015 for covering up his abuse of boys when he was a small-town high-school wrestling coach. There was no evidence presented that anyone else was involved in the abuse.[36] Cernovich went on: "I have no idea whether Comet Pizza is the center of this pedophile ring. The evidence isn't strong enough, which is why I have not named the parlor as being part of a sex trafficking ring."[37]

The excuse is disingenuous at best. During the time Cernovich was waging his "pizzagate" campaign, around 60,000 messages mentioning Comet Ping Pong were sent on Twitter alone. It's hard to figure out what else someone would have been referring to when talking about "pizzagate," if not the conspiracy theories swirling around the restaurant.

Cernovich wouldn't directly answer questions about his role in spreading the "pizzagate" rumors. Instead he told me via email: "Haters will always find a way to hate on me, so what they try to blame on me doesn't enter my consciousness. The media has covered up many pedophile scandals." Aware of my day job, he hit back with a script-flip familiar to me from the many people who emailed in the wake of my story on "pizzagate": the Jimmy Savile child abuse scandal that had rocked the BBC. The triggered conspiracy theorists argued that that shameful episode somehow detracted from my own credibility with regard to sex-trafficking allegations that had no basis in fact.[38] Cernovich blocked me on Twitter.

The conspiracy theory also found receptive ears within the Trump administration. Perhaps most notably, Michael Flynn Jr., the son of Donald Trump's one-time National Security Advisor, tweeted after the shooting: "Until #Pizzagate proven to be false, it'll remain a story. The left seems to forget #PodestaEmails and the many 'coincidences' tied to it." For that he jumped, or was pushed, from Trump's transition team.[39]

Flynn's father, who lasted less than a month in the national security job before being found out for dishonestly portraying his contacts with Russia, never mentioned "Pizzagate" or Comet Ping Pong, but he did tweet about a different made-up sex-crime conspiracy: "U decide - NYPD Blows Whistle on New Hillary Emails: Money Laundering, Sex Crimes w Children, etc...MUST READ!"[40]

Flynn Sr later deleted his tweet.

*　　*　　*

The rise of Trump has once again foregrounded the "paranoid style" in American politics. "American politics has often been an arena for angry minds," wrote Richard Hofstadter in his famous 1964 essay in *Harpers* which not only coined the phrase but eloquently traced its roots throughout the whole of American history.[41]

Hofstadter was concerned, in his moment, with far-right groups such as the John Birch Society, which was more or less cast out of mainstream conservativism by the establishment of the day.[42] But he found the tendency among all sorts of political movements on both the right and the left:

In the history of the United States one finds it, for example, in the anti-Masonic movement, the nativist and anti-Catholic movement, in certain spokesmen of abolitionism who regarded the United States as being in the grip of a slaveholders' conspiracy, in many alarmists about the Mormons, in some Greenback and Populist writers who constructed a great conspiracy of international bankers, in the exposure of a munitions makers' conspiracy of World War I, in the popular left-wing press, in the contemporary American right wing, and on both sides of the race controversy today, among White Citizens' Councils and Black Muslims.[43]

Today you can see the paranoid tendency at work at the political extremes, but its biggest engine is the alt-right, and its links go right to the White House.

* * *

It's worth mentioning another star in the alt-right firmament who pushed "pizzagate" but later tried to scrub his involvement—because Alex Jones is the most popular embodiment of the paranoid style in American politics today.

On November 27, Jones, a radio host and the founder of the website Infowars, spent half an hour of his radio show talking about "pizzagate," even telling his audience to "investigate it for yourself." "Let's go ahead and go to the report, 'Pizzagate Is Real,' he said. 'The question is: How real is it? What is it? Something's going on. Something's being covered up. It needs to be investigated. To just call it fake news—these are real Wikileaks. This is real stuff going on.'"[44]

During that same radio program Jones suggested that he would be "getting on a plane" to visit Comet Ping Pong. "I couldn't sleep last night and you know, people may look into it. I may take off a week and just only research this," he said, later commenting: "I don't have the self-control to be around these type of people. So you want us to cover pizzagate, we have covered it. We are covering it. And all I know is God help us, we're in the hands of pure evil."

Welch's Facebook profile indicated that he had "liked" Infowars and Jones, although after his arrest he was equivocal in an interview with the *New York Times*: "He's a bit eccentric ... He touches on some issues that are viable but goes off the deep end on some things." When it came to "pizzagate," Welch apparently thought Infowars viable enough to send a link to a friend while he was in the planning stages of his attack. The accompanying message told the friend to watch the video "PIZZAGATE: The Bigger Picture." Although no video from the time with that exact title remained on YouTube, the headline was used on an Infowars story,[45] and was also used by other accounts pushing the Infowars video.

After the Comet Ping Pong shoot-up, Infowars content on the story started disappearing from the internet. Jones's November 27 radio show was taken down from YouTube, as was the "Pizzagate is Real" report contained within it. His about-face was even more whiplash-inducing than Cernovich's. On December 15 he said that he had been the "most restrained" of all the voices in the alternative media looking into the story and that there was "probably nothing going on there."[46]

He even layered a conspiracy theory upon a conspiracy theory, saying that "pizzagate" was "probably setup," that he predicted the restaurant might come under fire and that he would be setup as a result. Powerful forces, he said, were plotting to remove him from the airwaves.[47]

*　*　*

Jones is America's most popular conspiracy theorist and a key inspiration for sections of the alt right and the alt-light. He was the original 9/11 "truther" and has spun narratives around the Boston Marathon bombing, the Oklahoma City bombing, terror attacks in France, Spain, Belgium, Norway, and elsewhere, as well as nearly every major mass shooting in the United States.[48] He complains he is unfairly treated by the mainstream media simply because he asks questions, and to some extent, he is correct— he rarely goes on the record declaring that some conspiracy theory or another is true. Instead, he brings onto his program conspiracy theorists and crackpots who are allowed to spin their stories at length to Jones's large, heavily engaged audience. By one estimate, Jones has a total listenership and viewership of around 8 million people,[49] which goes well beyond the hardcore alt-righters and reaches conservatives, the curious, and the conspiracy-minded on the left.

He began in the early 2000s broadcasting from his bedroom, complete with childish choo-choo train wallpaper and an Empire Strikes Back poster on the wall,[50] which belies the fact that his overriding worldview is that shadowy deep-state forces control society. He claims, for instance, that an elitist cabal wants to kill 80 percent of the world's population and enslave the rest.

In his hands, the nature of conspiracy theories themselves have changed, from paranormal or historical thought exercises—think Area 51, the moon landing, or the Loch Ness monster—to politically motivated, internet-ready bursts of misinformation and lies. Jones's emotive outbursts, while entertaining, have inspired the more unhinged members of his audience, like Edgar Welch, to action. Infowars fans had been involved in at least half a dozen shootings and terror attacks even before "pizzagate."[51]

And the focus of Jones's rages has also at times gone well beyond the shadowy forces of the "deep state." Ordinary people have been targeted—including the victims of shootings and terror attacks themselves.

*　*　*

I met Lenny Pozner in a pleasant, but undisclosed, location. He didn't want me to report any details about where he lives, other than it's somewhere in the United States. He had good reason to be concerned. One of the first things he did after me and my producer Sam Judah arrived at his apartment was show us a YouTube video.

It began with a clip of Pozner speaking to a news organization. He was filmed in silhouette, against the window of his balcony. Nothing is visible in the background except a few trees and a balcony railing. The video, which had no narration, switched to a shot of Google Street View, which showed the exterior of Pozner's home. The camera zoomed in on Lenny's balcony. A circle highlighted his balcony railing—a railing which, to my eyes, looked completely anodyne and unremarkable in the news clip, but which some unknown person used to identify exactly where he lived.

The video then showed more Google searches—of Lenny's address and of maps of the local area. There were no words or additional images, but the message was unmistakable: *This is where the guy lives. What's next, is up to you.*

Pozner had attracted conspiracy-minded stalkers stoked by Alex Jones because of his reaction to a horrible tragedy that visited him and his family. In December 2014, the Pozners were living in Newtown, Connecticut. His son, Noah, was a student at Sandy Hook Elementary School. He had just turned six years old when a young man rampaged through the school and shot him dead, along with 19 of his classmates and six teachers and school administrators. The shooter himself, through his immediate suicide, the murder of his mother, and a wrecked hard drive, managed to leave behind scant trace of his motivations or terminal mental state.

Incidentally, Lenny Pozner himself had an interest in conspiracy theories. He'd watched a few videos about whether the moon landings were faked, and was curious about myths like the Loch Ness monster. "It was science-fiction type stuff," he told me,

Something you would do at the end of a busy day, to see what kinds of questions people were asking, something for entertainment. I wanted to see what they had to say. It didn't take me too long to see they were really reaching. But I had an interest … some people take it seriously some people find it entertaining … But there are conspiracy theories and there are hoaxer narratives that target families and victims, and that is quite different.

Because of his interest, Lenny was an occasional Infowars listener. And because of *that*, he realized quite quickly after his son was murdered, that the horrific events at Sandy Hook were being turned into politically motivated fodder for Jones's conspiracy-minded listeners.

The claims of the conspiracy theorists were incredible even by the standards of Jones and the alt-right. The whole thing was faked, they were saying. The shootings were a drill, they alleged, which happened in a school which was abandoned, and the children were really alive and lived on under assumed names, and their graves were empty, and the whole town was in on it, and hundreds of people had signed non-disclosure agreements and were involved in a cover-up that went all the way to the Attorney General and the president, who were using the whole thing to push new gun-control laws (which, as it turns out, were never successfully passed by Congress).

Jones brought onto his show Wolfgang Halbig, a retired school-security consultant who became the focal point for the conspiracy theorists. Halbig raised tens of thousands of dollars to help "investigate" the cover-up, which consisted of filing court actions and Freedom of Information Act requests, gathering "evidence" and poring over the details of news footage. Jones popularized the theories on his show and, just as in "pizzagate," hundreds of videos flooded YouTube, thousands of messages flew around Twitter, and blog posts and fake news items popped up all over the place, including on a website owned by the Iranian government.[52]

And again, just as in "pizzagate," the rhetoric prompted some people into action. At least two were arrested for making threatening comments to parents of victims and other people in Sandy Hook. Among the Infowars audience, the delusion reached levels such that hatred was directed not only at the authorities allegedly involved in the made-up cover-up, but also at the grieving parents of murdered children.

Amidst this deluge of conspiracy, Lenny Pozner decided to fight back. He started by sending a short but polite note to Alex Jones, asking him to stop peddling lies. Jones took no notice. Eventually Pozner began filing copyright notices and complaints with every major social network, asking them to take down videos. He founded an organization, the HONR Network, with the aim of "stopping the continual and intentional torment of victims." He built a network of hundreds of volunteers who track the hoaxers and try to take down their content.

He told me he is worried about the alt-right and its influence in America. "What I started saying early on is that this little conspiracy theory is like a brushfire and it needs to get dealt with, it needs to get contained," he said. "It needs to get shaped, it needs to get directed—because without that it'll start burning and a brushfire can burn down a whole forest."

When confronted by trolls, people's reactions vary wildly. Some people ignore them—the "don't feed" option—and Lenny Pozner has heard from some Sandy Hook residents that that's what he should be doing. Sometimes people call out the trolls in public forums or try gingerly to work through social media companies to get results.

Lenny Pozner's strategy is impressive in its comprehensive-ness and single-minded purpose. And he has taken steps to fight the conspiracy theorists—some of whom, but not all, qualify as alt-righters—at great risk, both emotionally ("I have to be in the right frame of mind to tackle the videos," he told me) and personally, as evidenced by the creepy video he showed me when I first entered his home.

"I would like not to have to do this," he said. "I would like to just leave it alone and feel the memory of my child is sacred and other people are also treating it that way, but as long as they're not I feel I need to defend that memory."

* * *

Jones, meanwhile, is no longer a fringe player. Infowars, through its website and radio show, reaches millions of people each week. In between rants about the New World Order and paranoid interviews about the "deep state," Jones still sells his vitamins, survival gear, and wet wipes. But the brash, heavily commercial format appeals to conspiracy-minded fans and has given Jones a certain measure of influence.

In late 2015, he welcomed candidate Donald Trump onto Infowars, and Trump paid him a compliment he gives few media workers: "Your reputation is amazing. I will not let you down."[53] Trump ignored calls to disavow Jones, even after the *USA Today* newspaper published an open letter by the daughter of the murdered Sandy Hook Elementary School principal.[54] Infowars claims that it has close ties to the White House, although those claims are debatable.[55] For his part, when confronted with the evidence, Jones did his usual dissembling act. "I've always said I'm not sure what happened there, but there are a lot of anomalies, and there has been a cover-up of what did happen there," he said in a video with the headline "Alex Jones' final statement on Sandy Hook: Media attempting to demonize Infowars for questioning known liars."[56] "I know there are real mass shootings. I know people lose children, I'm a father, it hurts my heart. So I don't know what the truth is. All I know is, the official story of Sandy Hook has more holes in it than Swiss cheese."

The video segues into a series of Jones's greatest Sandy Hook hits, all of which cast doubt on the official narrative and the physical evidence which backs it up. Jones casts himself as a fearless truth-seeker, but even when signing off, he can't quite let it go, or resist a dig at the parents of murdered children: "If children were lost at Sandy Hook, my heart goes out to each and every parent, and those who say they're parents on the news. The only problem is, I've watched a lot of soap operas and I've seen actors before, and I know when I'm watching a movie and when I'm watching something real. Let's look into Sandy Hook."[57]

In April 2017, the conspiracy theorists formed an alliance. Cernovich was given a regular slot hosting Alex Jones's show.[58]

*   *   *

Jones runs the repeater station for 4chan and other conspiracy-minded corners of the alt-right internet, and his huge audience means that the ideas of the paranoid lunatic fringes spread outside of the circles of hardcore activists. He is, by one account, the conspiracy theorist "with the most far-reaching influence in the nation's history."[59] By his own account—or rather, the account of his lawyer during a fractious custody dispute—he's also a "performance artist playing a character."[60]

Clearly not all Infowars fans will pick up a gun and decide to "self-investigate"—many take Jones with a small mountain of salt, drawn in not by his alternative facts but by his bombast and emotion. But Jones and Infowars are a clear example of how alt-right tactics can infect public debate and bring emotional distress and physical violence on to innocent victims, even the grieving parents of murdered children.

Like the neo-Nazis of the Daily Stormer, Jones walks right up to the line of encouraging violent action. Bombast and bluster are his key operating modes, and although he never openly encourages specific acts of violence, various members of his audience have taken action, sometimes with deadly results. But the radical end of the alt-right spectrum isn't limited to mentally unstable people inspired to take action by crackpot theories. Even as it paints violent acts committed by minorities and radical Islamic terrorism as existential threats to Western white civilization, the culture of the alt-right is breeding its own brand of terrorists: socially isolated young men who are willing to kill.

10

The Violent Fringe

The horror of the moment the crowd in Charlottesville realized the car was not going to slow down was captured in a video posted online. As the speeding Dodge Challenger plowed into the crowd, protesters scrambled in panic as screams rose from the narrow street. A few of the demonstrators left in the wake of the attack hurled curses at the driver. But when the car quickly backed up, everyone on the street fled for cover. When it was over, a woman was dead and at least 19 others were injured.[1]

The driver was a 20-year-old man who had been photographed earlier in the day participating in white nationalist rallies in Charlottesville, along with hundreds of neo-Nazi and alt-right activists in what some described as the biggest far-right gathering in the United States for years.[2] James Alex Fields lived in northwest Ohio, and although he sported the "fashy" haircut that alt-righters had co-opted, the details of his life that leaked out after the attack sketched out a picture of a young man on the down-and-out rather than an erudite right-wing hipster. Reports described him as a loner,[3] fixated on the Nazis and Hitler,[4] who after a troubled childhood in Kentucky had tried and failed to join the US Army.[5] Fields had a history of violence directed at his disabled mother.[6] The day before the Charlottesville attack, he dropped his cat off at his mom's house, and texted her to say he was going to an alt-right rally.[7]

The attack in Charlottesville was a pivotal moment in the slowly building street-level conflict between the alt-right and its liberal and anti-fascist opponents. Protests and counter-protests had been building from Inauguration Day onwards, and had turned violent in several cities across the United States. Three days after the attack, the president angrily declared in front of a press conference that "you had some very fine people on both sides":

> What about the alt left that came charging at, as you say, at the alt right? Do they have any assemblage of guilt? What about the fact that they came charging with clubs in their hands swinging clubs? Do they have any problem? I think they do…
>
> You had a group on one side that was bad. You had a group on the other side that was also very violent. Nobody wants to say that. I'll say it right now. You had a group on the other side that came charging in without a permit and they were very, very violent.[8]

After the fractious press conference, Richard Spencer told *The Atlantic* that he was "really proud" of the president: "He bucked the narrative of alt-right violence, and made a statement that is fair and down to earth."[9]

While the Charlottesville attack made Americans—and the rest of the world—stand up and take fresh notice of the far right, it wasn't the first deadly attack carried out by those who had fallen under the sway of the alt-right. Violence had been a part of the movement for years.

* * *

It was a quiet Saturday afternoon at the end of August 2015. In between corralling my children and making dinner, I was sticking to the bad habit of checking my work emails on a weekend. Usually this was a low-risk activity that would uncover maybe an ignorable press release or some issue with a colleague that would have demanded a few minutes of my time the following Monday.

On this particular afternoon, however, my inbox included a bomb threat.

To: michael.wendling@bbc.co.uk
From: A*****@yahoo.com
Date: 30 Aug 2015

Hello, this is Australi Witness. You might know me for inspiring the attack in Garland, Texas earlier this year, where two mujahideen entered a "Draw Muhammad" (PBUH) event with intention to slaughter the kuffar inside of it.

Do real terrorists introduce themselves by listing their past attacks? And, thinking about it, do real terrorists use Yahoo accounts? Still, I was suddenly paying attention.

> I would like you to know that, on September 11, a pressure cooker bomb is going to be detonated in a large Midwestern US city (I won't say exactly which city for obvious reasons). The bomb will be filled with shrapnel, and the shrapnel will be covered in rat poison for maximum damage.

The writer rambled on for some time, finally signing off:

> The United States WILL pay for attacking the human rights of Muslims. This pressure cooker attack on 9/11 is NOTHING compared to what's coming in the future.
> That is all for now. I will tell you more once the attack happens.
> Sincerely,
> Australi Witness.

I read the email through a couple of times. Everyone who's worked in journalism is familiar with the "green ink brigade"— persistent, perhaps mentally ill letter-writers who ping reporters with conspiracy theories, rants and vague threats. In the days of dead trees they often used colored ink—perhaps green is cheaper when bought in volume—but in more recent times the hallmarks of the cuckoo brigade are odd fonts and nonstandard punctuation. The real nasty types use throwaway anonymous email services, but for most a random Google, Yahoo or Hotmail account will do. They collect journalists' email addresses to fire out their messages to hundreds at a time. I'm sure the response rate has not improved.

And yet this message seemed ever so slightly more credible than the usual missives. It was well composed. There were no spelling errors. The only suspicious note—and it was a big one— was the content of the message itself. What kind of terrorist would tip off a journalist? That *modus operandi* fitted no jihadist terror organization that I knew of.

The letter writer included other telling details—the name of a piece of encrypted chat software, for instance. But he also mentioned that he had been inspired by a liberal Muslim Australian human rights activist who wasn't exactly a household name, and claimed to have undertaken extensive work for "Amnesty International and other human rights organizations." Not only did this seem highly implausible, but it immediately struck me as a rather crude attempt to sling some dirt at a liberal campaigning organization.

There was another relevant clue. I looked up the attack in Texas. In May 2015 two jihadists from Arizona, jolted into action by online propaganda, drove to Garland, a suburb of Dallas, Texas.[10] At a civic center there, a number of groups including the American Freedom Defense Institute had organized an event dubbed the "First Annual Muhammad Art Exhibit and Contest." The AFDI has been called an anti-Muslim hate group by the Southern Poverty Law Center; its president Pamela Geller spoke at the art exhibition along with Geert Wilders, a far-right Dutch politician.[11]

The two jihadists drove up to the building and opened fire on police, hitting one security officer in the ankle before a SWAT team shot them both dead.[12]

The facts of the attack seemed clear cut. The perpetrators were dead; another man who helped them had been arrested. It was the first time ISIS had claimed responsibility for an attack on American soil. I flicked through a few more news reports. There was no mention of another missing co-conspirator, or a hunt for other attackers. The letter-writer seemed to be a crank.

Still, something about the message unnerved me. I notified my editor and the police. And I really didn't think much more of it until two weeks later, when a young man in Florida was arrested on terrorism charges related to the plot he had revealed to me in the email. An entire back story unraveled—involving another attack, a dizzying set of online personalities, and an obsession with free speech. This young man wasn't a Muslim extremist, but a mentally ill recluse who had become immersed in the world of the alt-right. After his arrest the strange, sad details of the story of Joshua Ryne Goldberg began to come out, and the reasons for his unnerving message became clear.

* * *

The alt-right backs up its obsession with absolute freedom of speech and its hatred of Islam with a joint argument: the former never hurts anybody, and the latter kills. It's a version of the playground chant: "Sticks and stones will break my bones but names will never hurt me." Sticks and stones, in this case, are wielded by the followers of Muhammad. The names, meanwhile, are the insults and abuse slung around Twitter. Anybody with a brain, they argue, can easily tell the difference.

This argument has a certain appeal to common sense in a world where Islamist terror operations are of high concern, and where attacks by groups like ISIS seem aimed at the very nature of Western democracy. In comparison, free speech seems not only harmless but absolutely vital, a life-affirming celebration of an open society.

When the argument is put forward by the alt-right, however, there is little room for nuance, and any critique of the absolutist position, or insistence on the necessity of dialogue as something more important than defending trolling, becomes an attack on Western values. Alt-right fans have flocked to alternative social networks like Gab and the Reddit-clone Voat, which function in a broadly similar way to mainstream networks but have much looser restrictions on what is and isn't allowed to be said. Those sites have become safe spaces for alt-right and other fringe groups. Users are able to say more or less whatever they want, but the discussion is limited to a narrow band of flavors of right-wing thought. The arguments that occur happen, if you like, within a very narrow "Overton Window."

In June 2017, one British 4channer posted the following: "I'm so fucked tired of London. I am genuinely thinking of going to the airport right now and starting a new life somewhere. Anywhere. Please, there must be anons that would suggest something or even hook me up with a job or something?" Although the original poster's later responses indicated that he was simply stressed out and looking for a better quality of life, 4channers interpreted his post through a racial lens:

> Literally move anywhere in the country side, 99% white in most places and comfy as fuck

> well America isn't much better but at least you can move innawoods in some very white state with guns and an internet connection if you really wanted

> I think everywhere in London shares the damage of immigration and cucks now, we really must escape.[13]

There are many similar examples out there. But for all its emphasis on online communication and written language, the most vocal supporters of the alt-right seem strangely unable to admit that words matter. They can convince. They can change minds. They can "red pill." They can drive people to kill.

*   *   *

According to local reports, 20-year-old Joshua Goldberg led a quiet life with his parents in Orange Park, a suburb of Jacksonville, Florida.[14] So quiet, in fact, that after his arrest local reporters interviewed some neighbors who didn't even realize he lived in a back bedroom in the house. When FBI agents staked out the house, they observed Goldberg's parents leaving and caught glimpses of shadows inside the home, and lights turning on and off. But they had to wait weeks for any sighting of Joshua Goldberg himself. He simply never went outside.[15]

Goldberg lived almost entirely online. Inside the Orange Park house, he created and controlled an interlocking web of dozens, maybe hundreds, of fictitious online identities. Many, although not all, were heavily political. Some, like the one that ran a message board on Reddit, were virulently racist. Using the pseudonym European88, he was a moderator of a "subreddit" called CoonTown. The board, as you can probably guess, was devoted to anti-black images and messages. Under the name "Michael Slay," Goldberg also posted articles on the Daily Stormer.

And yet other Goldberg sock puppets had very different political perspectives. One of his Twitter accounts ostensibly belonged to a feminist blogger, another to a female black conservative living in Washington. These were, in a sense, satire accounts, or just plain fakes. Reddit users can be quick to jump to conclusions, and they can occasionally organize misguided witch hunts like the one which misidentified the Boston Marathon bombers. But when obsessives on individual subreddits put their minds to it, they can uncover all sorts of information. Within days of Goldberg's arrest, redditors had uncovered dozens of his personas.[16]

Managing all of the different personas and coordinating, as he did, the fights and trolling between them, must have been exhausting. And Reddit was only one of the sites Goldberg was particularly active on. He had accounts on a range of social networks, message boards, and other websites, in addition to email addresses. For instance, several of his personas posted lengthy essays on the millennial confession hub Thought Catalog, and he was an active editor on Wikipedia.[17] Goldberg had so many online identities that it's possible some slipped through the net and might never be found or traced back to him.

*   *   *

As for how I came onto Goldberg's radar—and why he sent me the bomb warning—it appears I unwittingly first contacted him while reporting on a story connected with Dylann Roof's murderous rampage in Charleston in 2015. After the massacre, I had been looking at social media and hate speech—in particular, Reddit's decision to delete several sections of its site frequented by extremists.[18] I contacted several moderators of the subreddits in question. One of them was the "Michael Slay" Goldberg persona, who went by the handle European88. Slay/European/Goldberg was remarkably matter-of-fact when contacted. Would he be up for an interview, I asked? He responded with what sounded more like a job application letter than a white supremacist screed:

> Yes, I would be willing to answer any questions. I am a moderator of /r/CoonTown, and I have been since day one. I have also written extensively for The Daily Stormer, the most-visited White nationalist website in the world. In addition, I have recently begun to write for TheRightStuff.biz.[19]

He boasted about a Reddit post he'd written that at one point had been the stickied post at the top of "r/CoonTown." It was titled: "The only good nigger is a dead one."

"He was excited that you'd contacted him," said Luke McMahon, an Australian journalist. If I was the blindfolded man holding onto the tail of elephant Goldberg, McMahon was looking into the animal's eyes. He'd struck up a friendship, perhaps not with Goldberg himself (whatever that would even mean), but with one of his personas. McMahon later told me that Goldberg was not only elated but panicked by the fact that a reporter from a big international news organization had contacted him. It was a form of validation for his grand project. But the medium was the problem. He was so shy that he was afraid to talk on the radio.

A day after my message to European88, he emailed me: "I do not have access to Skype at the moment, as my laptop is currently broken and I'm using a different computer. Is there any other way?"[20] There are plenty of extremists in the world who are desperate for airtime, so even if you really want to ask them questions, it doesn't make much sense to bend over backwards to accommodate their technology problems. But this brief exchange had one crucial result. Goldberg, in his alt-right bubble, thought he had captured the attention of a reporter. And so when, using another one of his aliases, he wanted to sow fear about a terrorist plot, his email ended up in my inbox.

Shortly after Goldberg was arrested in 2015, McMahon told me: "It was immediately apparent to me that I was dealing with like a classic Internet troll, but one that was obviously quite sophisticated." "He was a very socially isolated individual," he continued.

> He was someone who found refuge on the internet and established connections with a community that he wasn't able to develop in the real world. Unfortunately that community that he became involved with is a very negative and destructive community.
>
> I'd often look at the weather in Florida … and it's like fantastic weather in Florida and I'm sitting here in freezing cold Melbourne. I said to him, "Why don't you go outside? Like why don't you go to the beach?" And he'd tell me these sort of intimate things about himself like the fact that he does suffer from depression and that he doesn't leave the house. I think it's really difficult to not empathize with someone who's in that situation.

Goldberg's mental illness was clearly the overriding factor in his scheming. But given all his contradictory personas, what's the evidence that his sympathies were with the alt-right rather than with (to take the preoccupation of another of his personas) intersectional feminism? After all, alt-right-friendly outlets such as Breitbart attempted to flip the script and paint him as a leftist once his story came to light. In several stories, Milo Yiannopoulos tried to make this connection, linking Goldberg to a feminist website[21] and the politics site DailyKos[22]—arguing that he was a liberal enemy, nothing to do with the far-right. Either the prospect of getting linked to a terror attack scared some alt-lighters, or they saw the chance to paint the plotter as a leftist. Most likely it was a bit of both.

But a proper examination of Goldberg's writing, as grim and confusing as such a task is, shows that he was no more a radical socialist, or an angry feminist, or a black conservative (all of which he posed as online) than he was a hooded member of the KKK. Both of those flavors of extremist personalities—and several others besides—were parodies of personas designed to service his ultimate obsession, one that comes direct from the alt-right: absolute free speech. For Goldberg, it seems, it wasn't just that people should have the right to say all sorts of repugnant things, but rather that people *should* say all sorts of repugnant things.

Take for instance an essay he posted using his "Tanya Cohen" persona, who fronted as an Australian feminist. Called "Here is Why it's Time to Get Tough on Hate Speech in America," it begins at a shrill pitch which gets consistently higher: "The United States refuses to protect even the most basic of human rights, firmly establishing itself as a pariah state that falls far behind the rest of the world in terms of protecting fundamental human rights and democratic freedoms."[23]

The story gets even more loopy as "Cohen" continues over the course of nearly 7,000 words, arguing that hate speech includes anything offensive, is akin to murder, and that those accused of it should be considered guilty until proven innocent and sent away to re-education camps: "Anyone guilty of hate speech—which should carry criminal penalties of 25 years to life—should be sent to special prisons designed to re-educate them and to instill values of tolerance, freedom, democracy, and human rights in them."

For a random post on Thought Catalog, an open-to-all-comers website, the Cohen essay generated a fair amount of chatter on social media and blogs, long before Goldberg's full story was known. Mike Masnick, an entrepreneur and the founder of the website Techdirt, saw the piece for what it was:

> It has to be satire. Not only that, but it's damn good satire, because it's just stupid enough at the beginning to drag you in and make you believe it, and then, slowly but surely, over the course of a very long writeup, it starts tossing out ever more ridiculous ideas—drip... drip... drip—that just, gently, turn up the outrage-o-meter, such that many people don't even realize that it's satire.[24]

The Cohen essay and others like it are exaggerated versions of what an alt-righter might think is going on inside the head of a progressive. Goldberg's tone was different—albeit, in the alt-right tradition, just as verbose—when he wrote under his own name. In one essay, "How Social Justice Warriors are Creating an Entire Generation of Fascists," he appears to write from personal experience and details a long list of crimes and misdemeanors committed by leftists. The language is pompous and contains sweeping generalizations, reading like a personal, ersatz version of Curtis Yarvin's Unqualified Reservations:

> SJWs—almost all of whom are white, upper-middle-class college students—picture themselves as persecuted, oppressed crusaders for peace and equality. But, upon any level of inspection, this claim immediately falls apart. I have been on

the Internet since I was a small child and I have perused some of the most extreme and disturbing corners of the web. I have had personal encounters with every manner of vile cretin—the sorts of people who would make even Charles Manson himself blush. With that said, never have I encountered anyone who was so giddy about their hatred than the people who make up the SJW community.[25]

Here Goldberg uses straight-up alt-right language ("SJW"), goes on to cite 4chan posts and talk about Stormfront (claiming that neo-Nazis are "nicer" than left-wingers), and engages in some classic script-flipping himself by throwing around the term "fascist."

Goldberg's writings under his own name garnered even more attention than his Cohen experiments. Yiannopoulos tweeted out a link to Goldberg's SJW essay which led to an email exchange between him and the alt-light champion:

Dear Milo,

This is Joshua Goldberg, a.k.a. Moon Metropolis. I have uncovered some evidence that notorious social justice activist Shaun King—who played a large role in stirring up division during Ferguson and Baltimore—is actually 100% white, much like Rachel Dolezal.

Yiannopoulos responded: "Hello. Enjoy your stuff. This is right up my alley. Do we have a line to the parents?"[26]

Goldberg's mental health problems led a court to determine he wasn't competent to stand trial.[27] A judge ordered him detained in a US federal medical facility. After undergoing treatment for two years, that ruling was reversed,[28] and he was ruled able to face a jury.

Goldberg was in some ways the ultimate troll plotter. He spun a confusing web of disinformation, planted extremist sock puppets, and had some limited success in making liberals look foolish. Had he not written under his real name, the sheer volume of his output would have made it impossible for his real views and extremist actions to be pinned down. If his machinations had worked, he would have been able to either take the credit for thwarting an Islamist plot—he indicated to investigators that this was his ultimate plan—or, alternatively, melt into the shadows in the aftermath of what would be painted as another Muslim attack. He was the ultimate nihilistic race warrior.

McMahon, I should point out, doesn't believe Goldberg's actions were meant to push an overtly alt-right agenda, even if that might have been the eventual outcome. "The thing that is hard for people to understand was that it was not really, in the sense of right or left, about ideology. Aside from the ideas around free speech," he told me later.[29] "He hated the alt-right and left equally."

"It was about terrain," he said, "and pushing ... [a] particular free speech argument to the absurd."

* * *

After his story unraveled, the alt-righters on 4chan could see a bit of Goldberg in themselves. One posted on the "Politically Incorrect" board: "tell me is he our guy?" Another message read:

I really can't wrap my head around how one schizo jew NEET[30] could be so productive. Also the fact that there is only two pictures of him in existence is odd.
    Did he believe in any of the things he did?
    Was it just for bantz?
    Was he used as a scapegoat for some grander scheme?
    Was he alone in his deeds?

"Master troll that got too arrogant and caught up in the game," one response said. Another commented (using a pejorative for Twitter): "He got caught because he got greedy (going on twatter). Better to lurk in the shadows and let the footsoldiers do the dirty work."[31] One extremist who was a co-moderator with Goldberg on the Reddit "CoonTown" board and who knew him a bit (in the internet sense) echoed those sentiments: "Goldberg had a lot of potential but hitting up FBI on twitter was pretty stupid. He should have just kept quiet and focused himself on dealing with white leftists."

For some of the more extreme elements of the alt-right, it wasn't Goldberg's actions that were to be condemned—it was the fact that he got caught.

* * *

Goldberg was perhaps the first case of an absolute free speecher inspired by the alt-right being charged under terror laws. But he certainly wasn't the only potentially violent criminal to be linked to the movement and its figureheads. The conspiracy-minded, Alex Jones wing has been linked to several deadly attacks, beginning long before the alt-right became a well-known phenomenon.

In 2009, a former Marine killed three police officers in Pittsburgh. Richard Poplawski had been posting on Stormfront and Infowars shortly before the shootings. Jones denied he had influenced Poplawski and said that the killer had actually come to Infowars to disagree with what was being said there. "If anybody should be blamed for this it's the Marines—they're the ones who trained him to kill," Jones said.[32]

In fact, Poplawski wanted Jones and Infowars to talk more about Jews, and talked about one of Jones's obsessions, the secret government plot to take away people's guns.[33] "For being such huge players in the endgame," he said in a message posted on the Infowars website on March 29, 2009, "too many 'infowarriors' are surprisingly unfamiliar with the Zionists." Another time he noted: "racial awareness is on the rise among the young white population."[34]

Beyond Poplawski, the "pizzagate" shooting, and the Sandy Hook harassment campaign, Infowars fans have gone on killing sprees, fired semi-automatic weapons at the White House, and have gotten involved in shoot-outs and attempted assassinations.[35] The site's readership even included one of the Boston Marathon bombers.[36]

While these connections are documented, it would be unfair to pin the blame for these attacks solely on Jones, or to say that he openly encourages violence. And when the shooting starts, or there's some intimation of trouble, Infowars moves swiftly to rid itself of any hint of blame. After James Alefantis hired a lawyer, Jones issued a non-apology apology, trying to distance himself from "pizzagate."[37]

There are other links between the far-right and politically and racially motivated violence and terror attacks, and the trickle turned into a gushing river as the alt-right gained prominence off of the back of the Trump campaign and presidency. I've touched on Dylann Roof, whose manifesto explicitly mentions the radicalization effect of the Council of Conservative Citizens, the organization whose spokesperson was alt-right hero Jared Taylor. Roof wrote that the Trayvon Martin case:

> prompted me to type in the words "black on White crime" into Google, and I have never been the same since that day. The first website I came to was the Council of Conservative Citizens. There were pages upon pages of these brutal black on White murders. I was in disbelief. At this moment I realized that something was very wrong. How could the news be blowing up the Trayvon Martin case while hundreds of these black on White murders got ignored?[38]

Joel Brown, a researcher at the University of Chicago, outlined what he described as striking similarities between Roof's manifesto and the ideology of Taylor and the alt-right, particularly in his obsession with IQ and the "preservation and protection of white culture."[39]

Later in 2015, a man named Allen Scarsella shot five people at a Black Lives Matter protest in Minneapolis. According to a police report, Scarsella had previously filmed BLM protests, exchanged words with protesters, and had written "angry internet posts on Reddit and 4chan." The police found what they called a "4Chan website e-mail string where participants discussed going to the BLM protests to 'stir things up' and 'cause commotion.'" The authorities also found a video made by Scarsella and his friends, where they "refer to African Americans in derogatory terms, say they are going to do some 'reverse cultural enriching' and 'make the fire rise.'"[40]

Unsurprisingly, Scarsella's racist posts show little sign of irony,[41] and he was convicted and sentenced to 15 years in prison for the shooting.[42] Some channers condemned Scarsella for failing to kill the people he shot, for apologizing in court, and (oddly) for trying to bring memes to life. "This dude is an idiot, but was obviously acting in self defense. Does anyone have that video of the dindus talking about chasing them down and giving them a beating?" read one of the milder responses to the case. Another commented: "It's not self-defense because he went there with the intention of provoking protesters into attacking him so that he could shoot them. Go read his text messages." Someone else shot back: "So if I leave a wallet on the ground and somebody steal the money out if it, there's no responsibility on the thieving nigger? I get it's my fault for leaving it there, but that isn't free reign to let niggers do whatever they please because liberals think they're too retarded to act civilized."[43]

The list of crimes attributed to those who have fallen under the influence of the alt-right keeps growing. In January 2017, Alexandre Bissonnette entered a Quebec City mosque and opened fire, killing six people and injuring 19 more. A friend described Bissonnette as "alt-right" and said that he shunned mainstream conservative groups, thinking they were too moderate.[44] Other accounts described Bissonnette as "an online troll" and as an "ultra nationalist white supremacist" who harbored "anti-immigration sentiment, especially toward Muslim refugees."[45]

In his online activities and flirtations with mainstream conservative groups, Bissonnette demonstrated the potential for young men to be radicalized online. The admin of a Facebook page which supported refugees recognized Bissonnette from comments he made on the page and elsewhere. François Deschamps, speaking to the *Globe and Mail*, made a distinction between the Bissonnette's comments and "outright hate": "He was someone who made frequent extreme comments in social media denigrating refugees and feminism. It wasn't outright hate, rather part of this new nationalist conservative identity movement that is more intolerant than hateful."[46]

Outlets including Breitbart and Fox News initially jumped on reports that a Moroccan man had been detained in connection with the attack, backtracking as the truth came to light. Alex Jones called the attack a "false flag" operation carried out by "jihadis killing other Muslims," a claim for which there was no evidence.[47]

In Seattle, a couple was charged with shooting a protester outside a Milo Yiannopoulos speech in January 2017. The day before Yiannopoulos was scheduled to talk at the University of Washington, Marc Hokoana messaged a friend on Facebook: "I can't wait for tomorrow. I'm going to the milo event and if the snowflakes get out off hand I'm going to wade through their ranks and start cracking skulls." The friend asked whether he was going to be carrying a gun. Hokoana said he wouldn't, but that his wife Elizabeth would be.[48] After the shooting, the pair were charged with assault. They claimed self-defense.[49]

The Seattle incident was the first major incident stemming from clashes between alt-right and "antifa" (anti-fascist) protesters in the United States after Trump assumed office. Both sides consistently blamed the other for instigating the violence, which flared up several times in 2017—most notably at the University of California at Berkeley, in conjunction with pro-Trump protest rallies and planned speeches by Yiannopoulos and right-wing media personality Ann Coulter.[50] It was a grim foreshadowing of what happened in Charlottesville.

And the violence continued. In March 2017, former US Army officer James Jackson took a bus from Baltimore to New York and stabbed an elderly black man he'd never met.[51] He turned himself in before carrying out the rest of his alleged plot; prosecutors said he planned to go on a rampage in Times Square.[52] Jackson was indicted on terror charges,[53] and his internet trail indicated that, in a short period before the killing, he had been immersed in the movement. The Daily Beast reported that "Jackson's internet use suggested recent radicalization by the alt-right" and that he liked videos with titles like "Blacks Know That Blacks are Violent so Why Does the White Media Pretend They are Not?" and "BLACK PERSON TALKS ABOUT ALT-RIGHT DESTROYED." He had subscribed to the YouTube channel of Richard Spencer's National Policy Institute and to others which pushed neo-Nazi and "human biodiversity" ideas.[54]

In May 2017 a man killed two people in Portland. The alleged murderer, Jeremy Joseph Christian, started shouting racial slurs at women on a train, and when two bystanders tried to intervene, he killed them. At his arraignment, Christian shouted about free-speech and antifas,[55] and was known to hang out with alt-righters, some of whom shunned him—but none of whom apparently thought to report him to the authorities when he went on neo-Nazi rants and showed up at free-speech rallies armed with a baseball bat.[56]

And then, in August 2017, came Charlottesville.

* * *

Alt-righters will argue that the threat from the far right is miniscule compared to the threat from terrorists motivated by

Islam. And considering the threats to the world posed by Islamic State and other radical Islamist groups, they may have a point. But here again is another version of the alt-right's favorite "you do it too" fallacy. Just because there is one prominent group of violent terrorists, doesn't mean another potentially deadly group doesn't deserve examination—or condemnation—as well.

The Islamist comparison is quite apt. Extremists identify young men, often ones who are frustrated and alienated, and draw them in with core messages about things they really care about. Once drawn in, they are conveyor-belted along a path of ever-more-extreme content, and slowly drawn into a radical bubble which warps their sense of reality. The alt-right experience is—like the movement as a whole—less organized, and 4channers have a sense of irony that is hard to detect in the ideological fanatics of the Islamic State. But the process is the same, and, as the cases I've outlined show, so are some of the results.

Just as extremists in (for instance) Raqqa have managed to inspire Muslims in the West to carry out terror attacks, alt-right influencers of various sorts have drawn young men into the web, stoked up their grievances, and provided a sense of community that may have been lacking elsewhere in their lives.[57] Is it any wonder that some psychologically troubled young men who have travelled this path end up perpetrating violence?

In the morass of the alt-right and far-right internets, people like Roof, Goldberg, Bissonnette, and Jackson found ideological strands that not only appeared to comport with their worldviews but also nudged them towards murder. Here lies the real and immediate physical danger of the alt-right online—not in its influence over electoral politics or even in its corrosive online abuse and general nastiness towards enemy groups, but in its potential to radicalize, to turn some people into killers.

11

The White House

Even in a US election year, the 4th of July weekend tends to be a slow news period, a time out which usually falls after the party nominees are clear, but before the formal set-piece nominating conventions. But of course "usual" was never a word used to describe the 2016 campaign, and while political journalists were looking forward to their holiday weekends, Donald Trump did his best to ruin everyone's plans.

On the morning of Saturday July 2, Trump tweeted out: "Crooked Hillary—Makes History!" alongside a meme which was a crude parody of the Clinton campaign's graphic design. "History Made" read the slogan on the accompanying graphic, over pictures of Clinton, a pile of cash, and a six-pointed star bearing the text "Most Corrupt Candidate Ever."[1]

Flicking through a timeline on Twitter, the message behind the tweet may have been easy to miss. There are no tails or grotesquely enlarged noses or any of the alt-right's other favored anti-Semitism tropes. But looked at in isolation and given a moment of contemplation, it was clear that the meme referenced not only Clinton, but—via the Star of David and the money pile—Jews. It didn't take very long at all for journalists to notice the dog whistle.

Trump's campaign team began backpedaling. Within two hours the tweet was deleted, and then reposted with one key difference—the Star of David had been transformed into a circle. Not that they were admitting there was anything wrong with the first image, mind you. The star could have just as well been a "sheriff's star," Trump declared. The shape is a common one, operatives argued, possibly plucked from the standard graphic templates that come with Microsoft Word. Trump tweeted out a picture of a sticker book devoted to the movie *Frozen*, showing a similar star on the cover. "Where is the outrage for this Disney book? Is this the 'Star of David' also?" he asked.[2] The media was out to get him, again.

But the proof of the meme's anti-Semitic, alt-right origins was out there.

In New York, Anthony Smith of the online news outlet Mic was one of those journalists getting ready to enjoy his holiday weekend. His reaction when he saw the tweet was an intensified form of eye-rolling. He later characterized it to me like this: "'Oh my God. I can't believe he actually did that.'" He tweeted about it himself, chalked it up to another stupid Trump miscue, and went out with some friends. That would have been about it, had he not got an anonymous tip in his inbox the following morning, telling him that the meme had started life on 8chan.

Given the previously mentioned difficulty in finding stuff in the 8chan archive, Smith said he was unsure that he would ever find the original image. He started combing through the haystack, searching for the needle. "I thought it would take me months," he admitted. But instead he came across it in about an hour. Smith quickly put the word out in a post titled: "Donald Trump's Star of David Hillary Clinton Meme Was Created by White Supremacists."

Smith linked the picture to a particularly crude Twitter account, one that regularly posted images of, for instance, black people as monkeys, refugees cutting off heads, and a Jewish journalist with a Photoshop-enlarged nose. He had discovered another prime example of the alt-right propaganda pipeline at work. The image had bubbled up from the chans, in a relatively short space of time—around two weeks, Smith estimated, from when it was first posted—wound its way through more mainstream sites, and eventually emerged on a future president's Twitter account.

Trump campaign social media director Dan Scavino denied knowledge of the source of the meme. In a statement he said it "was lifted from an anti-Hillary Twitter user where countless images appear ... As the Social Media Director for the campaign, I would never offend anyone and therefore chose to remove the image."

The incident marked the stirring of widespread interest in the links between Trump and the alt-right. But it was not an isolated case. Even before the Star of David incident, Trump had retweeted a number of people whose profiles prominently mentioned the "white genocide" conspiracy theory—one was even named @WhiteGenocideTM. Some hardcore race warriors were retweeted from his account multiple times.[3] An analysis by *Fortune* magazine found statistically significant connections between Trump and his campaign and the most influential people spreading the "white genocide" idea.[4]

There's no evidence that Trump himself believes in the "white genocide" conspiracy theory, but it's clear that the candidate and his campaign were swimming in alt-rightish social media waters. In another notable incident, Trump tweeted out a channer graphic which showed made up numbers put out by a fictional "Crime Statistics Bureau" which inflated the numbers of whites killed by blacks.[5] The fake stats were posted along with a suitably scary image of a black man with his face covered wielding a pistol in an upside-down grip. It was a crude attempt to make it look like America was in the throes of a race war. The person behind the account made his sympathies clear in his Twitter bio: "A detester of any kind of sick perverted dildo waving Marxism and liberalism, we Should have listened to the Austrian chap with the little moustache."[6]

*   *   *

Throughout the summer of 2016 the alt-right floated on, throwing its handfuls of red pills all over the place, becoming a steady and growing presence, an ever-louder buzz in the background of a campaign that was a sheer wall of noise. And one moment thrust the movement into the mainstream.

On August 25, 2016, Hillary Clinton took the stage at the Truckee Meadows Community College in Reno, Nevada. She was meant to give a speech about small businesses, but the original script was thrown out. A week before, Stephen Bannon had been appointed to run Trump's campaign. So instead of talking about mom-and-pop restaurants and business development grants, Clinton chose to gather together the links between Trump and the fringe extremists, and outline her opponents' ties to the alt-right:

> A man with a long history of racial discrimination, who traffics in dark conspiracy theories drawn from the pages of supermarket tabloids and the far, dark reaches of the internet, should never run our government or command our military....
>
> This is someone who retweets white supremacists online, like the user who goes by the name "WhiteGenocideTM." Trump took this fringe bigot with a few dozen followers and spread his message to 11 million people.
>
> His campaign famously posted an anti-Semitic image—a Star of David imposed over a sea of dollar bills—that first appeared on a white supremacist website....
>
> It's what happens when you listen to the radio host Alex Jones, who claims that 9/11 and the Oklahoma City bombings were inside jobs. He even said—and this really, is just so disgusting—he even said the victims of the Sandy Hook massacre were child actors and no one was actually killed there. I don't know what happens in somebody's mind or how dark their heart must be to say things like that.
>
> But Trump didn't challenge those lies. He actually went on Jones' show and said: "Your reputation is amazing. I will not let you down."
>
> This from the man wants to be president of the United States.[7]

Clinton went on to list a few Breitbart headlines, and she outlined what she saw as the key tenets of the movement, describing its increasing power on the right:

This is not conservatism as we have known it. This is not Republicanism as we have known it. These are race-baiting ideas, anti-Muslim and anti-immigrant ideas, anti-woman—all key tenets making up an emerging racist ideology known as the alt-right....

The de facto merger between Breitbart and the Trump campaign represents a landmark achievement for the alt-right. A fringe element has effectively taken over the Republican Party....

Of course there has always been a paranoid fringe in our politics, a lot of it rising from racial resentment. But it's never had the nominee of a major party stoking it, encouraging it, and giving it a national megaphone. Until now.[8]

The alt-right reacted to the Clinton speech with unbridled glee. Shouts of "praise Kek" were posted on all their usual hangouts.[9] One prankster inside the venue tried to interrupt Clinton's speech by shouting "Pepe" and "Infowars"—he duly stepped forward for a laudatory Breitbart interview.[10]

Far from an attack on their movement, the channers saw the Clinton speech as the ultimate vindication. They had managed to get under the skin of the biggest normie grandma of them all, one of their mortal enemies, and suddenly they were thrust into the national political conversation like never before. Memes circulated online. One of the most popular showed Clinton with the caption "OLD LADY YELLS AT INTERNET." Before Trump's election it may have been the alt-right's proudest moment.

* * *

Clinton had walked right into a trap. Despite the Star of David incident, and Trump's steady retweeting of alt-right figures, the movement hadn't made a huge impact on the public conscious-ness until then. Google Trends shows the relative popularity of search terms over time and serves as a useful proxy for general public interest. A simple query of the term "alt-right" throws up a mostly flat line until August 2016. There's an uptick after Bannon's appointment by Trump, but the real spike came after Clinton's Reno speech. Here was the burst of oxygen the activists had been waiting for.[11]

Donald Trump clearly did not believe in the hard alt-right goal of splitting the United States into separate ethnic enclaves. He wasn't praising Kek, discussing white nationalism or describing feminism as cancer. But his candidacy united several strains of thought within the movement and was pitched against a common enemy. Race obsessives approved of his focus on immigration, his proposal to ban Muslim visitors to the US and, of course, the idea of a Mexican border wall. The men's rights brigade saluted his macho swagger and his reported pick-up adventures. In personal terms, he was perhaps closest to the conspiracy theorists—popping up, as Clinton mentioned, on Alex Jones's show during the campaign, and being the prime promoter of the conspiracy theory that Barack Obama had not been born in the United States. And his use of social media inspired the channers and online pranksters. They saw a glimmer of themselves in him and excitedly spread the word whenever he retweeted one of their ranks.

By contrast, there could not have been a more perfect foil for the movement than Hillary Clinton: a feminist, globalist career politician, friendly to trade and migration, pursuing a hawkish foreign policy. The 2016 election was a sort of life-and-death battle which forges movements.[12]

For a brief moment, Trump settled a question that all radical political movements must answer: whether to stay on the fringes and agitate from outside the electoral system, or work within for change. Even though they may have had their doubts, alt-righters threw their support behind the candidate. Richard Spencer had previously oscillated between urging the Republican Party to focus its platform on immigration and shunning traditional American electoral politics altogether. He enthusiastically saluted Trump, as described in Chapter 1.[13]

Matthew Heimbach, an identitarian who began a "White Students Union" at his university and who later set up an organization called the Traditionalist Youth Network, wrote:

> While Donald Trump is neither a Traditionalist nor a White nationalist, he is a threat to the economic and social powers of the international Jew. For this reason alone as long as Trump stands strong on deportation and immigration enforcement we should support his candidacy insofar as we can use it to push more hardcore positions on immigration and Identity. Donald Trump is not the savior of Whites in America, he is however a booming salvo across the bow of the Left and Jewish power to tell them that White America is awakening, and we are tired of business as usual.
>
> The march to victory will not be won by Donald Trump in 2016, but this could be the stepping stone we need to then radicalize millions of White working and middle class families to the call to truly begin a struggle for Faith, family and folk.[14]

Heimbach was of course wrong about the ultimate outcome of the election, but Trump was getting a bevy of endorsements from prominent alt-righters. Spencer bragged that dozens of his sympathizers were at the Republican National Convention in Cleveland. "We feel an investment in the Trump campaign," he told the Associated Press. "Trump thinks like me … Do you think it's a coincidence that everybody like me loves Trump and supports him?"[15]

Three weeks after Clinton's speech in Reno, Trump tweeted an image of himself as Pepe the frog.[16] The channers nearly exploded with joy.

* * *

The alt-right came out in full force to support Donald Trump, but ascribing any actual electoral benefit to him because of the movement is impossible. We've already learned that the demographics of the alt-right are more or less unknowable, and the actual impact of the movement on the election is hazy.

It's also clear that while Trump's Twitter feed garnered big headlines, his campaign efforts were focused on that much bigger network, Facebook. On Facebook, fundraising and micro-targeting of supporters and potential supporters in swing states were most likely both more effective and less visible than tweets or TV ads.[17]

The "fake news" phenomenon also fed Trump's fan base, but the real power may have come not from those false stories— made-up piffle which claimed, for instance, that the Pope had endorsed Trump, or that a Bill Clinton sex tape had been leaked— but rather from the venues in which they were widely circulating. There were thousands of pro-Trump Facebook groups, many of them closed (in other words, you needed permission from the administrators to join).[18]

Fake news items, often dreamt up by Macedonian teenagers[19] or others looking to make a quick buck, circulated inside these groups, but so did real news items given a partisan spin, and plain old clickbait propaganda designed to game social media algorithms ("Want a halt to Muslim immigration? Click 'Like' if you agree"). The issues that excited these boards—immigration and crime among them—had some overlap with the alt-right, but they had nothing really to do with the movement. Pepe didn't feature in their memes, and there was no backwards justification to paleoconservative intellectuals—or in fact to intellectuals of any stripe. As shown in the "pizzagate" saga and the fake terror victim trend, alt-righters eagerly shared fake news or misinfor- mation—sometimes "ironically," seeming to mock not only their leftist opponents but also the gullible subset of Trump supporters who actually believed that stuff—but the volume of this material was only a fraction of the highly partisan content circulating in those groups.

Again, the effects of individual networks or campaign strategies are difficult to unravel, but it is, at the least, quite clear that the average voter in a key Midwestern state was much more likely to come into contact with Facebook, or someone who'd been on Facebook, than they were to be "red-pilled" by 4chan.

When we talk about real tangible effects on the campaign, however, the alt-right rabble did have one noticeable impact in the closing stages race, and it came on Twitter.[20] In particular, alt-right activists were highly effective at focusing attention on bad news about Hillary Clinton and, in particular, highlighting the drip-drip of emails from two major hacks—the Podesta hack, and the hack of the Democratic National Committee. Wikileaks' release of the emails prompted periodic publicity campaigns by alt-right figures which boosted related hashtags with tweetstorms. Throughout October 2016, as Wikileaks released the emails in batches, a sequential series of hashtags trended on Twitter: #PodestaEmails, #PodestaEmails2, #PodestaEmails3, etc. On the chans and Reddit, the emails were picked through and strategies for promoting certain bits of information were discussed. Many journalists pay close attention to Twitter, and concurrently with the release of the leaks, Google searches for Wikileaks rose.[21]

Coincidentally, while investigating the alleged links between Russia and the Trump campaign, I had a conversation with the hacker, or the front for the team of hackers, who claimed responsibility for the DNC and Podesta hacks.[22] Western intelligence agencies and security researchers eventually reached the conclusion that "Guccifer 2.0" was covering for a hacking team with ties to Russia's military intelligence apparatus—APT28 or, as it is more popularly known, "Fancy Bear."

My Twitter direct messages with Guccifer were largely inconclusive as to his real origins—he denied he was Russian and stuck to his story, that he was a Romanian hacker who was dedicated to a fuzzily described notion of freedom along with a dash of the lolz.[23] "Together with [Wikileaks founder Julian] assange, we'll make america great again," he joked.

The investigation into Russian interference in the US election continues, and given the tumultuous early months of the Trump administration on that score, there will likely be further revelations after this book goes to print. But the closing stages of the 2016 election gave us the first indications of a technical and philosophical alliance between the alt-right and pro-Putin activists online. The connections were forged in the white heat of that bitter campaign, as some saw a common enemy in the form of Hillary Clinton. Just as opposition to Clinton united the alt-right—and a broader swathe of conservatives and isolationists—pro-Russian factions and opponents of interventionist foreign policy abroad threw their lot in with Trump.

But the agreement between the current Russian elite and the alt-right goes deeper than a marriage of convenience. Within the movement, there is a widespread view that Putin is a strong, virtuous, white leader practicing a paternalistic, nationalist form of capitalism, and defending his country from radical Islam and the liberal Western forces of political correctness.[24]

Richard Spencer once commented that Russia is the "sole white power" in the world.[25] His wife Nina Kouprianova was born in the Soviet Union and is the translator of Alexander Dugin, a far-right political scientist.[26] Dugin has been described as "a leading Russian political analyst" by the state-funded website Sputnik. An enthusiastic supporter of Russia's interventions in Georgia and Ukraine, he predicted in 2008 that the United States would split into six different parts loosely based on ethnic spheres of influence.[27]

Dugin's influence within Russia itself is the subject of debate, but it's clear why his theories might appeal to the alt-right. The journalist and historian Owen Matthews describes the intellectual ties between Dugin and Steve Bannon like this:

They both believe global elites have conspired against ordinary people. Their enemies: secularism, multicultural-ism, egalitarianism. In both Bannon's and Dugin's worldview, the true global ideological struggle is not between Russia and the United States but between culturally homogenous groups founded on Judeo-Christian values practicing humane capitalism on one side and, on the other, an international crony-capitalist network of bankers and big business.[28]

Clinton herself, in the Reno speech, made the link between Russia and Trump's alt-right-friendly tendencies, calling Putin "the grand godfather of this global brand of extreme nationalism."[29]

The idea of Russia as a red-pilled Muslim- and PC-free zone inspires paeans on 4chan and plenty of idle channer dreams about emigration. "I don't know /pol/, it's getting pretty bad here," said one typical post of this genre, dating from December 2016 and apparently posted by an American. The message was titled: "Should I move to Russia or stay here?"[30]

The links between the alt-right and Russia aren't limited to philosophical ideas or mutual admiration. Parts of Russia's foreign policy apparatus have also put out alt-right messages. Take for instance Sputnik, which opened offices in Washington, Beijing, and the UK. In the months before the US presidential election Cassandra Fairbanks, one of the "pizzagate" dissem-inators, gained a huge following and more than a little bit of notoriety by swinging her support very publicly from Bernie Sanders to Donald Trump. Prior to coming out for Trump, she'd been heavily active in left-wing and libertarian causes, writing for a combination of fringe, often left-leaning websites, along with mainstream outlets such as *Teen Vogue*.

Switching from Sanders to Trump was unusual but certainly not unique, given the two candidates' outsider statuses and positions on trade. What was more unusual was that during the election campaign, Fairbanks was employed writing news articles in Washington for Sputnik at the same time as pumping out alt-right-flavored pro-Trump tweets to her tens of thousands of followers on Twitter.

Russia's official channels also have fun playing with alt-right themes. In January 2017, the Russian Embassy in London tweeted out a Pepe meme as part of a dig at British Prime Minister Theresa May. When I wrote a story about the tweet for the BBC website, the embassy refused to answer questions about the meme, snippily telling me: "We would be grateful if [the] BBC actually investigated who wants [the] UK to stand in the way of better US-Russia relations." The embassy routinely tags journalists it views as hostile in its Twitter output and has so far refused to comment on who exactly writes its tweets.[31]

The 2016 election also provided a template for one of the most puzzling and perhaps most frightening political developments of recent times. Shadowy hacker groups working in conjunction with automated and propaganda accounts, amplified by alt-right social media and others, work to undermine liberal and leftist politicians and sow discord with the aim of backing a broader anti-globalist agenda. The Wikileaks DNC/Podesta revelations and their enthusiastic promotion by alt-right Twitter were the first manifestation of this, but if there were any lingering doubts that pro-Russian hacking groups and alt-right forces were working together in a loose online alliance, they were thoroughly dismantled by a telling incident in the hours before the final round of the May 2016 French presidential election.

Just hours before French reporting restrictions were due to kick in, a mysterious hacker posted a link on 4chan to 9 gigabytes—around 700,000 pages—of emails from the campaign of Emmanuel Macron.[32] Alt-right activists had been targeting the French election for months, hoping to boost the Front National leader Marine Le Pen.[33]

Perhaps to an even greater degree than Trump, Le Pen seemed to speak directly to the alt-right, dividing France into "patriots" and "globalists" and campaigning on an anti-Islam platform: "Financial globalization and Islamist globalization are helping each other out ... Those two ideologies want to bring France to its knees."[34] Le Pen's party got a loan from a bank with ties to the Kremlin and she even took time out from the campaign trail to hold talks with Vladimir Putin.[35]

So perhaps it's only natural that when the Macron email leaks surfaced, suspicion immediately fell on the Russian state. The modus operandi appeared to be similar to the DNC/Podesta hacks, and Western security firms found some circumstantial evidence that the hack was again the work of "Fancy Bear."[36] As in the US case, definitive proof was lacking and the investigation and debate would go on for some time. But what's interesting in this case is how the leaks spread. Alt-right activists, boosted by the Wikileaks Twitter account, managed to circumvent the French reporting restrictions in a last-ditch effort to try to influence the ultimate vote.

Just minutes after the links to the documents were posted on 4chan, Jack Posobiec alerted his Twitter followers to a "Massive doc dump on /pol/" and used the hashtag "#MacronLeaks." He told me he had been alerted by the poster of doctored anti-Macron documents which had surfaced several days earlier on 4chan,[37] and which had prompted an official legal complaint by the Macron campaign.[38] "The same poster of the financial documents said to stay tuned tomorrow for a bigger story—so I pretty much spent the next 24 hours hitting refresh on the site," he told me via Twitter.

Would the emails, like the previously doctored documents, turn out to be Photoshopped hoaxes? At that point, it didn't really matter. Posobiec's tweet was retweeted 87 times within five minutes. Some of the spreaders were automated bots; many were alt-righters included in Posobiec's large (more than 100,000) Twitter following.

The news began taking off, mostly in English, and mostly among alt-righters outside of France. Posobiec himself hadn't really noticed—he was at a party hosted by Milo Yiannopoulos. "I had actually left my phone for a few hours while conducting interviews ... and didn't realize it had gotten so big until later when someone at the party was talking about 'Posobiec's hashtag' without realizing I was standing right there!" he told me.

The story had been given a boost by Wikileaks. If Posobiec was big on Twitter, Wikileaks—with its 4 million plus followers—was absolutely enormous. They waded in, initially with a cautious tweet saying that the leaks "could be a 4chan practical joke," the first of a series of messages highlighting the leaked documents. On the chat app Discord, which had recently gotten traction among alt-right activists, there were active discussions about how to propagate the MacronLeaks hashtag and, crucially, get it in front of French readers as the election coverage window was closing. Before too long, MacronLeaks was a top trending topic in France.

The ruse didn't work, of course, assuming the aim was to get Marine Le Pen elected. But here again the propaganda pipeline that had been developed during the US election was deployed with lightning speed. Hackers targeted "globalist" candidates and revealed their leaks to the channer obsessives. From /pol/ the information was signal-boosted to Twitter, where it was picked up by activists and others. And from there it became news—the word spreading to people who had never even heard of 4chan.[39]

The alt-right pipeline had helped to spawn a new and somewhat mysterious source of huge political influence—the potential for unknown and perhaps unknowable groups to use "public interest hacks," spread by a network of activists, to influence election processes in real time.[40] It was a mechanism that, while ostensibly based in facts—real email messages—relied more on deadline-driven rumor and spin to cast suspicion on anyone perceived to be pushing the "globalist agenda."[41]

But just as this new and powerful source of political influence was coming into existence, the very movement that had spawned it was starting to tear itself apart.

* * *

In the days after the US election, there was a feeling on the chans and Reddit reminiscent of the last scene of *The Graduate*: a mixture of giddy excitement, forward-looking trepidation, and a dawning realization that the shit just got real.

"I'm fucking trembling out of excitement brahs," one channer wrote, alongside a drawing of Pepe the Frog.[42] "We actually elected a meme as president." "TRUMP IS THE GOD EMPEROR," wrote another, "someone tell me this isn't a dream." "We did it. /pol/ saved America"[43]

Days later, when Trump made gestures towards the mainstream media—giving interviews to programs like CBS's *60 Minutes*, and disavowing some of the extreme elements of his support—alt-righters on Reddit immediately felt betrayed: "You are fooled if you think Trump was going to give us some sort of permission slip to start cleansing America," one commented. Another asked: "Anyone here feeling bamboozled by the Donald?"[44]

It was the beginning of the end.

12
Downfall

The strands of the alt-right that found each other quickly and knotted together in the fight against Hillary Clinton, didn't start unravelling when Richard Spencer was punched on Inauguration Day. The process was actually well underway by then. In the wake of Trump's victory, activists propelling a movement which thrived on opposition and contradiction were forced to contemplate a future at or near the seats of power, and the intense media scrutiny that came with it.

Attention naturally gravitated towards the intellectuals and media stars. But even within those circles there was an apparent contradiction. Did the movement belong to the alt-light, the new conspiracy-spreading activist-journalists? Did it belong to the intellectuals who wanted to march to Constantinople and create nation-sized ethnic enclaves? And what about the neo-Nazis? How would the nastier trollish elements react to Jared Kushner and Ivanka Trump, two Jews who were now at the heart of the White House (and one a woman to boot)? What did they actually want, now that their man was president?

In the wake of the election, there was a new sense of seriousness about the far right, one which concentrated minds and was at odds with the entire nature of the movement. That Google Trends chart line which showed a huge spike in searches for "alt-right" after Clinton's Reno speech now spiked again, reaching a peak twice as high in the two weeks after the vote. News events took on new gravity. The Spencer salute[1]—which in a less febrile climate might have drawn outrage from a slice of the left, and chortling shouts of "triggered" from the channers—became instead a significant media event, and one which laid bare the divisions in the movement. Some alt-lighters were disgusted at the display and immediately moved to distance themselves from the term "alt-right." There were others who thought it distasteful and damaging to the cause but understood the sentiment behind it. Another group gleefully reveled in the controversy it caused. And then of course there were the authentic neo-Nazis. It was a recipe for the breakup not of a republic, but of a movement.

In the short term Spencer and some of the other intellectuals were best placed to seize the momentum and publicity opportunities. They, after all, had come up with the name of the movement and had done the work of developing its core beliefs. They had also been working to create proto-institutions while wandering in the wilderness during the Obama years, and like Trump himself knew how to court the mainstream media while remaining sharply critical of it.

Of course, not everyone associated with the alt-right was pleased about this turn of events, and the cracks that would turn into huge rifts were nowhere more evident than at a party held on the eve of the inauguration. It was dubbed the "Deploraball," an awkward portmanteau which riffed on Clinton's similarly clumsy description of some Trump supporters as a "basket of deplorables."[2]

The literature promoting the Deploraball left no doubt about the type of alt-righter it was meant to celebrate: "We're not bragging when we say we memed a President into office. We also did the grunt work. We enlisted the help of meme magicians and content distributors across all social networks and we decorated cities overnight." But event organizers almost immediately ran into the difficult business of deciding which deplorables were fit to attend and which ones were, well, just too deplorable. Accusations and counter-claims created a rift between the original group of volunteers, who organized events across the country, and those who promoted the biggest such event, a party in Washington. For instance, D.C. ball organizer Mike Cernovich and alt-right Twitter personality Anthime Gionet (who went by the online alias "Baked Alaska") got into a public spat[3] over the latter's anti-Semitic tweets.[4]

Gionet was uninvited, which irritated Spencer, who called the organizers "alt-light." He didn't mean it as a compliment. The Daily Stormer also weighed in, calling the event "sanitized, cuckolded, pro-Jew." In the wake of Gionet's uninvitation, Yiannopoulos was enlisted—but never showed up, reportedly over a dispute about whether he would be put at the top of the bill.[5] The ball purged the more radical end of the alt-right and at the same time turned off the movement's ego-driven alt-lightish celebrities.

On the night itself, attendees ran a gauntlet of anti-Nazi protesters outside the event. There was the odd punch-up[6] and a bloodied protester sat on the pavement.[7] Spencer was spotted lurking outside, trying to engage with people who didn't really want him to be there.[8] The scenes were a mild foreshadowing of the later unrest in Charlottesville, Portland, Berkeley, and elsewhere.

Inside the ballroom, the guests included Cassandra Fairbanks, millennial alt-righter Lauren Southern, and *Vice* founder Gavin McInnes. Peter Thiel made a brief appearance. Martin Shkreli, the guy who became famous for jacking up the price of a lifesaving drug and who was later convicted of securities fraud, was also in attendance.[9] There's no doubt that at least a few of the attendees had some fun, but if the alt-right was really hoping to spawn a fabulous new counterculture, this certainly wasn't the event to do it. The *New York Post* described the ball as "actually kind of tame."

"It's good to see everyone from Twitter!" Cernovich told the crowd.[10] "This is a show of force, and I want to be very transparent in that regard: You think we don't exist, you want to marginalize us, you think we won't show up." "If the GOP opposes Trump, what are we going to do in 2018?" he said. "We're taking it over! We'll take it over! We'll get rid of all of them!"[11] At one point a woman pulled out an acoustic guitar and began to sing that classic left-wing protest song "The Times They Are a-Changin.'"

"The scene was pure establishment," wrote Issie Lapowsky of *Wired* magazine. Lapowsky questioned whether attendees had thought much about what they really wanted now that their man was about to become president. "Until they're willing and able to define what they will and won't stand for, the rest of the country will do it for them."[12] And, oddly enough, after the night was over some unknown person posted a strange, ungrammatical recap on the Deploraball's official website. The rant criticized the big event in Washington—the only gathering that the media had really noticed:

> The formerly alt-rightish MAGA3X Event at the [National Press Club] was mistakenly scrubbed clean of it's deplorables. Instead catering to an archaic form of Republican no one wants to be. It's success and sold-out ticket sales were precisely because we had billed it as the Bad Boy's of the Internet tribal convention. ...
>
> The organizers continued to fight aggressively for normie status, creating an entire event with the feel of a business networking function. This was part of our original pitch ... a networking event followed by a riotous party, the latter never materialized.
>
> Instead Pepe and Richard Spencer were silently banned, in beta dad mode....
>
> The Press who did attend, stood through the self congratulatory speeches repurposed to reflect the latest iteration of what a bore this type of establishment Trumpist is. Instead of the cool kids, the event was filled with over 40's hoping to rub elbows with edgy guests who never appeared [all *sic*].[13]

The trolls were starting to eat themselves.

*   *   *

Reflecting on the alt-light several months later, Richard Spencer refused to chuck anyone off of the movement bus, but also had some barbed criticism for the alt-right's moderate wing: "Mike Cernovich is kind of a genius in his way in jumping on news stories and maybe doing a little fake news himself," he told me.

That being said, I don't know what Mike Cernovich thinks about politics. I don't know what he ultimately believes, about anything really. The alt-light seems to be a hastily assembled rag-tag group of people who are a little bit edgy or a little bit unusual but who like Trump. And I don't see that going anywhere.... They cannot take us away from the essence of racialism that is at the heart of the alt-right. The other funny thing is that they have hitched their bandwagon to free speech.... But they themselves, because they are not able to talk about these deeply important matters that I and others are willing to talk about, they ultimately have to censor speech.

Their refusal to full-throatedly embrace race-based politics made them ideologically inconsistent, he said, and they would refuse to address or even acknowledge what Spencer and his cohorts had consistently been arguing all along. The alt-light insisted on defending American or Western values, and tried to deflect racial questions; Spencer, in contrast, was talking about a homeland for white people. The movement was breaking down according to a simple question: Should politics be defined by race? Spencer then delivered a verbal death blow. "Ultimately," he said of the alt-light, "they have to cuck."[14]

* * *

Humor and satire thrives in opposition. With their man in the White House, in charge of the US nuclear arsenal and much else besides, the alt-righter memes mocking Hillary and campus snowflakes suddenly seemed drained of their power. Movement leaders were studied for their reaction to every breaking news event. Their line was clear when, for instance, the president was accused of revealing classified information to Russian officials—attack and shout "fake news."

But the activists were less impressed with other presidential moves—like Trump's decision in April 2017 to launch cruise missiles at the Syrian Army. Here was a key foreign policy difference between neoconservatives and neoreactionaries—the latter are entirely opposed to foreign entanglements, and the Syria conflict was exactly the kind of morass that they feared getting involved in. At the very least, the alt-righters argued, any Syria-directed firepower should be directed exclusively at the Islamic State group, and not at the forces of Bashar al-Assad, who many in the movement considered not just tolerable or benign, but positively heroic for standing up to the alphabet soup of various Syrian rebel groups.[15]

Spencer tweeted "I absolutely condemn Washington's military strike against Syria. #Syria #NoMoreWar"[16] and "If Bannon does not resign, I will have lost a tremendous amount of respect for him. #NoWarInSyria."[17] Bannon, of course, did not resign then and there, but he was out of the White House by August 2017.

Cernovich, who sparked a new conspiracy theory by claiming that the chemical weapons strike which prompted the missile attack was a hoax,[18] condemned the US military action and live-streamed for ten hours straight.[19] In the coming months, Trump would disappoint the alt-right again and again, with decisions about staffing, foreign policy, and the slightest hint of compromise on the questions of the makeup and timeline of his proposed border wall. "/pol/ hates Trump now. What happened?" one channer lamented.[20]

*   *   *

The more media-savvy alt-righters began making the most of the newfound attention on the movement, but others were tuning out. With ethno-nationalists like Spencer and conspiracy theorists like Jones and Cernovich increasingly competing to becoming the faces of the alt-right, some were jumping ship. Paul Gottfried, for example, rued ever having been linked with the movement. "My presumed association with the alt-right has contributed to my professional isolation," he told me via email. "In the last six months literary agents and publishers have begun to treat my communications as SPAM and have made it abundantly clear that they want nothing to do with me. As a septuagenarian scholar who has published thirteen books, most of which are read in translation, I am appalled by this reaction."[21]

Gottfried was also distancing himself from Spencer, who he said was involved in organizing the Mencken Club but "only stayed on for a few years before dropping out":

> One of the incidents that may have suggested to him that the group would not suit his purpose was the ready acceptance for membership of a black applicant who had been faithfully coming to our meetings. Although as a member of the board he objected, his objection went nowhere with the other board members.
>
> Critical points on which I disagree with Richard, as his views have become more crystallized, are his leftist social views ... and his saddling of non-whites with responsibility for what white Westerners have done. For me it seems ridiculous to go after black or brown people for the multicultural, PC plague that is afflicting the West. It's whites who have done this to themselves.

Although he had lauded the intellectuals as "dangerously bright," Yiannopoulos was keen to avoid them a year later. He ran a mile from a *Politico* interview request: "Not interested in appearing in any piece alongside Spencer et al. ... We have nothing in common."[22] Influential alt-righters were also increasingly becoming the targets of the movement's own tactics, turned against them by enemies on both the right and the left. "Mike Enoch," founder of the Daily Shoah podcast, was unmasked as a New York website developer named Mike Peinovich. His credibility among his hardcore fandom was destroyed when he was doxxed and it was revealed his wife was Jewish.[23]

Reporters chased down a popular British alt-right vlogger who went by the name Millennial Woes, uncovering the mundane reality of a chubby 30-something broadcasting from his dad's house.[24] And, as noted earlier, Yiannopoulos found himself in the middle of a pedophilia scandal of his own making, when a teenage libertarian dug up old tapes of him seeming to defend sexual relationships between adults and children, and hinting that he may have witnessed statutory rape without doing anything about it.[25] Yiannopoulos resigned from his job at Breitbart, lost a book deal, and was uninvited from the Conservative Political Action Conference.

Richard Spencer wrote of Yiannopoulos: "Ignore him. Don't participate in anything he does. Distance yourself from him."

Milo rode the Alt-Right wave for a while, but he is not Alt-Right or an identitarian or nationalist of any kind. Why should we demonstrate loyalty or kindness to a man who fundamentally does not agree with our basic premises? Even when Milo was most sympathetic towards us last spring, such as in his rather lame and poorly written essay on the Alt-Right, he clearly never even understood us.

I believe Milo did act as a bridge between the mainstream and the Alt-Right for a time. But that bridge has been burned, by Milo and us both.[26]

And by mid-2017, Breitbart, his former employers, were kicking back against any insinuation that their site was affiliated with the alt-right. The term itself was becoming toxic.

Alex Jones, meanwhile, after being outed by his own lawyer as a performance artist, found himself subjected to intense scrutiny over his conspiracy mongering, particularly about Sandy Hook. Infowars steadfastly ignored my interview requests, and apparently hoped to get an easier ride by agreeing to an interview with NBC's Megyn Kelly. When she didn't play ball, Jones engaged in some classic alt-right script-flipping and whined about being a victim.[27]

The other strands of the alt-right tended to retreat into their own closed systems. Men's rights blogs slunk back into their message of misandry, complaining about microaggressions such as fashionable T-shirts which read "More issues than Vogue,"[28] and how girls supposedly get to drink longer at water fountains.[29]

Gamergate-themed message boards stabilized and pumped out their usual steady diet of anti-SJW outrage, with no shortage of news stories about feminism and transgender rights (among other things) to continue to fuel their rage. Breitbart mostly stopped talking about video games, and traffic to a whole host of favorite Gamergate sites levelled off, decreased or cratered. Many gamers, it appears, went back to playing games.

When it came to Trump himself, though, many still held out hope. Even in the rocky early months of his administration, some fans could find a bit of succor in his decision-making. Channers often spoke of the president playing "4D chess" or "10D chess"—in other words, crediting him with working on a higher plane than mere mortals shuffling along on a 3D board. The idea was most often trotted out to explain otherwise baffling actions which seemed drastically opposed to alt-right or identitarian goals—the Syria cruise-missile strike being a prime example.

"We've been pragmatic," Iain Davis, the English alt-righter, told me. "We're putting up with him doing that because he's Donald Trump. We still trust him, and in a way we expect him to be playing that 4D chess all the time. I see the subtle things he's doing, like reducing immigration." I put to Davis that politically, Trump was in deep trouble, having difficulties accomplishing any of his stated goals, and that impeachment over the issue of Russia was a real possibility. "We talk about that a lot," he said. "You'd see an awful lot of violence from the right if that happened. Because they'd feel like all hope is lost and they'd have to rely on the Second Amendment to defend themselves. I don't think you'd get a civil war but you'd get something like it."

4chan continued to bleed rumor and paranoia, nudged along in that direction by those Russia entanglements, alt-right-friendly media sources getting fed little bits of information from the Trump administration, and pure speculation. At times, the fear (or celebration) of the impending end times overwhelmed 4chan. One thread excitedly warned of "the greatest happening of our time"—charges being filed against Trump, Vice President Mike Pence, Reince Priebus, Paul Ryan, and others. Among the responses:

> this feels like campaign season but instead of excitement about hillary's poll numbers, i'm excited about an almost inversion of that; trump's downward spiral- his violent and wretched descent into oblivion.

> I actually hope this is true. This is a coup, and is very similar to when corporate business men attempted to establish a fascist government in the USA. The kikes are going all out on this one.

> I wanted to see everything burn and get lots of happenings. I'm glad Trump is delivering. I just hope he declares a war before he goes.[30]

It seemed like a movement exhausted and looking forward to the end times—if not the end of the world, then the flame-out of its own political moment.

* * *

It would have been unheard of six months before, but by mid-2017 posts like this one began popping up on 4chan with increasing regularity:

Holy shit. As someone who supported Trump in November, kept faith through February, was in denial in March, this is the final fucking straw.

It became clear day 1 Trump and crew have no fucking idea how politics work, are willing to sacrifice the people for profit, and are puting party and person before country. If that was not enough, this is the writing on the wall all but confirming that Trump is

a) destroying American values of transparency, check&balances, and due process of law for his own leadership

b) was complicit in some illegal transaction and interaction during the election

I have voted Right most my life and see myself who was duped. The entire right has been duped. This isnt conservatism, this isnt freedom, this isnt what we were promised. This is how dictatorships are born. For the first time in a long time, Im afraid [all *sic*].[31]

Faith in "meme magic" was waning, and, after Charlottesville, the supposedly ironic stance of the channers suddenly seemed dated and off-key.

In August 2017, shortly after the car attack, the blogger Eliot Higgins discovered a classic script-flipping alt-right smear campaign. Activists circulated faked pictures of bruised women, claiming they had been beaten up by antifa thugs because they harbored right-wing views. Higgins called the campaign— which used pictures of famous actresses featured in high-profile anti-domestic-violence campaigns—"pretty clumsy," and, after BBC Trending and other outlets covered the story,[32] many on 4chan seemed woefully to agree.

"The left is really starting to get on our tactics. Has Kek's power left us finally?" Others chimed in: "honestly this campaign was obviously a smear. any idiot could tell."[33] A detailed, though confusing and angry, discussion about methods and tactics followed. The thread included inchoate chatter about whether any publicity is good publicity. The channers were realizing that the spotlight was on them, and they almost seemed to be emerging blinking into the world, like sheepish teenagers crawling out of their bedrooms:

> Well duh, you guys realize they browse here all the time, right?

> When you've got your plans up for everyone to see it's pretty fucking obvious.

On the irony point, journalist and alt-right critic Angela Nagle observed that "Charlottesville marks the end of a significant phase of the alt-right," and that "ironic dodges" were no longer available to activists. She warned: "The alt-right in the strict sense will now become more isolated, more focused and unambiguous—and perhaps more militant."[34]

* * *

Long-term political predictions are usually a bad idea, and particularly so in the world as it stands today. But examining the history of the alt-right, their strategies and tactics, and their stated intentions, I think it's reasonable to try to set out a road map of where this loose confederation is headed in the years ahead.

Here's one big issue. Compared to doxxing Hollywood stars, spasmodic private "investigations," or giddily memeing a presidential candidate who may actually retweet your stuff, day-to-day politics is boring. And most of the rank-and-file channer-level alt-righters are energized not by the long plod that wins ground wars, but by big online battles. Post-Trump, they promptly went on a losing streak in big elections in other Western democracies, such as Holland, France, and Britain, showing up their weakness and relative geographic isolation.

At the most basic level, the mostly American and British meme warriors failed to grasp the politics of the foreign countries they

219

targeted, and woefully lacked the language and cultural skills needed to come up with messages that hit home. After their chosen candidates disappointed in those votes, the movement's mass mind quickly moved on, looking for the next scrap.

The dream of "taking over the Republican Party" with flash mobs and 24/7 streaming video of candidates' lives—ideas that were once seriously discussed in the wake of Trump's victory— were, only a few short months into the new administration, already beginning to evaporate like a fever dream from a much stranger time.[35] Bannon was out of the White House, and the so-called nationalist wing of the Trump administration, the faction whose values seemed to most align with the alt-right, was on the wane.

The next big set-piece in US politics is the 2018 mid-term elections, and while it's not hard to imagine that, at least online, a head of steam could gather around challengers running against "cuckservative" Republican establishment politicians, there's little indication that activists are up for the stodgy tasks of backing primary candidates, with all the boring tasks—signature collection, fundraising, and so on—which that entails.

The intra-movement fighting that characterized the alt-right around the time of the inauguration wasn't necessarily a fatal flaw, but the distillation of the movement and the primacy of its fringier elements—the white nationalists and conspiracy theorists—limited its broader political appeal.

In some limited spheres, on the other hand, a critical mass of energy still remains. It may well be that university campuses are where the ghosts of the alt-right live on, in trollish challenges to their hated sacred cows: safe spaces, trigger warnings, political correctness at large. And surely, the failure of identity-flavored, Clinton-style establishment politics to provide any real notion of unity or to deliver a victory means that a big slice of the left is on the defensive.

Yet by early 2017 there were already signs that a counter-insurgency (or perhaps a counter-counter-insurgency) was on

Downfall

the way on this front as well, in parallel to grassroots movements designed to stifle President Trump. The sometimes violent and often counter-productive antifa protests were part of this, as were the massive peaceful counter-demonstrations in the wake of Charlottesville. But more subtle strategies were also being formulated, designed to capitalize on the inherent contradictions and hypocrisies of the alt-right itself. Consider, for example, a short missive in the *Portland Mercury*—an alternative newspaper serving the ground zero of hipsterdom on the US West Coast. Despite its reputation as a liberal paradise, in 2017 Portland became the unexpected location of a series of alt-right/antifa protests and street battles. In true Breitbart style the *Mercury* article was headlined "TRIGGERED SNOWFLAKES!!" and was penned by an anonymous contributor:

> I call on all non-alt-right whackos to start labeling alt-right whackos with the same labels they apply to us. When the orange-haired-monster-in-chief runs to Twitter in a fit of rage, he's been triggered. When Richard Spencer and his small group of hillbilly white nationalists protest the removal of a confederate statue, they've also been triggered and are trying to preserve their safe space....
>
> 90% of the time all you'll get is a thumbs down ... it stops them in their tracks. They're not used to being called "Snowflakes" or being accused of being "TRIGGERED" and it forces them to crawl back under the filthy rock from which they emerged.[36]

And so as street battles raged, violent outbursts that only seemed to play into the hands of the alt-right, a somewhat savvier opposition were reclaiming the prankster tradition—for instance, tricking alt-righters into believing that antifa groups were planning to destroy Confederate monuments in Texas or gravestones in Georgia.[37] The pranks encouraged groups of far-right activists to turn up, and journalists pointed out

221

the presence of KKK and white nationalist extreme elements among the crowds—but the supposedly violent leftists intent on vandalism were nowhere to be found.

The appeal of the alt-lightish warriors relies to a great deal on their insistence that they are the fun, ironic counterculture and that the left is entirely devoid of humor or joy. It's an argument that on the face of it—say, to an 18-year-old, freshly enlisted at a university and encountering committed feminists for the first time—has a certain common-sense logic, even if it's ultimately absurd. But such reasoning breaks down pretty damn quick if and when those Portlander campus liberals pick up the joke and start to poke fun at the Republican stooges for what they see as their ironic love of bad music, speech-stifling arguing style, and creepy hero-worship of a billionaire Republican president skimming across the surface of a swamp, constantly trailed by the whiff of scandal.

For all its genuine rage, the alt-right's broad appeal was built around humor, irony, and mockery—and they're not the only team that can play that game.

*   *   *

In 2017 we witnessed the snuffing out of a brief and frightening glimmer of possibility, that the alt-right could grow into something resembling a conventional political force. But in its tactics, ideas, and personalities, it has opened up and shown to the world a box of assorted deplorables and long-dormant ideas which will have deep and unpredictable effects for years.

The movement's first phase is over. In fact, by the time you read these words, it will no doubt have morphed into something completely different—a rump of serious white nationalists perhaps, or the last remnants of a toxic paranoid fringe endlessly circulating YouTube videos among themselves. The campus warriors might succeed in changing their ecosystem and ushering in a new conservative cultural wave—although before that happens they probably need to get some decent tunes.

Who knows—against all odds, the giddy dream of building a viable political force off the back of obnoxious trolling might somehow be revived, and through political grunt work, the movement may move into the mainstream, getting sucked into the Beltway funnel that it spent so much effort trying to destroy.

A more likely scenario is that this Frankenstein of a political group will continue to fall apart, with energetic elements shooting off in all sorts of directions. The only questions that matter might be, what will replace the alt-right? How big will it be? And how much wreckage will it leave in its wake?

Notes

All URLs accessed June–August 2017

Introduction

1. Antonia Malchik, "The town that white supremacist Richard Spencer calls home," *Los Angeles Times*, December 16, 2016, www.latimes.com/opinion/op-ed/la-oe-malchik-richard-spencer-whitefish-20161216-story.html.

2. More on Breitbart comes later, but for a summary, shortly after Trump's election I spelled Breitbart's ethical foundations—or lack thereof. See Mike Wendling, "Breitbart: The web that connects Trump and Farage," BBC News, November 20, 2016, www.bbc.co.uk/news/election-us-2016-38005983.

3. Allum Bokhari and Milo Yiannopoulos, "An establishment conservative's guide to the alt-right," Breitbart, March 29, 2016, www.breitbart.com/tech/2016/03/29/an-establishment-conservatives-guide-to-the-alt-right.

4. Sarah Posner, "How Donald Trump's new campaign chief created an online haven for white nationalists," *Mother Jones*, August 22, 2016, www.motherjones.com/politics/2016/08/stephen-bannon-donald-trump-alt-right-breitbart-news.

5. Amalie C. Nash, "White nationalist Richard Spencer punched during D.C. protests," *USA Today*, January 20, 2017, www.usatoday.com/story/news/politics/2017/01/20/white-nationalist-richard-spencer-punched-during-dc-protests/96859496.

6. The interview was conducted by the Australian Broadcasting Corporation. Various YouTubers posted the raw footage, including at www.youtube.com/watch?v=9rh1dhur4aI.

7. Just for the avoidance of doubt, here's the group description from the now-deleted "alt-right" message board or "subreddit" on the discussion website Reddit, preserved at http://rationalwiki.org/wiki/Alt-right: "The Alt-Right, unlike the dominant ideology of the 20th Century (Liberalism/Conservatism), examines the world through a lens of realism. Rather than continue to look at the world through

the ideological blinders that Liberalism imposes in its dogmatic evangelism of the Equalitarian religion, we prefer to look & examine social relations & demographics from a perspective of what's real. Thus, racial & sexual realism is a key component of the Alt-Right—perhaps the key component that ties the diverse factions within it together. Another core principle of the Alt-Right is Identitarianism. Identitarianism is the prioritization of social identity, regardless of political persuasion. Thus, the Alt-Right promotes White Identity and White Nationalism."

8. Or Whataboutism, or "the pot calling the kettle black," or *tu quoque*, https://en.wikipedia.org/wiki/Tu_quoque

9. And, indeed, they may have a point, even if that point is tangential to the argument at hand. As we'll see, alt-righters, particularly the more serious ones, love tangents—the longer the digression, the better.

10. Milo Yiannopoulos, "MILO: How I forced GLAMOUR magazine to admit I'm not a 'white supremacist,'" Breitbart, January 27, 2017, www.breitbart.com/milo/2017/01/27/forced-glamour-magazine-admit-im-not-white-supremacist.

11. Mike Wendling, "Trump's shock troops: Who are the 'alt-right'?," BBC News, August 26, 2016, www.bbc.co.uk/news/magazine-37021991.

12. This certainly won't be the last baffling contradiction you will encounter in this book.

13. J. Lester Feder, "This is how Steve Bannon sees the entire world," Buzzfeed, November 15, 2016, www.buzzfeed.com/lesterfeder/this-is-how-steve-bannon-sees-the-entire-world?utm_term=.xpoZEXrMe#.wkgjpVMaQ.

14. Court documents from Bannon's divorce proceedings produced stories with headlines such as "Anti-Semitic Trump campaign CEO Stephen Bannon not a big fan of 'whiny brat' Jews, ex-wife says" (*New York Daily News*, August 27, 2016, www.nydailynews.com/news/election/trump-campaign-ceo-bannon-complained-jews-daughters-school-article-1.2767615), and prompted Breitbart to retort "Stephen K. Bannon: friend of the Jewish people, defender of Israel" (November 14, 2016, www.breitbart.com/big-government/2016/11/14/stephen-k-bannon-friend-jewish-people-defender-israel).

15. This figure is an increase from 4 percent in 1990, and will rise to 8 percent by 2020, according to Conrad Hackett, "5 facts about the Muslim population in Europe," Pew Research, July 19, 2016, www.

pewresearch.org/fact-tank/2016/07/19/5-facts-about-the-muslim-population-in-europe.

16. Like many political movements, the far-right likes to think it is capturing the imaginations of vast swathes of young people, and that demography will take care of the rest. Young Americans are actually getting slightly more liberal, according to research including Clara Hendrickson and William A. Galston, "How Millennials voted this election," Brookings Institution, November 21, 2016, www.brookings.edu/blog/fixgov/2016/11/21/how-millennials-voted.

17. Oliver Lee, "Understanding Trump's troll army," Vice, March 13, 2016, https://motherboard.vice.com/en_us/article/understanding-trumps-troll-army, and quoted in Wendling, "Trump's shock troops."

18. Steve Sailer, "Political punk rock," Taki's Magazine, September 7, 2016, http://takimag.com/article/political_punk_rock_steve_sailer/print#ixzz4JYdGrcjx.

19. Ben Schreckinger, "World war meme," Politico Magazine, March/April 2017, www.politico.com/magazine/story/2017/03/memes-4chan-trump-supporters-trolls-internet-214856.

20. Reddit board ("subreddit") r/The_Donald, generally acknowledged to be the biggest alt-right message board on the site, is one of the top 200 or so such subreddits. At the time of writing it had more than 400,000 subscribers. The site's most popular subreddits have millions of subscribers, according to the website Reddit Metrics: http://redditmetrics.com/top/offset/100.

21. Like the man who invented the term "alt-right," Paul Gottfried—for instance in a personal interview and in Jacob Siegel, "The Alt-right's Jewish godfather," Tablet, November 29, 2016, www.tabletmag.com/jewish-news-and-politics/218712/spencer-gottfried-alt-right.

22. Urizenus Sklar, "Interview with alt-right Pepemancer and Kek/Trump supporter, weev," Alphaville Herald, September 22, 2016, http://alphavilleherald.com/2016/09/interview-with-alt-right-pepemancer-and-kektrump-supporter-weev.html. The white nationalist/supremacist question has, above all of the issues preoccupying the alt-right, been the one that has most flummoxed the mainstream media, with different organizations offering different descriptions. For instance the Associated Press says: "Whenever 'alt-right' is used in a story, be sure to include a definition: 'an offshoot of conservatism mixing racism, white nationalism and populism,' or, more simply, 'a white nationalist

movement.'" (John Daniszewski, "Writing about the 'alt-right'," The Definitive Source blog, November 28, 2016, https://blog.ap.org/behind-the-news/writing-about-the-alt-right. But meanwhile the *Guardian* sounded a note of caution in rejecting pleas to ban the phrase for its "sanitising effect": "Avoid defining the 'alt-right' simply as a white nationalist group not because it isn't, but because: a) That's not all it is: it can also be anti-globalization, anti-establishment, antisemitic, racist, misogynist etc, and, b) People within the movement are not all of those things: some would associate themselves with the group simply because they want to protect US jobs/industry; others because they have had enough of the political, media and business elite pulling the strings, and would not consider themselves to be white supremacists, racists etc." "'Alt-right': Why the *Guardian* decided not to ban use of the term," *Guardian*, November 30, 2016, www.theguardian.com/world/mind-your-language/2016/nov/30/alt-right-why-the-guardian-decided-not-to-ban-use-of-the-term.

23. For example, a 4chan /pol/ thread "What is degeneracy?" from 5 February 5, 2017, archived at https://yuki.la/pol/123720208. But really pretty much any random /pol/ thread on any random day; don't say I didn't warn you.

24. Examples were collected in: Kaitlyn Tiffany, "Right-wing extremist Richard Spencer got punched, but it was memes that bruised his ego," The Verge, January 23, 2017, www.theverge.com/2017/1/23/14356306/richard-spencer-punch-internet-memes-alt-right, and (perhaps interestingly, in the Jared Kushner-owned *Observer*): John Bonazzo, "11 of the most creative remixes of a white nationalist getting punched in the face," *Observer*, January 21, 2017, http://observer.com/2017/01/richard-spencer-punch-inauguration-twitter.

25. For a good overview of the discussion see German Lopez, "The debate over punching white nationalist Richard Spencer in the face, explained," Vox, January 26, 2017, www.vox.com/identities/2017/1/26/14369388/richard-spencer-punched-alt-right-trump.

26. Clayton Purdom, "Here come more video games about punching Nazis and hitting them with stuff," AV Club, February 8, 2017, www.avclub.com/article/here-come-more-video-games-about-punching-nazis-an-249983.

27. Jim Treacher, "Is it okay to punch a New York Times reporter?," Daily Caller, January 23, 2017, http://dailycaller.com/2017/01/23/is-it-okay-to-punch-a-new-york-times-reporter.

28. The crowdfunding drive raised more than $5,000 but, as of writing, nobody had been arrested for the punch; www.wesearchr.com/ bounties/expose-the-antifa-who-sucker-punched-richard-spencer.

29. Alt-righters are technically correct when they argue that there are vanishingly few far-right activists who belong to longstanding groups such as the Ku Klux Klan in the United States today, and that they have little influence. At the same time, there has been a recent explosion in other types of far-right groups. See Mark Potok, "The 'Patriot' movement explodes," Intelligence Report, Southern Poverty Law Center, March 1, 2012, www.splcenter.org/fighting-hate/ intelligence-report/2012/patriot-movement-explodes.

30. Lorraine Ali, "The media's challenge in the time of Trump: Where to draw the line between free speech and dangerous rhetoric," *Los Angeles Times*, December 9, 2016, www.latimes.com/entertainment/ tv/la-ca-st-trump-alt-right-hate-media-white-nationalism- 20161121-story.html.

31. The footage was filmed by *The Atlantic*; www.youtube.com/ watch?v=106-bi3jlxk.

32. Gideon Resnick, "White nationalist to alt-right leader: 'Knock it off!' with the Nazi stuff," The Daily Beast, November 22, 2016, www.thedailybeast.com/articles/2016/11/22/white-nationalist-to- alt-right-leader-knock-it-off-with-the-nazi-stuff.html.

33. Ben Schreckinger, "The alt-right comes to Washington," *Politico Magazine*, January/February 2017, www.politico.com/magazine/ story/2017/01/alt-right-trump-washington-dc-power-milo-214629.

Chapter 1

1. Paul Gottfried, "Some observations from the man who created alt-right," Frontpage Mag, August 30, 2016, www.frontpagemag. com/fpm/263988/some-observations-man-who-created-alt-right- paul-gottfried.

2. "About," website of the H.L. Mencken Club, http://hlmenckenclub. org/about.

3. Lydia Saad, "Bush Presidency Closes With 34% Approval, 61% Disapproval," Gallup, January 19, 2008, www.gallup.com/poll/ 113770/bush-presidency-closes-34-approval-61-disapproval.aspx.

4. W. Wesley McDonald, "Russell Kirk and the prospects for conservatism," *Humanitas*, Vol. 12, 1999, www.nhinet.org/humsub/ mcdon12-1.pdf.

Notes

5. Michael Foley, *American Credo: The Place of Ideas in US Politics*,Oxford University Press, 2007, p. 318.

6. Buchanan famously received an unusual amount of votes in Palm
   Beach County, Florida, where the infamous "butterfly ballot" was
   used. Buchanan's name was listed opposite Democrat Al Gore's.
   Buchanan himself said it was likely many Gore voters mistakenly
   voted for him, quite possibly costing Gore the presidency. See "Pat
   Buchanan on NBC's Today," The American Presidency Project,
   www.presidency.ucsb.edu/showflorida2000.php?fileid=
   buchanan11-09, and John Nichols, *Jews for Buchanan: Did You Hear
   the One About the Theft of the American Presidency?*, The New
   Press, 2001.

7. Larry Keller, "Prominent racists attend inaugural H.L. Mencken
   Club gathering," Hatewatch/Southern Poverty Law Center,
   November 26, 2008, www.splcenter.org/hatewatch/2008/11/26/
   prominent-racists-attend-inaugural-hl-mencken-club-gathering.

8. Gottfried's speech was published online on a minor right-wing
   website: The Unz Review, December 1, 2008, www.unz.com/article/
   the-decline-and-rise-of-the-alternative-right.

9. Ibid.

10. Personal Interview, May 2017.

11. Spencer's personal webpage, http://richardbspencer.com/about.

12. Siegel, "The alt-right's Jewish godfather."

13. "About us" page from AlternativeRight.com, as it appeared in 2010,
    archived at https://web.archive.org/web/20100504201511/www.
    alternativeright.com/about-us. AlternativeRight.com has since
    changed hands. Spencer's original articles were archived on
    radixjournal.com, although at one point in 2017 the Radix domain
    appeared to have expired, resulting in dead links. The references to
    Radix come via Internet Archive.

14. Richard B. Spencer, "Oh no he di'int," Radix Journal, May 19, 2011,
    http://web.archive.org/web/20150202063939/www.radixjournal.
    com/altright-archive/altright-archive/main/blogs/hbd/no-he-diint;
    and Richard B. Spencer, "The coming gentrification wars," Radix
    Journal, July 15, 2011, http://web.archive.org/web/20170106050002/
    www.radixjournal.com/altright-archive/altright-archive/main/
    blogs/zeitgeist/the-coming-gentrification-wars.

15. Richard B. Spencer, "The toxic safe haven," Radix Journal, August 9,
    2011, http://web.archive.org/web/20170106044648/http://www.
    radixjournal.com/altright-archive/altright-archive/main/blogs/
    malinvestments/the-toxic-safe-haven. All of Spencer's writings from

this time can be found at http://web.archive.org/web/20170107
114615/http://www.radixjournal.com/altright-archive/?offset=131
6677493000&author=500f7134c4aad0680ce5d4a0.

16. Richard B. Spencer, "The dawn of idiocracy (Part 1)," Radix Journal,
April 7, 2010, http://web.archive.org/web/20170106043805/http://
www.radixjournal.com/altright-archive/altright-archive/main/
blogs/zeitgeist/the-dawn-of-idiocracy-part-1.

17. Richard B. Spencer, "Epic tram lady," Radix Journal, November 29,
2011, http://web.archive.org/web/20170106044149/http://www.
radixjournal.com/altright-archive/altright-archive/main/blogs/
zeitgeist/epic-tram-lady.

18. There is a voluminous amount of material online which purports to
back up HBD theory, much of which riffs off of recent advances in
genetic science, even though research has shown that all humans
have about 99.5% of DNA in common. See Samuel Levy et al., "The
diploid genome sequence of an individual human," PLOS Biology,
September 4, 2007, http://journals.plos.org/plosbiology/article?id=
10.1371/journal.pbio.0050254#s2. For critical perspectives see "Is
human biodiversity a respected scientific theory," www.quora.com/
Is-human-biodiversity-a-respected-scientific-theory, and
Erasmussimo, "Racism has a new name: HBD," Daily Kos, January
12, 2013, www.dailykos.com/story/2013/01/12/1178414/-Racism-
has-a-new-name-HBD#.

19. Personal interview, May 2017.

20. Personal interview, May 2017.

21. Richard B. Spencer, "Facing the future as a minority," Radix Journal,
September 28, 2016, http://web.archive.org/web/20170216034050/
www.radixjournal.com/journal/2016/9/28/facing-the-future-as-a-
minority.

22. Richard B. Spencer, "The political ideas of Anders Behring Breivik,"
Radix Journal, July 23, 2011, http://web.archive.org/web/20170106
043723/http://www.radixjournal.com/altright-archive/altright-
archive/main/blogs/untimely-observations/the-political-ideas-
of-anders-behring-breivik.

23. Kevin MacDonald, "Understanding Jewish influence I: Background
traits for Jewish activism," The Occidental Quarterly, archive
captured on February 20, 2008 and preserved at http://web.archive.
org/web/20080210053629/http://theoccidentalquarterly.com/
archives/vol3no2/km-understanding.html.

Notes

24. "The occidental observer: Online anti-Semitism's new voice," Anti-Defamation League, December 12, 2012, www.adl.org/news/article/the-occidental-observer-online-anti-semitisms-new-voice.

25. Kevin MacDonald, "The political ideas of Anders Behring Breivik," The Occidental Observer, July 23, 2011, www.theoccidentalobserver.net/2011/07/the-political-ideas-of-anders-behring-breivik.

26. Spencer, "The political ideas of Anders Behring Breivik."

27. Butler established a compound in Idaho and held annual gatherings of white nationalists which were some of the largest far-right gatherings of the past few decades—until the march in Charlottesville in August 2017. He lost the property through civil legal action backed by the Southern Poverty Law Center in 2000, and died in 2004.

28. Tristan Scott, "Whitefish council adopts resolution supporting diversity, tolerance," Flathead Beacon, December 2, 2014, http://flatheadbeacon.com/2014/12/02/whitefish-council-adopts-resolution-supporting-diversity-tolerance.

29. By the time the alt-right had become big news, during the 2016 presidential campaign, Yarvin was behind a startup called Urbit, "a secure peer-to-peer network of personal servers, built on a clean-slate system software stack," www.urbit.org.

30. "About me," http://unqualified-reservations.blogspot.co.uk.

31. Curtis Yarvin, writing as Mencius Moldbug, "A formalist manifesto," Unqualified Reservations (blog), April 23, 2007, http://unqualified-reservations.blogspot.co.uk/2007/04/formalist-manifesto-originally-posted.html.

32. Ibid.

33. Among other places, discussion of the "red pill" idea can be found on 4chan here: http://4chandata.org/lit/What-does-it-mean-to-be-red-pilled-Have-such-people-come-to-reality-as-it-really-is-a320303.

34. Curtis Yarvin, writing as Mencius Moldbug, "The case against democracy: ten red pills," Unqualified Reservations (blog), April 24, 2007, http://unqualified-reservations.blogspot.co.uk/2007/04/case-against-democracy-ten-red-pills.html.

35. Ibid.

36. Curtis Yarvin, writing as Mencius Moldbug, "Nosedive," Unqualified Reservations (blog), December 12, 2008, http://unqualified-reservations.blogspot.com/2008/12/nosedive.html.

37. Curtis Yarvin, writing as Mencius Moldbug, "Bad poem of the week: 'Vanitas Mundi' by Robin Ekiss," Unqualified Reservations (blog),

May 8, 2007, http://unqualified-reservations.blogspot.com/2007/05/bad-poem-of-week-vanitas-mundi-by-robin.html.

38. Curtis Yarvin, writing as Mencius Moldbug, "The Laphroaig is unawarded," Unqualified Reservations (blog), May 15, 2007, http://unqualified-reservations.blogspot.com/2007/05/laphroaig-is-unawarded.html.

39. Curtis Yarvin, writing as Mencius Moldbug, "Why I am not a white nationalist," Unqualified Reservations (blog), November 22, 2007, http://unqualified-reservations.blogspot.com/2007/11/why-i-am-not-white-nationalist.html.

40. Rosie Gray, "Behind the internet's anti-democracy movement," *The Atlantic*, February 10, 2017, www.theatlantic.com/politics/archive/2017/02/behind-the-internets-dark-anti-democracy-movement/516243.

41. Klint Finley, "Geeks for monarchy: The rise of the neoreactionaries," Techcrunch, November 22, 2013, https://techcrunch.com/2013/11/22/geeks-for-monarchy.

42. Curtis Yarvin, writing as Mencius Moldbug, "A gentle introduction to Unqualified Reservations (part 1)," Unqualified Reservations (blog), January 8, 2009, http://unqualified-reservations.blogspot.co.uk/2009/01/gentle-introduction-to-unqualified.html.

43. Ibid. Italics in original.

44. Ibid.

45. Ibid.

46. The idea is named after its originator, Joseph Overton, a former vice president of an obscure libertarian think-tank. See "Does the Mackinac Center Have a Point of View?," www.mackinac.org/12894.

47. Curtis Yarvin, writing as Mencius Moldbug, "Why I am not a white nationalist," Unqualified Reservations (blog), November 22, 2007, http://unqualified-reservations.blogspot.co.uk/2007/11/why-i-am-not-white-nationalist.html.

48. Ibid.

49. Klint, "Geeks for monarchy."

50. Peter Thiel, "The education of a libertarian," Cato Unbound, April 13, 2009, www.cato-unbound.org/2009/04/13/peter-thiel/education-libertarian.

51. Eliana Johnson and Eli Stokols, "What Steve Bannon wants you to read," *Politico Magazine*, February 7, 2017, www.politico.com/magazine/story/2017/02/steve-bannon-books-reading-list-214745.

52. Dylan Matthews, "Neo-monarchist blogger denies he's chatting with Steve Bannon," Vox, February 7, 2017, www.vox.com/policy-and-

politics/2017/2/7/14533876/mencius-moldbug-steve-bannon-neoreactionary-curtis-yarvin.

53. Personal interview, for BBC Radio 4, Analysis, May 2017.

54. The home page of the CCRU's primitive website still exists, as of writing, at www.ccru.net.

55. Mark Fisher, "Nick Land: mind games," Dazed Digital, www.dazeddigital.com/artsandculture/article/10459/1/nick-land-mind-games.

56. Nick Land, "Twitter cut," Xenosystems (blog), February 24, 2017, www.xenosystems.net/twitter-cut.

57. Nick Land, "Quote note (#299)," Xenosystems (blog), November 3, 2016, www.xenosystems.net/quote-note-299.

58. Nick Land, "IQ shredders," Xenosystems (blog), July 17, 2014, www.xcnosystems.net/iq-shredders.

59. Personal interview, May 2017.

60. Nick Land, "What is the alt-right? III," Xenosystems (blog), March 3, 2017, www.xenosystems.net/what-is-the-alt-right/#more-6218.

Chapter 2

1. Jessica Elgot, "Civil rights activist Rachel Dolezal misrepresented herself as black, claim parents," Guardian, June 12, 2015, www.theguardian.com/world/2015/jun/12/civil-rights-activist-rachel-dolezal-misrepresented-herself-as-black-claim-parents.

2. Justin Wm Moyer, "'Are you an African American?' Why an NAACP official isn't saying," Washington Post, June 12, 2015, www.washingtonpost.com/news/morning-mix/wp/2015/06/12/spokane-naacp-president-rachel-dolezal-may-be-white/?utm_term=.50a031f144a6.

3. See www.youtube.com/watch?v=oKRj_h7vmMM. By mid-2017 the raw footage had been watched more than 2.6 million times; most of KXLY's other news clips had only a few hundred views each.

4. Samantha Allen, "Dolezal's damaging 'transracial' game," The Daily Beast, June 16, 2015, www.thedailybeast.com/articles/2015/06/16/dolezal-s-damaging-transracial-game; there are many other examples.

5. See https://twitter.com/wginfonetorg/status/661333486175784960.

6. Milo Yiannopoulos, "Passing for black: Top tips from transracial icon Rachel Dolezal," Breitbart, June 13, 2015, www.breitbart.com/big-journalism/2015/06/13/passing-for-black-top-tips-from-transracial-icon-rachel-dolezal.

7. Mike Wendling, "I met Rachel Dolezal—and never doubted her black roots," BBC News, BBC Trending blog, June 12, 2015, www.bbc.co.uk/news/blogs-trending-33109866.

8. Thomas Clouse, "Investigation of Kevin Harpham's 2011 planned MLK March bombing in Spokane turned terrorism into an FBI case study," The Spokesman-Review, January 15, 2017, www.spokesman.com/stories/2017/jan/15/five-years-after-conviction-harpham-bomb-investiga.

9. Meghann M. Cuniff, "Postings reveal bomb suspect's views," The Spokesman-Review, March 13, 2011, www.spokesman.com/stories/2011/mar/13/postings-reveal-suspects-views. To give some idea of how obsessed people on VNN are about the idea, a search of vnnforum.com uncovers hundreds of posts mentioning the phrase.

10. Wikipedia, "White genocide conspiracy theory," https://en.wikipedia.org/wiki/White_genocide_conspiracy_theory.

11. "Noble lies are for children," johnderbyshire.com, December 23, 2010, www.johnderbyshire.com/Opinions/NationalQuestion/taylorqa.html.

12. See https://twitter.com/GirlsOfEuropa/status/831188861225103360.

13. Curt Devine, Drew Griffin, and Scott Bronstein, "White supremacist group stands by racist ideology," CNN, June 24, 2015, http://edition.cnn.com/2015/06/23/us/white-supremacist-group-dylann-roof.

14. Public Intelligence, "Anders Behring Breivik's complete manifesto '2083—A European Declaration of Independence,'" posted July 28, 2011, https://publicintelligence.net/anders-behring-breiviks-complete-manifesto-2083-a-european-declaration-of-independence.

15. Personal interview, April 2017. Beale was referring to Islamist terror attacks in France and the influx of refugees into Europe, but, contrary to his assertion, the news hasn't put tourists off. In 2016, Paris was the third-most visited city in the world with 18 million international visitors, beaten only by London (another place alt-righters frequently portray as a cesspool overrun by immigrants and crime—"Londonistan") and Singapore. Allison Millington, "These are the world's most visited cities in 2016," Business Insider/World Economic Forum, September 28, 2016, www.weforum.org/agenda/2016/09/these-are-the-worlds-most-visited-cities-in-2016.

16. Ibid.

17. Thomas Clouse, "MLK bomb maker gets 32 years in prison," The Spokesman-Review, December 20, 2011, www.spokesman.com/stories/2011/dec/20/mlk-parade-bomber-seeks-guilty-plea-withdrawal.

Chapter 3

1. The US public radio programme On the Media has a "Breaking news consumer's handbook" which often circulates in the wake of attacks and tragedies. It includes tips such as "In the immediate aftermath, news outlets will get it wrong," and "Big news brings out the fakers. And Photoshoppers," www.wnyc.org/story/breaking-news-consumers-handbook-pdf.

2. 4chan, "Brit/pol/ - 2nd London happening edition rightly So," June 3, 2017, archived at https://archive.4plebs.org/pol/thread/128322 413/#q128325930.

3. 4chan, June 3, 2017, archived at https://archive.4plebs.org/pol/thread/128322196/#128322196.

4. See Lamia Estatie, "Misinformation and fake photos shared after London attack," BBC News, BBC Trending blog, June 5, 2017, www.bbc.co.uk/news/blogs-trending-40158469, and Jim Waterson and Hannah Al-Othman, "This is the fake news being spread about the London Bridge terror attack," Buzzfeed, June 4, 2017, www.buzzfeed.com/jimwaterson/this-is-the-fake-news-being-spread-about-the-london-bridge?utm_term=.isWq2pMYg#.nsaPNYldm.

5. This section is heavily informed by interviews with Gabriella Coleman, author of *Hacker, Hoaxer, Whistleblower, Spy: The Many Faces of Anonymous* (Verso, 2014), and Angela Nagle, author of *Kill All Normies: Online Culture Wars From 4Chan and Tumblr to Trump and the Alt-Right* (Zero Books, 2017), which featured on "What is 4Chan?," BBC Trending radio, BBC World Service, June 2, 2017, www.bbc.co.uk/programmes/p05402xs.

6. 4chan citations in this book come from third-party websites which archive the site and from various journalists and others who have spotted and screengrabbed material. 4chan's structure makes it easy, even mandatory, for anons to shuck off their past—and it's almost impossible to pin posts on any particular real-world person—but sometimes things are saved elsewhere for posterity. An outline of the board's rules can be found at www.4chan.org/rules—but to extend the metaphor, this is something like getting an impression of Disney World by reading the back of your ticket.

7. 4chan, "New nigger hate thread," posted March 21, 2017, archived at http://archive.is/AMbVK.

8. Know Your Meme, "Rickroll," http://knowyourmeme.com/memes/rickroll.

9. Know Your Meme, "LOLcats," http://knowyourmeme.com/memes/lolcats.

10. "What is 4Chan?," BBC Trending.

11. Christopher Poole, writing as "moot," "Why were /r9k/ and /new/ removed?," 4chan, August 20, 2011, archived at www.webcitation.org/6159jR9pC.

12. "Rules - /pol/ - politically incorrect," www.4chan.org/rules#pol.

13. See the next chapter for more on Gamergate and the online men's movement.

14. Gabriel Emile Hine et al., "Kek, cucks, and God Emperor Trump: A measurement study of 4chan's politically incorrect forum and its effects on the Web," International AAAI Conference on Web and Social Media 2017, https://aaai.org/ocs/index.php/ICWSM/ICWSM17/paper/view/15670/14790.

15. Ibid.

16. Archived at http://archive.is/AMbVK.

17. I'm not going to descend into an argument over penis size, but for more information see: D. Veale et al., "Am I normal? A systematic review and construction of nomograms for flaccid and erect penis length and circumference in up to 15 521 men," *BJU International*, 115 (6), 2015, 978–86; K.R. Wylie I. and Eardley, "Penile size and the 'small penis syndrome'," *BJU International*, 99 (6), 2007, 1449–55; J.C. Orakwe and G.U. Ebuh, "'Oversized' penile length in the black people; myth or reality?," *Tropical Journal of Medical Research*, 11 (1), 2007, 16–18.

18. 4chan post, "23andme—anyone satisfied with it?," archived at https://yuki.la/pol/101703431; and Reddit, r/WhiteRights, "Finally got around to checking my privledge," www.reddit.com/r/WhiteRights/comments/28lp4n/finally_got_around_to_checking_my_privilege. See also Elspeth Reeve, "White nonsense: Alt-right trolls are arguing over genetic tests they think 'prove' their whiteness," Vice, October 9, 2016, https://news.vice.com/story/alt-right-trolls-are-getting-23andme-genetic-tests-to-prove-their-whiteness; and Sarah Zhang, "Will the alt-right promote a new kind of racist genetics," *The Atlantic*, December 29, 2016, www.theatlantic.com/science/archive/2016/12/genetics-race-ancestry-tests/510962.

19. www.reddit.com/r/The_Donald/comments/6os1bd/literally_had_a_lib_friend_of_mine_tell_me_i_dont.

20. www.reddit.com/r/The_Donald/comments/6orlfi/hey_fbi_im_one_of_60_million_bots_that_putin.

21. www.reddit.com/r/The_Donald/comments/6ophb6/bombshell_report_dropped_in_france_33_of_young/?utm_content=comments&utm_medium=hot&utm_source=reddit&utm_name=The_Donald.

22. For instance, a chart ranking recent presidential candidates according to how much tax they paid, www.reddit.com/r/The_Donald/comments/5zjl17/who_paid_the_most_federal_income_tax_and_the_least.

23. Among many other things, Trump wrote: "I have been very concerned about media bias and the total dishonesty of the press. I think new media is a great way to get out the truth," www.reddit.com/r/The_Donald/comments/4uxdbn/im_donald_j_trump_and_im_your_next_president_of.

24. Alex Dackevych, "'CNN wrestling' tweet came from extreme Reddit user," BBC News, BBC Trending blog, July 3, 2017, www.bbc.co.uk/news/blogs-trending-40483914.

25. Alex Griswald, "No that Trump/Russia dossier isn't an elaborate 4chan hoax," Mediaite, January 27, 2017, www.mediaite.com/online/no-that-trumprussia-dossier-isnt-an-elaborate-4chan-hoax.

Chapter 4

1. Bonnie Robinson et al., "Santa Barbara killer Elliot Rodger, son of Hollywood director, vowed to 'slaughter' women who rejected him," *New York Daily News*, May 27, 2014, www.nydailynews.com/news/crime/deranged-santa-barbara-california-killer-tied-premeditated-youtube-video-reports-article-1.1804354. Rodger's manifesto, "My Twisted World," was saved at www.documentcloud.org/documents/1173808-elliot-rodger-manifesto.html.

2. Alan Duke, "California killer's family struggled with money, court documents show," CNN, May 28, 2014, http://edition.cnn.com/2014/05/27/justice/california-elliot-rodger-wealth.

3. Anthony Zurcher, "Are 'pick-up artists' to blame for Isla Vista shooting?," BBC News, May 27, 2014, www.bbc.co.uk/news/blogs-echochambers-27553254.

4. I reported on the story, including in "The extreme misogyny of pick-up artist hate," BBC News, BBC Trending blog, May 31, 2014, www.bbc.co.uk/news/blogs-trending-27640474.

5. PUAhate.com went offline shortly after the Isla Vista shooting, and many users migrated to a similar site called Sluthate.com. See the thesis by Mary Lilly, "'The World is Not a Safe Place for Men': The

Representational Politics of the Manosphere," University of Ottawa, 2016, https://ruor.uottawa.ca/bitstream/10393/35055/1/Lilly_Mary_2016_thesis.pdf.

6. Josh Glasstetter, "Elliot Rodger, Isla Vista shooting suspect, posted racist messages on misogynistic website," Hatewatch, Southern Poverty Law Center, May 23, 2014, www.splcenter.org/hatewatch/2014/05/24/elliot-rodger-isla-vista-shooting-suspect-posted-racist-messages-misogynistic-website.

7. Rodger's manifesto.

8. BBC News, "The extreme misogyny of pick-up artist hate."

9. For an example of the liberal and often pro-feminist manosphere, see The Good Men Project, https://goodmenproject.com.

10. Larry Copeland, "Life expectancy in the USA hits a record high," *USA Today*, October 8, 2014, www.usatoday.com/story/news/nation/2014/10/08/us-life-expectancy-hits-record-high/16874039.

11. Hannah Richardson, "Why do more women than men go to university?," BBC News, August 18, 2016, www.bbc.co.uk/news/education-37107208.

12. Featured post on front page of "MGTOW," www.mgtow.com, captured March 23, 2017.

13. Gjoni wrote and added to the post in August and September 2014: https://thezoepost.wordpress.com.

14. Ibid.

15. Cathy Young, "GamerGate's Eron Gjoni breaks silence, talks about infamous Zoe Quinn post, 'Five Guys' joke," Heatstreet, August 15, 2016, https://heatst.com/culture-wars/gamergates-eron-gjoni-breaks-silence-talks-about-infamous-zoe-quinn-post-five-guys-joke.

16. Although Gjoni detailed a relationship Quinn had with a journalist, his rambling post never made the allegation that she received favorable coverage in exchange for sex, and in fact he praised her professional skills. The journalist in question never reviewed Quinn's game and and—notably—received about a tenth of the amount of abuse that was directed at Quinn, according to Aja Romano, "The battle of Gamergate and the future of video games," The Kernel, December 28, 2014, http://kernelmag.dailydot.com/issue-sections/features-issue-sections/11195/battle-of-gamergate-2014.

17. Jesse Singal, "Gamergate should stop lying to journalists—and itself," *New York Magazine*, October 20, 2014, http://nymag.com/scienceofus/2014/10/gamergate-should-stop-lying-to-itself.html. The idea that Gamergate was an ethical crusade became so widely

mocked online that it spawned its own memes, see Know Your Meme, "Actually It's About Ethics," http://knowyourmeme.com/memes/actually-it-s-about-ethics.

18. A thread on the main Gamergate subreddit attracted a grand total of 12 comments: www.reddit.com/r/KotakuInAction/comments/2is2uo/my_thoughts_on_the_shadow_of_mordor_controversy. See also Eric Kain, "'Middle-Earth: Shadow Of Mordor' paid branding deals should have #GamerGate up in arms," Forbes, October 8, 2014; and for a direct link to alt-right luminaries, Zaid Jilani, "Gamergate's fickle hero: The dark opportunism of Breitbart's Milo Yiannopoulos," Salon, October 29, 2014, www.salon.com/2014/10/28/gamergates_fickle_hero_the_dark_opportunism_of_breitbarts_milo_yiannopoulos.

19. Jean Burgess and Ariadna Matamoros-Fernández, "Mapping sociocultural controversies across digital media platforms: one week of #gamergate on Twitter, YouTube, and Tumblr," *Communication Research and Practice* 2 (1), 2016, 79–96. After an examination of a slice of Gamergate posts the authors emphatically state: "GamerGate's issue publics are absolutely not concerned only or even primarily with 'ethics in games journalism.'"

20. Alex Mazey, "#GamerGate: Why do we even listen to feminist criticism of video games?," Rebel Media (blog), February 16, 2016, www.therebel.media/_gamergate_why_do_we_even_listen_to_feminist_criticism_of_video_games.

21. Jim Edwards, "FBI's 'Gamergate' file says prosecutors declined to charge men believed to have sent death threats—even when they confessed on video," Business Insider, February 16, 2017, www.businessinsider.com/gamergate-fbi-file-2017-2?r=UK&IR=T. The heavily redacted FBI file on Gamergate is archived at https://vault.fbi.gov/gamergate/Gamergate%20Part%2001%20of%2001/view.

22. Matt Lees, "What Gamergate should have taught us about the 'alt-right'," *Guardian*, December 1, 2016, www.theguardian.com/technology/2016/dec/01/gamergate-alt-right-hate-trump.

23. "Kotaku" is a reference the Gawker-owned video-game website that Gamergaters accused of being one of the bastions of Cathedral-dwelling social justice warriors.

24. Casey Johnston, "Chat logs show how 4chan users created #GamerGate controversy," Ars Technica, September 10, 2014, https://arstechnica.com/gaming/2014/09/new-chat-logs-show-how-4chan-users-pushed-gamergate-into-the-national-spotlight. At a very basic level, Twitter bots are very easy to create; with no

technical know-how you can Google instructions and set one up in about ten minutes.

25. Lees, "What Gamergate should have taught us."

26. Milo Yiannopoulos, "Am I too old for video games?," The Kernel, September 17, 2013, http://kernelmag.dailydot.com/comment/column/5344/am-i-too-old-for-video-games.

27. Milo Yiannopoulos, "Exposed: The secret mailing list of the gaming journalism elite," Breitbart, September 17, 2014, www.breitbart.com/london/2014/09/17/exposed-the-secret-mailing-list-of-the-gaming-journalism-elite.

28. "Return of Kings—About," www.returnofkings.com/about; Nathan Wyatt, "A sex tourist swallows the red pill," Taki's Magazine, January 13, 2013, http://takimag.com/article/a_sex_tourist_swallows_the_red_pill_nathan_wyatt/print#axzz2NipbnmQ7.

29. Michael Seville, "Why men are intellectually superior to women," Return of Kings, February 25, 2014, www.returnofkings.com/29112/the-intellectual-inferiority-of-women.

30. Steve McMahon, "Women should not be allowed to vote," Return of Kings, May 15, 2014, www.returnofkings.com/34330/women-should-not-be-allowed-to-vote.

31. This post by Valizadeh himself is for some reason gone from the Return of Kings site, but archived at https://webcache.googleusercontent.com/search?q=cache:KqrKMkpHJWUJ:www.rooshvforum.com/thread-25884.html+&cd=1&hl=en&ct=clnk&gl=us.

32. L.D. Hume, "Women belong at home, not at the office," Return of Kings, February 5, 2014, www.returnofkings.com/28600/women-belong-at-home-not-at-the-office.

33. Dawn Pine, "The story of how female Viagra got approved to fight 'sexism,'" Return of Kings, July 31, 2017, www.returnofkings.com/126744/the-story-of-how-female-viagra-got-approved-to-fight-sexism.

34. Michael Sebastian, "4 ways that western women are ruining themselves," Return of Kings, March 23, 2017, www.returnofkings.com/117494/4-ways-that-western-women-are-ruining-themselves.

35. Roosh Valizadeh, "How to stop rape," Rooshv.com, February 16, 2015, www.rooshv.com/how-to-stop-rape.

36. For instance, Christopher Leonid, "The problem of false rape accusations is not going away," Return of Kings, April 1, 2017, www.returnofkings.com/116992/the-problem-of-false-rape-accusations-is-not-going-away. The reality is that fake claims do exist; repeated

studies have shown that they make up a very small proportion of reports to law enforcement. Owen Bowcott, "Rape investigations 'undermined by belief that false accusations are rife,'" *Guardian*, March 13, 2013, www.theguardian.com/society/2013/mar/13/rape-investigations-belief-false-accusations.

37. Lloyd Grove, "Why did Fox News welcome date rape apologist Mike Cernovich?," The Daily Beast, August 9, 2016, www.thedailybeast.com/articles/2016/08/09/why-did-fox-news-welcome-date-rape-apologist-mike-cernovich.html.

38. Andrew Marantz, "Trolls for Trump," *The New Yorker*, October 31, 2016, www.newyorker.com/magazine/2016/10/31/trolls-for-trump.

39. That particular thread used to live at http://boards.4chan.org/pol/thread/118844792/if-you-think-women-should-be-allowed-to-vote-you, but it was not archived; you're just going to have to trust me on this one.

40. Roosh Valizadeh, "The White European culture is dead," RooshV.com, March 16, 2017, www.rooshv.com/the-white-european-culture-is-dead.

41. 4chan post from January 26, 2017, screengrab captured at https://twitter.com/4chansbest/status/824796660412846080

Chapter 5

1. Tse Yin Lee, "Love for Louis Tomlinson and Trump supporters say dump Star Wars," BBC News, BBC Trending blog, December 9, 2016, www.bbc.co.uk/news/blogs-trending-38261402; Emma Gray Ellis, "The alt-right hates Rogue One, because of course it does," Wired, December 14, 2016, www.wired.com/2016/12/rogue-one-alt-right-boycott; Luke Graham, "Some Trump supporters threaten to boycott 'Star Wars' on rumors Disney flatly denies," CNBC, December 9, 2016, www.cnbc.com/2016/12/09/trump-supports-threaten-to-boycott-star-wars.html.

2. Justin Carissimo, "Rogue One: Alt-right supporters create #DumpStarWars to boycott film," *Independent*, December 9, 2016, www.independent.co.uk/arts-entertainment/films/star-wars-rogue-one-alt-right-boycott-a7464806.html.

3. Dave McNary, "'Rogue One: A Star Wars Story' hits $1 billion at worldwide box office," Variety, January 22, 2017, http://variety.com/2017/film/news/rogue-one-a-star-wars-story-worldwide-box-office-1201966453.

4. www.google.co.uk/?gfe_rd=cr&ei=fKHcWI7_A8_O8geVv5aw
   BA#q=dumpstarwars&tbm=nws&*.
5. Emma Wilson, "Why do trolls go after feminists?," BBC News, BBC
   Trending blog, December 6, 2015, www.bbc.co.uk/news/blogs-
   trending-35009045.
6. The tactic is of course not confined to the right. Influential activists
   and thinkers including Saul Alinsky and Gene Sharp advocated the
   "political jiu-jitsu" tactic. See Brian Martin, "The Politics of Gene
   Sharp," *Gandhi Marg Quarterly*, 35(2): 201–30, July–September
   2013, http://www.bmartin.cc/pubs/13gm.pdf.
7. Rush Limbaugh, *The Way Things Ought to Be*, Pocket Books, 1992,
   p. 193: "I prefer to call the most obnoxious feminists what they
   really are: feminazis."
8. Emma Green, "Make trolling great again," *The Atlantic*, September
   26, 2016, www.theatlantic.com/politics/archive/2016/09/make-
   trolling-great-again/499523.
9. Antonia Okafor, "College deems 'white genocide' a joke when it
   declines to punish prof for tweets it claims are 'satire'," Independent
   Journal Review, January 2017, http://ijr.com/2017/01/768271-
   college-deems-white-genocide-a-joke-when-it-declines-to-punish-
   prof-for-tweets-it-claims-are-satire.
10. Corey Robin, "Defend George Cicciariello-Maher," Jacobin
    Magazine, December 27, 2016, www.jacobinmag.com/2016/12/
    drexel-free-speech-academic-freedom-alt-right.
11. "Anyone at Drexel able to bring me to speak to the student body?"
    Spencer's tweet read. "Contact me." No invitation was forthcoming,
    https://twitter.com/RichardBSpencer/status/813422459525468160.
12. Elizabeth Preza, "'This is what winning looks like': Neo-Nazis set
    sights on destroying Drexel professor who mocked them," Raw
    Story, December 27, 2017, www.rawstory.com/2016/12/this-is-
    what-winning-looks-like-neo-nazis-set-sights-on-destroying-
    drexel-professor-who-mocked-them.
13. Brian Palmer, "White supremacists by the numbers," Slate Magazine,
    October 29, 2008, www.slate.com/articles/news_and_politics/
    explainer/2008/10/white_supremacists_by_the_numbers.html.
14. Andrew Anglin, "A normie's guide to the alt-right," The Daily
    Stormer, October 31, 2016, archived at http://web.archive.org/
    web/20170814204318/www.dailystormer.com/a-normies-guide-
    to-the-alt-right.
15. Personal communication, April 2017.

16. A typical anti-Semitic meme shared on the anonymous app Whisper: http://whisper.sh/whisper/050e0c1a4cba73185779 b5c6f2d9a060c5f610/Oy-vey-its-anudda-shoah. Sometimes the mocking takes in "hilarious" targets like actual Holocaust survivors, for instance in a thread "trump is like anudda shoah," from March 30, 2017, archived at https://archive.4plebs.org/pol/thread/ 118857216.

17. J.M. Berger, "How white nationalists learned to love Donald Trump," *Politico Magazine*, October 25, 2016, www.politico.com/magazine/ story/2016/10/donald-trump-2016-white-nationalists-alt-right- 214388.

18. Robert Whitaker, "The white mantra," Whitaker Online, www. whitakeronline.org/blog/the-white-mantra.

19. RationalWiki—which crowdsources debunkings of pseudoscience, documents "the full range of crank ideas," and pulls together takedowns of totalitarians and fundamentalists—has a number of carefully sourced dissections of alt-right ideas, in this case, "Anti-racist is a code word for anti-white," http://rationalwiki.org/ wiki/Anti-racist_is_a_code_word_for_anti-white.

20. ADL, "Anti-racist is a code for anti-white," www.adl.org/education/ references/hate-symbols/anti-racist-is-a-code-for-anti-white.

21. Bret Schulte, "The alt-right of the Ozarks," Slate Magazine, April 3, 2017, www.slate.com/articles/news_and_politics/politics/2017/04/ what_harrison_arkansas_fight_with_the_kkk_says_about_the_alt_ right.html?wpsrc=sh_all_mob_fb_bot.

22. Theodore Beale, writing as Vox Day, "What the alt-right is," Vox Populi blog, August 24, 2016, http://voxday.blogspot.co.uk/2016/08/ what-alt-right-is.html.

23. Even to describe the entire movement, for instance Lawrence Murray, "The fight for the alt-right: the rising tide of ideological autism against big-tent supremacy," The Right Stuff, March 6, 2016, http://therightstuff.biz/2016/03/06/big-tentism.

24. Roderick Kaine, "Autism and the extreme male brain," AltRight. com, December 22, 2016, https://altright.com/2016/12/22/autism- and-the-extreme-male-brain.

25. 4chan, "Can we have an autistic screeching thread?," December 3, 2016, https://archive.4plebs.org/pol/thread/101386152.

26. The YouTube video "You can't stump the Trump (volume 4)" has been watched more than 1.4 million times, www.youtube.com/ watch?v=MKH6PAoUuDo.

27. Urban Dictionary, "Chimpout," www.urbandictionary.com/tags. php?tag=chimpout.

28. Anonymous, writing as "Shalom Shekelberg," "Ben Garrison movie poster parodies on display in Texas," The Daily Stormer, July 12, 2014, archived at http://web.archive.org/web/20170814133113/ www.dailystormer.com/ben-garrison-movie-poster-parodies-on-display-in-texas.

29. Joel Pollak, "Blue state blues: The crybullies who claim Donald Trump is bad for the Jews," Breitbart, May 20, 2016, www.breitbart. com/big-government/2016/05/20/blue-state-blues-crybullies-say-donald-trump-bad-jews.

30. Dana Schwartz, "Why angry white men love calling people cucks," GQ, August 1, 2016, www.gq.com/story/why-angry-white-men-love-calling-people-cucks.

31. Reddit r/The_Donald, "LMAO they just said cuck on Fox News while talking about the alt-right," August 24, 2016, www.reddit. com/r/The_Donald/comments/4zf4x7/lmao_they_just_said_cuck_on_fox_news_while.

32. Eric Striker, "The Jews behind pro-globalist Super Bowl advertisements," The Daily Stormer, February 7, 2017, archived at http://web.archive.org/web/20170729093428/www.dailystormer. com/the-jews-behind-pro-globalist-super-bowl-advertisements.

33. Paul Dacre, "The BBC's cultural Marxism will trigger an American-style backlash," Guardian, January 24, 2007, www.theguardian.com/ commentisfree/2007/jan/24/comment.comment.

34. Matthew Feldman and Roger Griffin (eds), Fascism: Vol III, Fascism and Culture, Routledge, 2003, p. 343.

35. Perhaps the best synopsis of this came from Scott Oliver, "Unwrapping the 'Cultural Marxism' nonsense the alt-right loves," Vice, February 23, 2017, www.vice.com/en_us/article/unwrapping-the-conspiracy-theory-that-drives-the-alt-right

36. Richard Spencer, "The god of white dispossession," Radix Journal, January 20, 2014, http://web.archive.org/web/20170610203527/ http://www.radixjournal.com/journal/2014/1/20/the-god-of-white-dispossession.

37. The Right Stuff "TRS Lexicon," http://therightstuff.biz/trs-lexicon.

38. Jonathan Weisman, "The Nazi tweets of 'Trump God Emperor,'" New York Times, May 26, 2016, www.nytimes.com/2016/05/29/ opinion/sunday/the-nazi-tweets-of-trump-god-emperor. html?smid=tw-share&_r=0.

39. Cooper Fleishman and Anthony Smith, "(((Echoes))), exposed: The secret symbol neo-Nazis use to target Jews online," Mic, June 1, 2016, https://mic.com/articles/144228/echoes-exposed-the-secret-symbol-neo-nazis-use-to-target-jews-online#.Yz2h8Al49.

40. Bokhari and Yiannopoulos, "An establishment conservative's guide."

41. Reddit r/The_Donald, "Alt-right sounds like a great term to me," November 25, 2016, www.reddit.com/r/The_Donald/comments/5eux9j/alt_right_sounds_like_a_great_term_to_me_its_the.

42. Daniel Spaulding, "Classical nihilism," AlternativeRight (blog), August 2015, http://alternative-right.blogspot.com/2015/08/classical-nihilism.html.

43. Heben Nigatu, "Why the "fake geek girl" meme needs to die," Buzzfeed, January 4, 2013, www.buzzfeed.com/hnigatu/why-the-fake-geek-girl-meme-needs-to-die?utm_term=.knQmY6kNZ#.vlNKO4qmn.

44. Monica Hesse and Dan Zak, "Does this haircut make me look like a Nazi?," *Washington Post*, November 20, 2016, www.washingtonpost.com/news/arts-and-entertainment/wp/2016/11/30/does-this-haircut-make-me-look-like-a-nazi/?utm_term=.dcedd2f6e410.

45. Anna Silman, "For the alt-right, dapper suits are a propaganda tool," *New York Magazine*, November 23, 2016, http://nymag.com/thecut/2016/11/how-the-alt-right-uses-style-as-a-propaganda-tool.html.

46. For a full range, just Google: www.google.com/search?q=god+emperor+trump.

47. Wikipedia, "Talk:Scientific Racism," https://en.wikipedia.org/wiki/Talk:Scientific_racism#Disputed_tag.

48. Ari Feldman, "Human biodiversity: The pseudoscientific racism of the Alt-right," Forward, August 5, 2016, http://forward.com/opinion/national/346533/human-biodiversity-the-pseudoscientific-racism-of-the-alt-right.

49. 4Chan, April 5, 2017, archived at https://yuki.la/pol/119615095.

50. "Ex-Army" blog, "HuWhite identity," October 9, 2015, http://ex-army.blogspot.co.uk/2015/10/huwhite-identity.html.

51. They've copied a number of stories from me and my BBC colleagues, for instance www.amren.com/news/2015/10/is-this-manga-cartoon-of-a-six-year-old-syrian-girl-racist/ (archived at https://web.archive.org/web/20170218013114/www.amren.com/news/2015/10/is-this-manga-cartoon-of-a-six-year-old-syrian-girl-racist) is word-for-word Mike Wendling, "Is this manga cartoon of

a six-year-old Syrian girl racist?," BBC News, BBC Trending blog, October 8, 2015, www.bbc.co.uk/news/blogs-trending-34460325.

52. Jared Taylor, "Africa in our midst: Lessons from Katrina," American Renaissance, October 2005, archived at https://web.archive.org/web/20051024025504/www.amren.com/mtnews/archives/2005/09/africa_in_our_m.php.

53. Council of Conservative Citizens, "Media interviews with the CofCC," archived at https://web.archive.org/web/20150624161010/http://conservative-headlines.com/2015/06/media-interviews-with-the-cofcc.

54. E. A. Wallis Budge, *The Gods of the Egyptians: Or, Studies in Egyptian Mythology*, 1, Methuen & Co, 1904, pp. 241.

55. Know Your Meme, "Kekistani," http://knowyourmeme.com/memes/kekistan.

56. Know Your Meme, "Shadilay," http://knowyourmeme.com/memes/shadilay.

57. Urban Dictionary "Libtard," www.urbandictionary.com/define.php?term=Libtard.

58. Whitney Phillips, Jessica Beyer, and Gabriella Coleman, "Trolling scholars debunk the idea that the alt-right's shitposters have magic powers," Motherboard, March 22, 2017, https://motherboard.vice.com/en_us/article/trolling-scholars-debunk-the-idea-that-the-alt-rights-trolls-have-magic-powers.

59. BBC World Service, BBC Trending, "How the 'Great Meme War' moved to France," April 9, 2017, www.bbc.co.uk/programmes/po4ykfnj.

60. Jon Huang, Samuel Jacoby, Michael Strickland, and K.K. Rebecca Lai, "Election 2016: Exit polls," *New York Times*, November 8, 2016, www.nytimes.com/interactive/2016/11/08/us/politics/election-exit-polls.html?_r=0, and Galston and Hendrickson, "How millennials voted."

61. Michael W. Kirst, "Women earn more degrees than men, gap keeps increasing," The College Puzzle (blog), May 28, 2013, https://collegepuzzle.stanford.edu/?tag=women-exceed-men-in-college-graduation.

62. Maeve Duggan, "Online harassment," Pew Research Center, October 22, 2014, www.pewinternet.org/2014/10/22/online-harassment.

63. Dan Bloom, "'Alt-right' activist Milo Yiannopoulos calls gender pay gap a 'conspiracy theory' in fiery TV clash," *Mirror*, November 18,

2016, www.mirror.co.uk/news/uk-news/alt-right-activist-milo-yiannopoulos-9286278.

64. Laurie Penny, "Fear of a feminist future," The Baffler, October 17, 2016, http://thebaffler.com/war-of-nerves/fear-feminist-future-laurie-penny.

65. E.W., "Women and the alt-right," *The Economist*, February 1, 2017, www.economist.com/blogs/democracyinamerica/2017/02/no-women-s-march. With a response (of sorts) published in Cecilia Davenport, "A woman's touch," Radix Journal, February 2, 2017, http://web.archive.org/web/20170606080916/http://www.radixjournal.com/blog/2017/2/2/a-womans-touch.

66. There are some notable examples in Andy Nowicki, "Fifty shades of misandry," AlternativeRight (blog), April 17, 2016, http://alternative-right.blogspot.com/2016/04/fifty-shades-of-misandry.html; Owen Strachan, "The alt-right is what happens when society marginalizes men," The Federalist, March 21, 2017, http://thefederalist.com/2017/03/21/alt-right-happens-society-marginalizes-men.

67. Lorna Shaddick, "We're the establishment now": 'alt-right' in the spotlight," Oxford Dictionaries (blog), November 16, 2016, http://blog.oxforddictionaries.com/2016/11/alt-right.

68. Beyond memes, 4chan and YouTube videos, the alt-right has very little cultural production of its own, and thus has to try to appropriate other stuff. Mitchell Sunderland, "Can't shake it off: How Taylor Swift became a Nazi idol," Broadly, May 23, 2016, https://broadly.vice.com/en_us/article/ae5x8a/cant-shake-it-off-how-taylor-swift-became-a-nazi-idol.

69. Nick Pell, "The alt-right movement: everything you need to know," *The Irish Times*, January 4, 2017, www.irishtimes.com/opinion/the-alt-right-movement-everything-you-need-to-know-1.2924658.

70. Mike Pearl, "How to tell if your alt-right relative is trying to redpill you at thanksgiving," Vice, November 23, 2016, www.vice.com/en_us/article/how-to-tell-if-your-alt-right-relative-is-trying-to-redpill-you-at-thanksgiving.

71. The anti-smoking radicals actually got more than they wanted; in the UK and other countries those plain cigarette packets are adorned with scary pictures of cancerous tumors and diseased organs.

72. John Lanchester, "Brexit Blues," *London Review of Books*, July 28, 2016, www.lrb.co.uk/v38/n15/john-lanchester/brexit-blues.

73. Joe Brewer, "Overton Window presents distorted view," Cognitive Policy Works, August 2, 2007, www.cognitivepolicyworks.com/resource-center/thinking-points/overton-window-presents-distorted-view; Laura March, "The flaws of the Overton Window theory," *New Republic*, October 27, 2016, https://newrepublic.com/article/138003/flaws-overton-window-theory.

74. Marsh, "The flaws of the Overton Window theory."

75. Ibid.

76. Nick Barlow, "Closing the Overton Window," What you can get away with (blog), October 2, 2016, www.nickbarlow.com/blog/?p=4630.

77. Ibid.

78. Anti-Defamation League, "Pepe the frog," www.adl.org/education/references/hate-symbols/pepe-the-frog.

79. See https://twitter.com/realdonaldtrump/status/653856168402681856?lang=en.

80. ADL, "Pepe the frog."

81. Like YouTuber Sargon of Akkad: https://twitter.com/Sargon_of_Akkad/status/850821330584973313.

82. Furie initially tried to reclaim, then tried to "kill off" Pepe, without, it must be said, much luck. "Pepe the Frog 'is killed off to avoid being a hate symbol'," BBC News, May 8, 2017, www.bbc.co.uk/news/world-us-canada-39843468.

83. Paul Dempsey, "Real-world politics torpedo Facebook's virtual pioneer," Engineering and Technology, September 27, 2016, https://eandt.theiet.org/content/articles/2016/09/view-from-washington-palmer-luckey.

84. Stephen Marche, "Why Canada can't laugh at America anymore," *Esquire*, November 7, 2016, www.esquire.com/news-politics/a50327/why-us-election-2016-is-not-funny.

85. Ben Yagoda, "Who you calling 'snowflake'," *The Chronicle of Higher Education*, December 4, 2016, www.chronicle.com/blogs/linguafranca/2016/12/04/who-you-calling-snowflake.

86. For examples in the wild, see Know Your Meme, "Social justice warrior," http://knowyourmeme.com/memes/social-justice-warrior.

87. Abby Ohlheiser, "Why 'social justice warrior,' a Gamergate insult, is now a dictionary entry," *Washington Post*, October 7, 2015, www.washingtonpost.com/news/the-intersect/wp/2015/10/07/why-social-justice-warrior-a-gamergate-insult-is-now-a-dictionary-entry/?utm_term=.98c822e0779c.

88. Fred Clark, "What 'SJW' really means," Patheos, September 13, 2016, www.patheos.com/blogs/slacktivist/2016/09/13/what-sjw-really-means.

89. Remso W. Martinez, "No one wins in the alt-right vs. SJW conflict," Being Libertarian, January 29, 2017, https://beinglibertarian.com/no-one-wins-alt-right-vs-sjw-conflict.

90. Mitchel Blatt, "Only difference between SJWs and alt-righters is which identities they hate," The Federalist, August 27, 2016, http://thefederalist.com/2016/08/27/progressives-sjws-alt-righters-two-sides-identity-politics-coin. For a more succinct and meme-y take, Know Your Meme, "Alt-right—alt-right vs social justice warriors," http://knowyourmeme.com/photos/1164559-alt-right.

91. Greg Lukianoff and Jonathan Haidt, "The coddling of the American mind," The Atlantic, September 2015, www.theatlantic.com/magazine/archive/2015/09/the-coddling-of-the-american-mind/399356.

92. Know Your Meme, "Trigger," http://knowyourmeme.com/memes/trigger.

93. Danielle DeCourcey, "#TheTriggering is spreading hateful messages in defense of free speech," attn: Magazine, March 10, 2016, www.attn.com/stories/6496/the-triggering-racist-sexist-twitter-movement; Josh Feldman, "Anti-PC effort #TheTriggering explodes on Twitter," Mediaite, March 9, 2016, www.mediaite.com/online/anti-pc-effort-thetriggering-explodes-on-twitter.

94. Angela Nagle, Kill All Normies: Online Culture Wars from Tumblr and 4chan to the Alt-right and Trump, Zero Books, 2017, p. 8.

95. Reddit, r/TumblrInAction, www.reddit.com/r/TumblrInAction/wiki/tags.

96. For instance this video clip from Conservative Review featuring blogger Michelle Malkin asks "Is the Muslim rapefugee crisis coming to America?," www.facebook.com/475549362567960/videos/1165238713599018.

97. Kate Connolly, "Tensions rise in Germany over handling of mass sexual assaults in Cologne," Guardian, January 7, 2016, www.theguardian.com/world/2016/jan/06/tensions-rise-in-germany-over-handling-of-mass-sexual-assaults-in-cologne.

98. Crofton Black and Abigail Fielding-Smith, "German alt-right loves this fake 'refugee crime' map," The Daily Beast, February 27, 2017, www.thedailybeast.com/articles/2017/02/27/german-alt-right-loves-this-fake-refugee-crime-map.html.

99. See https://twitter.com/idiotator/status/852000072111869952.

100. James Shultz, "Questioning the rape narrative in Cologne, Germany," A Voice for Men, January 14, 2016, www.avoiceformen. com/mens-rights/false-rape-culture/questioning-the-rape-narrative-in-cologne-germany.

101. Andrew Anglin, "Feminists ignoring Cologne proves feminism is an anti-white hoax," The Daily Stormer, January 9, 2016, archived at http://web.archive.org/web/20170611154158/www.dailystormer. com/feminists-ignoring-cologne-proves-feminism-is-an-anti-white-hoax; or, for a meninist rather than neo-Nazi take, Roosh Valizadeh, "Germany proves that "rape culture" is merely a political weapon against western men," Return of Kings, January 8, 2016, www.returnofkings.com/77129/germany-proves-that-rape-culture-is-merely-a-political-weapon-against-western-men.

102. Phil McCausland, "Donald Trump explains Sweden terror comment that baffled a nation," NBC News, February 20, 2017, www. nbcnews.com/news/us-news/donald-trump-explains-sweden-terror-comment-baffled-nation-n723006.

103. Maajid Nawaz, *Radical: My Journey Out of Islamist Extremism*, W.H. Allen, 2012; also a video: Maajid Nawaz, "Je suis Muslim: How universal secular rights protect Muslim communities the most," Big Think, November 18, 2015, http://bigthink.com/videos/maajid-nawaz-on-islamic-reform.

104. Joel Bernstein, "The rise of the #Regressiveleft hashtag," Buzzfeed, March 15, 2016, www.buzzfeed.com/josephbernstein/the-rise-of-the-regressiveleft-hashtag?utm_term=.npJp7wWvz#.mrJn3VzO9.

105. "Audi is going for the gold in the #VSOlympics with their Super Bowl commercial," tweeted @VirtueOlympics, https://twitter.com/VirtueOlympics/status/828418089544998915.

106. Joseph Bulbulia and Uffe Schjoedt, "Religious culture and cooperative prediction under risk: Perspectives from social neuroscience," in Ilkka Pyysaianen (ed.), *Religion, Economy, and Cooperation*, Mouton de Gruyter, 2010, pp. 37–9.

107. Helen Lewis, "The echo chamber of social media is luring the left into cosy delusion and dangerous insularity," *New Statesman*, January 22, 2015, www.newstatesman.com/helen-lewis/2015/07/echo-chamber-social-media-luring-left-cosy-delusion-and-dangerous-insularity.

108. Mark Peters, "Virtue signaling and other inane platitudes," *The Boston Globe*, December 24, 2015, www.bostonglobe.com/ideas/2015/12/24/virtue-signaling-and-other-inane-platitudes/YrJRcvxYMofMcCfgORUcFO/story.html.

109. David Shariatmadari, "'Virtue-signalling'—the putdown that has passed its sell-by date," *Guardian*, January 20, 2016, www.theguardian.com/commentisfree/2016/jan/20/virtue-signalling-putdown-passed-sell-by-date.
110. For instance the squeals (or "autistic screeches") of delight when "THE BBC NORMIES HAVE DISCOVERED THE GREAT MEME WAR IN FRANCE," 4chan, April 9, 2017, archived at https://archive.4plebs.org/pol/thread/120271363.
111. Viewed in this way, "cuck" could be the internet version of "Rassenschande," the Nazi era taboo—then law—against inter-racial relationships. There are many other examples.
112. Stephen Petrow, "The coded language of the alt-right is helping to power its rise," *Washington Post*, April 10, 2017, www.washingtonpost.com/lifestyle/style/the-coded-language-of-the-alt-right-is-helping-to-power-its-rise/2017/04/07/5f269a82-1ba4-11e7-bcc2-7d1a0973e7b2_story.html?utm_term=.51861a15d890.

Chapter 6

1. The original interview posted at www.facebook.com/Breitbart/videos/10158592546820354/ was deleted, but the internet rarely forgets, and copies survive, for instance at https://twitter.com/ashleyfeinberg/status/829855768434397187.
2. Callum Borchers, "Sean Spicer's Facebook Live interview with Breitbart News is the most awkward thing ever," *Washington Post*, February 10, 2017, www.washingtonpost.com/news/the-fix/wp/2017/02/10/sean-spicers-facebook-live-interview-with-breitbart-news-is-the-most-awkward-thing-ever/?tid=sm_tw_pp&utm_term=.f91aff5766c4&wprss=rss_the.fix.
3. Andy Cush, "Breitbart's Facebook Live interview with Sean Spicer is the bleakest video you've ever seen," Spin, February 10, 2017, www.spin.com/2017/02/breitbarts-facebook-live-interview-with-sean-spicer-is-the-bleakest-video-youve-ever-seen.
4. Posner, "How Donald Trump's new campaign chief created an online haven for white nationalists."
5. Harriet Sinclair, "Breitbart claims it is not alt-right and neither is Steve Bannon," *Newsweek,* August 20, 2017, www.newsweek.com/breitbart-claims-it-not-alt-right-and-neither-steve-bannon-652518.
6. BBC News, "How Breitbart became Donald Trump's favourite news site," November 14, 2016, www.bbc.co.uk/news/world-us-canada-37109970.

7. "An independent governance assessment of ACORN: The path to meaningful reform," Proskauer, December 7, 2009, www.proskauer. com/files/uploads/report2.pdf.

8. Susan Kinzie, "Duo release another video of their meeting with ACORN worker," *Washington Post*, October 22, 2009, www. washingtonpost.com/wp-dyn/content/article/2009/10/21/AR2009 102103284_pf.html.

9. Andrew Breitbart, "Video proof: The NAACP Awards racism–2010," BigGovernment, July 19, 2010, archived at www.webcitation. org/5rbhsjhzR?url=http://biggovernment.com/abreitbart/2010/ 07/19/video-proof-the-naacp-awards-racism2010.

10. Conor Friedersdorf, "Andrew Breitbart's legacy: credit and blame where it's due," *The Atlantic*, March 8, 2012, www.theatlantic.com/ politics/archive/2012/03/andrew-breitbarts-legacy-credit-and-blame-where-its-due/253953.

11. See https://twitter.com/andrewbreitbart.

12. Joel B. Pollak, "The Vetting—exclusive—Obama's literary agent in 1991 booklet: 'Born in Kenya and raised in Indonesia and Hawaii,'" Breitbart, May 17, 2012, www.breitbart.com/big-government/ 2012/05/17/the-vetting-barack-obama-literary-agent-1991-born-in-kenya-raised-indonesia-hawaii.

13. Friedersdorf, "Andrew Breitbart's legacy."

14. McKay Coppins, "Breitbart's inheritors battle over his legacy," Buzzfeed, October 22, 2012, www.buzzfeed.com/mckaycoppins/ breitbarts-inheritors-battle-over-his-legacy?utm_term=.eve6 AxrDN#.qqnOLYBmD.

15. A chart of Breitbart's traffic figures can be found at www. rank2traffic.com/breitbart.com. It's no coincidence that they really start to increase following Trump's entry into the presidential campaign in mid-2015. Further analysis at Claire Malone, "Trump made Breitbart great again," FiveThirtyEight, August 18, 2016, https://fivethirtyeight.com/features/trump-made-breitbart-great-again.

16. Willa Frej, "Breitbart's greatest hit (pieces): Some of the website's most disgusting headlines," Huffington Post, November 14, 2016, www.huffingtonpost.com/entry/breitbart-headlines_us_5829 ba13e4b060adb56f1bdb; Saul Heather, "Steve Bannon: Some of the worst Breitbart headlines published under Donald Trump's chief strategist," *Independent*, November 14, 2016, www.independent. co.uk/news/people/steve-bannon-breitbart-donald-trumps-chief-

strategist-a7416606.html; and yes, Wendling, "Breitbart: The web that connects Trump and Farage."
17. Breitbart, February 19, 2016.
18. Breitbart, December 8, 2015.
19. As with a lot of what Yiannopoulos does, it's hard to tell when he's serious and when he's not—about which, more later.
20. Bannon never publicly explained this comment or, as of writing, repeated it.
21. Wendling, "Breitbart: The web that connects."
22. Soon after, he led a new media startup called Big League Politics, which hired a few alt-right sympathetic writers and ran, for instance, conspiracy-laden stories about a murdered Democratic National Committee staffer. See Patrick Howley, "Seth Rich police chief hobnobbed with clinton Campaign and DNC officials (PHOTOS)," Big League Politics, May 21, 2017, http://bigleague politics.com/seth-rich-police-chief-hobnobbed-clinton-campaign-dnc-officials-photos, for one such example.
23. Wendling, "Breitbart: The web that connects."
24. Michael Patrick Leahy, "TB spiked 500 percent in Twin Falls during 2012, as Chobani Yogurt opened plant," Breitbart, August 26, 2016, www.breitbart.com/big-government/2016/08/26/tb-spiked-500-percent-twin-falls-2012-year-chobani-opened-local-plant.
25. By chance, I briefly met Ulukaya in 2013 at a business conference in Monaco; we chatted a bit about upstate New York—where I'm from and where his original yogurt plant was located. I produced an interview by the BBC business correspondent Peter Day which was broadcast on the BBC World Service, "Global business: Entrepreneur of the year," July 18, 2013, www.bbc.co.uk/programmes/p01brr6n.
26. Associated Press and Louise Boyle, "Chobani founder signs up to Bill Gates' Giving Pledge and promises to donate most of his self-made $1.4bn fortune," Mail Online, May 29, 2015, www.dailymail.co.uk/news/article-3102668/Chobani-CEO-pledges-donate-1-4bn-wealth.html.
27. Clinton Foundation, "One-on-one conversation with President Bill Clinton and Hamdi Ulukaya," February 4, 2016, www.clintonfoundation.org/clinton-global-initiative/meetings/winter-meeting/2016/webcasts/day-1.
28. David Gelles, "For helping immigrants, Chobani's founder draws threats," New York Times, October 31, 2016, www.nytimes.com/

2016/11/01/business/for-helping-immigrants-chobanis-founder-draws-threats.html?_r=0.

29. Lee Stranahan, "Twin Falls refugee rape special report: Why are the refugees moving in?," Breitbart, August 10, 2016, www.breitbart.com/big-government/2016/08/10/twin-falls-refugee-rape-special-report-refugees.

30. Chobani press release, "CHOBANI CELEBRATES GRAND OPENING OF WORLD'S LARGEST YOGURT MANUFACTURING PLANT IN TWIN FALLS, IDAHO," December 17, 2012, www.chobani.com/blog/2012/12/chobani-celebrates-grand-opening-of-worlds-largest-yogurt-manufacturing-plant-in-twin-falls-idaho.

31. Gelles, "For helping immigrants."

32. Leahy and others who reported about Chobani didn't respond to my questions about their reporting at the time when I initially wrote about Twin Falls in November 2016, nor did they respond to requests for comment for this book.

33. Breitbart London, "Labour MP Jo Cox killed on street—suspected attacker 'mental health problems'," June 16, 2016, www.breitbart.com/london/2016/06/16/breaking-labour-mp-jo-cox-shot-stabbed-constituency-surgery-yorkshire.

34. Ibid.

35. Roy Greenslade, "Pro-Brexit papers' coverage of Jo Cox killing raises questions," *Guardian*, June 17, 2016, www.theguardian.com/uk-news/2016/jun/17/pro-brexit-papers-coverage-of-jo-cox-killing-raises-questions.

36. Breitbart, "Tag: Jo Cox," www.breitbart.com/tag/jo-cox.

37. Breitbart, "Remain campaigners rush to blame Brexit for MP attack," June 16, 2016, www.breitbart.com/london/2016/06/16/remain-campaigners-rush-blame-brexit.

38. Raheem Kassam, "EXCLUSIVE—Jo Cox friend and eyewitness: 'Immoral' for her to be used as referendum 'token'," Breitbart, June 17, 2016, www.breitbart.com/london/2016/06/17/exclusive-jo-cox-friend-eyewitness-immoral-used-referendum-token.

39. Donna Rachel Edmunds, "Official Remain campaign tells supporters: Use Jo Cox death to attack Brexit," Breitbart, June 20, 2016, www.breitbart.com/london/2016/06/20/official-remain-campaign-tells-supporters-use-jo-cox-death-attack-brexit.

40. Breitbart, "Thomas Mair guilty of murdering MP Jo Cox," November 23, 2016, www.breitbart.com/london/2016/11/23/thomas-mair-guilty-murdering-mp-jo-cox.

41. James Delingpole, "Times columnist Aaronovitch: Brexit campaigners kinda, sorta killed Jo Cox MP...," Breitbart, November 24, 2016, www.breitbart.com/london/2016/11/24/times-columnist-aaronovitch-brexit-campaigners-kinda-sorta-killed-jo-cox-mp.

42. Dominic Casciani and Daniel De Simone, "Thomas Mair: Extremist loner who targeted Jo Cox," BBC News, November 23, 2016, www.bbc.co.uk/news/uk-38071894.

43. Charles Arthur, "The Kernel to close as debts stay unpaid," Guardian, March 5, 2013, www.theguardian.com/media/2013/mar/05/kernel-close-debts-unpaid-sentinel-media.

44. Milo Yiannopoulos, "Did Black Lives Matter organizer Shaun King mislead Oprah Winfrey by pretending to be biracial?," Breitbart, August 19, 2015, www.breitbart.com/big-government/2015/08/19/did-black-lives-matter-organiser-shaun-king-mislead-oprah-winfrey-by-pretending-to-be-biracial.

45. Milo Yiannopoulos, "Leading GamerGate critic Sarah Nyberg claimed to be a pedophile, apologized for white nationalism," Breitbart, September 11, 2015, www.breitbart.com/big-journalism/2015/09/11/leading-gamergate-critic-sarah-nyberg-claimed-to-be-a-pedophile-apologised-for-white-nationalism.

46. Jelani Cobb, "The mistake the Berkeley protesters made about Milo Yiannopoulos," The New Yorker, 15 February 2017, https://www.newyorker.com/news/daily-comment/the-mistake-the-berkeley-protesters-made-about-milo-yiannopoulos.

47. BBC Radio 4, "The Briefing Room: Milo Yiannopoulos and the alt-right," August 26, 2016, www.bbc.co.uk/programmes/b07pjb9y.

48. Bokhari declined to be interviewed for this book; Yiannopoulos did not respond to multiple requests. I later interviewed him for the BBC in Berkeley in September 2017.

49. Bokhari and Yiannopoulos, "An establishment conservative's guide."

50. Ibid.

51. Ibid.

52. Bokhari and Yiannopoulos, "An establishment conservative's guide."

53. In a sense, their focus on culture and great works is actually alien to the alt-right, which tends to gauge success not on the nebulous fields of art and architecture but on more measurable or immediately obvious indicators such as economics and social order. Singapore is much cleaner than London; you'd be hard pressed to argue that it has a better music scene. Nick Land suggested that the "IQ shredder" city states of East Asia would prove to be "far more competent" over time than democracies, but again, it's the criteria that counts.

54. Bokhari and Yiannopoulos, "An establishment conservative's guide."
55. Ibid.
56. "Ramzpaul," "American History Z," YouTube, February 18, 2013, www.youtube.com/watch?v=CmQoT81NbE8.
57. Southern Poverty Law Center, "American Renaissance speakers call for white homeland," April 7, 2013, www.splcenter.org/hatewatch/2013/04/07/american-renaissance-speakers-call-white-homeland; the SPLC has more about Ramzpaul's views: "Ramsey calls himself a 'satirist,' a kind of far-right Jon Stewart, but he is more importantly an ideologue and a hero to much of the radical right." Southern Poverty Law Center, "Paul Ray Ramsey," undated, www.splcenter.org/fighting-hate/extremist-files/individual/paul-ray-ramsey.
58. Milo Yiannopoulos, "FULL TEXT: 'How to destroy the alt Right' By MILO," Breitbart, September 19, 2016, www.breitbart.com/milo/2016/09/19/milo-destroy-alt-right-speech.
59. Gavin McInnes, the Vice co-founder who went on to become a conservative raconteur, was just one who picked up the theme, for instance in Rebel Media, "Gavin McInnes: What is the alt-right?," YouTube, April 7, 2017, www.youtube.com/watch?v=UQCZ9izaCa4.
60. For instance, Depeche Mode rejecting praise bestowed by Richard Spencer; see Jason Newman, "Depeche Mode reject alt-right leader's band praise," *Rolling Stone*, February 23, 2017, www.rollingstone.com/music/news/depeche-mode-reject-alt-right-leaders-band-praise-w468558. Or attempts like a blog titled "Hail to the thief—the pro-Trump, alt-right protest album we needed, but didn't deserve," The Author's Files, June 7, 2017, http://theauthorsfiles.blogspot.co.uk/2017/06/hail-to-the-thief-pro-trump-alt-right-protest-album.html. Radiohead also made their views on the alt-right clear; at a California gig just after the Berkeley riot, Thom Yorke asked the audience: "How many alt-right members are there in the audience tonight? ... Because you can fuck right off." See Nick Miller, "REVIEW: Radiohead marvels sold-out crowd, comments on Coachella hiccups and Saturday's alt-right brawl, during its first night in Berkeley," *East Bay Express*, April 18, 2017, www.eastbayexpress.com/oakland/review-radiohead-marvels-sold-out-crowd-comments-on-coachella-hiccups-and-saturdays-alt-right-brawl-during-its-first-night-in-berkeley/Content?oid=6387527.
61. For example, although exit polls are a work in progress, and political scientists are still studying the motivating factors of the 2016 election, it's clear that economic issues galvanized many Republican

voters. CNN Politics, "Exit polls," November 23, 2016, http://edition.cnn.com/election/results/exit-polls.

62. Personal communication, June 2017.

63. Joseph Bernstein, "Inside the alt-right's campaign to smear Trump protesters as anarchists," Buzzfeed, January 11, 2017, www.buzzfeed.com/josephbernstein/inside-the-alt-rights-campaign-to-smear-trump-protesters-as?utm_term=.sveN74k8y#.ts3G93yQK.

64. Marantz, "Trolls for Trump."

65. Personal email. Cernovich has denied being part of the alt-right, saying there's too much "drama" in political movements. Mike Cernovich, "Is Mike Cernovich part of the alt-right?," Danger and Play, August 31, 2016, www.dangerandplay.com/2016/08/31/is-mike-cernovich-part-of-the-alt-right.

66. Andrew Marantz, "The far right American nationalist who tweeted #MacronLeaks," The New Yorker, May 7, 2017, www.newyorker.com/news/news-desk/the-far-right-american-nationalist-who-tweeted-macronleaks.

67. See https://twitter.com/jackposobiec/status/861604501517725701?lang=en.

Chapter 7

1. Andrew Anglin, "Breitbart's alt-right analysis is the product of a degenerate homosexual and an ethnic mongrel," The Daily Stormer, March 31, 2016, archived at http://web.archive.org/web/20170610023156/www.dailystormer.com/breitbarts-alt-right-analysis-is-the-product-of-a-degenerate-homosexual-and-an-ethnic-mongrel. After the rally and terror attack in Charlottesville in August 2017, the Daily Stormer came under renewed scrutiny for mocking victim Heather Heyer. The resulting publicity led several web-hosting companies in a number of countries to ban the Stormer, thus all links to Stormer content will be listed via the Internet Archive.

2. Ibid.

3. Andrew Anglin, "A normie's guide to the alt-right," The Daily Stormer, August 31, 2016, archived at http://web.archive.org/web/20170814204318/www.dailystormer.com/a-normies-guide-to-the-alt-right.

4. Dennis E. Showalter, "Jews, Nazis and the law: The case of Julius Streicher," Museum of Tolerance Online/Simon Wiesenthal Center, Annual 6, Chapter 6, http://motlc.wiesenthal.com/site/pp.asp?c=gvKVLcMVIuG&b=395155.

5. Joel Oliphint and Andy Downing, "The white nationalist from Worthington," Columbus Alive, February 8, 2017, www.columbusalive.com/entertainment/20170208/white-nationalist-from-worthington.

6. The Daily Stormer cites Amazon's Alexa rankings in support of its claim: Andrew Anglin, "Support the Daily Stormer," November 22, 2016, archived at http://web.archive.org/web/20170814170159/www.dailystormer.com/support-the-daily-stormer. This despite previously calling the company "a complete joke which can never be taken seriously again: Andrew Anglin, "Alexa ranking manipulation: Alex Jones discovers actual real life conspiracy," November 21, 2014, archived at http://web.archive.org/web/20170613175215/www.dailystormer.com/alexa-ranking-manipulation-alex-jones-discovers-actual-real-life-conspiracy. The criticism came after it measured a huge drop in the Stormer's own stats, of course. In 2016, rival ranking firm Comscore put the Daily Stormer's figures well behind Stormfront's, and at times dipping so low that they could not be accurately measured. Josh Harkinson, "White supremacist sites claim their traffic is booming. Actually, no," Mother Jones, November 23, 2016.

7. The Stormer front page from the time is archived at http://web.archive.org/web/20160627121940/dailystormer.com.

8. "Far-right group National Action to be banned under terror laws," BBC News, December 12, 2016, www.bbc.co.uk/news/uk-38286708.

9. "Nazi sympathiser jailed for four weeks over 'grossly offensive' anti-Semitic tweet sent to Labour MP," Daily Mail, October 21, 2014, www.dailymail.co.uk/news/article-2800945/nazi-sympathiser-jailed-four-weeks-grossly-offensive-anti-semitic-tweet-sent-labour-mp.html.

10. Andrew Anglin, "Operation: Filthy Jew Bitch—A National Action soldier has been jailed for calling a Jew a Jew, and we must resist," The Daily Stormer, October 21, 2014, archived at http://web.archive.org/web/20170611123807/www.dailystormer.com/operation-filthy-jew-bitch-a-national-action-solider-has-been-jailed-for-calling-a-jew-a-jew-and-we-must-resist.

11. Daily Hansard, Debate, House of Commons, October 29, 2014, c311, www.publications.parliament.uk/pa/cm201415/cmhansrd/cm141029/debtext/141029-0001.htm#141029-0001.htm_spnew71.

12. Emma Barnett, "Twitter must block anti-Semitic words, says abused Labour MP," Telegraph, December 18, 2014, www.telegraph.co.uk/women/womens-life/11302428/Anti-semitic-abuse-Twitter-must-

block-racist-words-says-Labour-MP.html; "MP wants action over 'vitriolic' Twitter abuse of colleague," BBC News, October 29, 2014, www.bbc.co.uk/news/uk-politics-29821693.

13. Anglin, "Operation...."

14. Marcus Dysch, "Neo-Nazi gave out internet abuse tips in campaign against MP," *Jewish Chronicle*, October 30, 2014, www.thejc.com/news/uk-news/neo-nazi-gave-out-internet-abuse-tips-in-campaign-against-luciana-berger-1.60174.

15. Press Association, "Racist troll guilty of harassing Labour MP with antisemitic posts," December 7, 2016, www.theguardian.com/uk-news/2016/dec/07/racist-troll-guilty-harassing-labour-mp-luciana-berger-joshua-bonehill-paine.

16. Andrew Anglin, "Fat Luciana Berger claims another scalp: Troll jailed over alleged 'anti-Semitic death threat'," The Daily Stormer, February 11, 2017, archived at http://web.archive.org/web/20170724082944/www.dailystormer.com/fat-luciana-berger-claims-another-scalp-troll-jailed-over-alleged-anti-semitic-death-threat.

17. Hilary Whiteman, "I will not be silenced: Australian Muslim fights Twitter 'troll army'," CNN, February 28, 2015, http://edition.cnn.com/2015/02/27/asia/australia-muslim-twitter-campaign.

18. Keith Stuart, "Nintendo denies Alison Rapp firing is linked to harassment campaign," *Guardian*, March 31, 2016, www.theguardian.com/technology/2016/mar/31/nintendo-denies-alison-rapp-firing-is-linked-to-harassment-campaign.

19. Lauren Gambino, "Journalist who profiled Melania Trump hit with barrage of antisemitic abuse," *Guardian*, April 29, 2016, www.theguardian.com/us-news/2016/apr/28/julia-ioffe-journalist-melania-trump-antisemitic-abuse.

20. Although he once claimed to be living in Nigeria, it's most likely that in 2016 and 2017 he was living in Russia or Ukraine. Ohio voting records show that he mailed in an absentee ballot for the 2016 presidential election from Krasnodar, a city in western Russia. Jesse Balmert, "Daily Stormer neo-Nazi website owner once registered to vote at fake address," *Cincinnati Enquirer*, August 31, 2017, www.cincinnati.com/story/news/politics/2017/08/31/daily-stormer-neo-nazi-website-owner-fake-address/616755001. See also Keegan Hankes, "Eye of the Stormer," February 9, 2017, Intelligence Report, Southern Poverty Law Center, www.splcenter.org/fighting-hate/intelligence-report/2017/eye-stormer.

21. Sherry Spencer, "Does love really live here?," Medium, December 15, 2016, https://medium.com/@recnepss/does-love-really-live-here-fff159563ba3.

22. Andrew Anglin, "Jews targeting Richard Spencer's mother for harassment and extortion—TAKE ACTION!," The Daily Stormer, December 16, 2016, archived at http://web.archive.org/web/201708 14125402/www.dailystormer.com/jews-targeting-richard-spencers-mother-for-harassment-and-extortion-take-action.
23. S. Spencer, "Does love really live here?"
24. Lynnette Hintze, "Whitefish woman sues neo-Nazi for online assault," The Daily Inter Lake, February 18, 2017, www.daily interlake.com/article/20170418/ARTICLE/170419855.
25. Andrew Blake, "Anti-Semitic march in Montana town to coincide with Martin Luther King Day: Report," *Washington Times*, January 3, 2017, www.washingtontimes.com/news/2017/jan/3/anti-semitic-march-in-montana-town-to-coincide-wit.
26. Dillon Tabish, "Neo-Nazi website postpones armed march in Whitefish," Flathead Beacon, January 11, 2017, http://flathead beacon.com/2017/01/11/neo-nazi-website-postpones-armed-march-whitefish.
27. Brian Byrne, "Daily Stormer's Andrew Anglin, still on the run, served lawsuit via Ohio newspaper," The Daily Dot, September 18, 2017, www.dailydot.com/layer8/andrew-anglin-daily-stormer-lawsuit-newspaper.
28. Michael Kunzelman, "Target of online trolls suing neo-Nazi website's publisher," Associated Press, April 18, 2017, archived at www.chicagotribune.com/news/nationworld/ct-daily-stormer-intimidation-lawsuit-20170418-story.html.
29. For instance: "The Daily Stormer just demonises nationalism by making it look as stupid as possible," wrote one commenter on a Stormfront hate thread. "There's no sensible politics whatsoever there; its as if the whole thing is a parody with the silly artwork and stories," www.stormfront.org/forum/t1165766.
30. Jacob Siegel, "Dylann Roof, 4chan, and the new online racism," The Daily Beast, June 29, 2015, www.thedailybeast.com/articles/2015/06/29/dylann-roof-4chan-and-the-new-online-racism.html.
31. Matt Pearce, "What happens when a millennial goes fascist? He starts up a neo-Nazi site," *Los Angeles Times*, June 24, 2015, www.latimes.com/nation/la-na-daily-stormer-interview-20150624-story.html.
32. Paul Ramsey, writing as RAMZPAUL, "White nationalism is a cult," RAMZPAUL blog, April 2, 2016, archived at www.ramzpaul.com/2016/04/white-nationalism-is-cult.html.

33. David Kravets, "Appeals court reverses hacker/troll 'weev' conviction and sentence," Ars Technica, November 4, 2014, https://arstechnica.com/tech-policy/2014/04/appeals-court-reverses-hackertroll-weev-conviction-and-sentence.

34. Andrew Auernheimer, "What I learned from my time in prison," The Daily Stormer, October 1, 2014, archived at http://web.archive.org/web/20170723115752/www.dailystormer.com/what-i-learned-from-my-time-in-prison.

35. Ibid.

36. Abigail Tracey, "Hacker weev could face punishment for 'mass printer trolling' under junk fax law," Forbes, April 6, 2016, www.forbes.com/sites/abigailtracy/2016/04/06/hacker-weev-troll-daily-stormer-college-printers-fax-law-hacking-security/#1a1f24e64daf.

37. Andrew Aurenheimer, "'Women in tech', doxing, Kathy Sierra, and the koolaid," weev Livejournal blog, October 8, 2014, archived at https://web.archive.org/web/20141012000213/http://weev.livejournal.com/409913.html?thread=6193977. The post includes the tell-tale alt-righter victimhood line: "Now white men are the vulnerable minority."

38. In January 2017, he wrote a blog post detailing that he was living in Ukraine and saying that he had won a lot of money betting on a Trump presidency. Andrew Aurenheimer, "To all my friends in Ukraine: Time grows short, act now," Livejournal blog, January 20, 2017, http://weev.livejournal.com/417066.html.

39. Personal communication; via email Aurenheimer (either jokingly or laughably) wrote: "I am available at the standard SAG/AFTRA day rate for special guest stars, which currently sits at $1026.40."

40. Keegan Hankes, "Dylann Roof may have been a regular commenter at neo-Nazi website The Daily Stormer," Southern Poverty Law Center, June 21, 2015, www.splcenter.org/hatewatch/2015/06/22/dylann-roof-may-have-been-regular-commenter-neo-nazi-website-daily-stormer.

41. Siegel, "Dylann Roof, 4chan, and the new online racism."

42. "The recent spree shooting by Dylann Storm Roof is a travesty that cannot be rationalized. Barging into a Church and firing on defenceless elderly people taking part in Bible study is not something that fits into the basic moral system of the vast majority of nationalists, whether they are Christians, National Socialists, secessionists, or anything else." Eric Striker, Charleston shooting: A tale of two narratives," The Daily Stormer, June 24, 2015, archived at

http://web.archive.org/web/20170612030554/www.dailystormer.com/charleston-shooting-a-tale-of-two-narratives.

43. Andrew Anglin, "DyRo trial is set to begin," The Daily Stormer, December 7, 2016, archived at http://web.archive.org/web/20170720020210/www.dailystormer.com/dyro-trial-is-set-to-begin.

44. Andrew Anglin, "Wacko Jew terrorist Joshua Goldberg attempted to infiltrate the Daily Stormer," The Daily Stormer, September 11, 2015, archived at http://web.archive.org/web/20170612115442/www.dailystormer.com/wacko-jew-terrorist-joshua-goldberg-attempted-to-infiltrate-the-daily-stormer.

45. Andrew Anglin, "#ProjectGermany: feminist hag stabbed in the neck over invasionist positions," The Daily Stormer, October 17, 2015, archived at http://web.archive.org/web/20170814134721/www.dailystormer.com/projectgermany-feminist-hag-stabbed-in-the-neck-over-invasionist-positions.

46. Andrew Anglin, "Brexit: Jo Cox' death was not a tragedy and the world is a better place without her," The Daily Stormer, June 23, 2016, archived at http://web.archive.org/web/20170609231559/www.dailystormer.com/brexit-jo-cox-death-was-not-a-tragedy-and-the-world-is-a-better-place-without-her.

47. Nazia Parveen, "Teenager who praised killer of Jo Cox guilty of making pipebomb," Guardian, January 27, 2017, www.theguardian.com/uk-news/2017/jan/27/bradford-teenager-pipe-bomb-not-guilty-terror-charge-leeds-crown-court.

48. For a first-hand account see Tanya Gersh, as told to Lois Beckett, "I was the target of a neo-Nazi 'troll storm'," Guardian, April 20, 2017, www.theguardian.com/us-news/2017/apr/20/tanya-gersh-daily-stormer-richard-spencer-whitefish-montana.

49. Aja Romano, "Milo Yiannopoulos's Twitter ban, explained," Vox, July 20, 2016, www.vox.com/2016/7/20/12226070/milo-yiannopoulus-twitter-ban-explained.

50. Matthew Dunn, "Milo Yiannopoulos banned from Twitter, which highlights double standards of the platform," News.com.au, July 21, 2016, www.news.com.au/technology/online/social/milo-yiannopoulos-banned-from-twitter-which-highlights-double-standards-of-the-platform/news-story/5245dd1c1cf06671f254d0fd9472ed11. Kristen Brown, "How a racist, sexist hate mob forced Leslie Jones off Twitter," Fusion, July 19, 2017, http://fusion.net/how-a-racist-sexist-hate-mob-forced-leslie-jones-off-t-1793860398.

51. Twitter never comments directly on individual accounts—a stance that arguably inflames alt-right criticism—so there's always some

speculation as to what prompts a ban, but in a statement on the troll storm the company said "our rules prohibit inciting or engaging in the targeted abuse or harassment of others ... We've seen an uptick in the number of accounts violating these policies and have taken enforcement actions against these accounts, ranging from warnings that also require the deletion of tweets violating our policies to permanent suspension." Mike Isaac, "Twitter bars Milo Yiannopoulos in wake of Leslie Jones's reports of abuse," *New York Times*, July 20, 2016, www.nytimes.com/2016/07/20/technology/twitter-bars-milo-yiannopoulos-in-crackdown-on-abusive-comments.html?_r=1.

52. Ben Kew, "Milo suspended permanently by Twitter minutes before 'Gays for Trump' party at RNC," Breitbart, July 19, 2016, www.breitbart.com/milo/2016/07/19/breaking-milo-suspended-twitter-20-minutes-party.

53. There's little evidence that people actually did this, a fact which means Yiannopoulos was either breathtakingly ignorant, or deliberately obtuse. Chiderah Monde, "Justin Bieber fans draw shock, outrage with gruesome 'Cut4Bieber' trending topic," *New York Daily News*, January 8, 2013, www.nydailynews.com/entertainment/gossip/cut4bieber-trending-topic-draws-shock-outrage-article-1.1235624; Know your meme, "Cutting for Bieber," http://knowyourmeme.com/memes/cuttingforbieber.

54. Andrew DeGrandpre, "The man who disparaged the Charlottesville victim is 'amused' by death threats," *Washington Post*, August 15, 2017, www.washingtonpost.com/news/post-nation/wp/2017/08/15/the-man-who-disparaged-the-charlottesville-victim-is-amused-by-death-threats.

Chapter 8

1. Mike Wendling and Will Yates, "Gab: Free speech haven or alt-right safe space?," BBC News, BBC Trending blog, December 14, 2016, www.bbc.co.uk/news/blogs-trending-38305402.

2. Ibid.

3. Abby Ohlheiser, "Banned from Twitter? This site promises you can say whatever you want," *Washington Post*, November 29, 2016, www.washingtonpost.com/news/the-intersect/wp/2016/11/29/banned-from-twitter-this-site-promises-you-can-say-whatever-you-want/?utm_term=.f00700fa7a74.

4. "I will smite all your territory with frogs" (Exodus 8:2). The frogs are the second plague sent by God via Moses against the Egyptians. When Pharaoh promises to let the Israelites go, the frogs die off and Egypt starts to stink. As to what all this has to do with free speech and social networking, your guess is as good as mine.

5. These and other interviews with people on Gab were conducted via email.

6. Oliver Lee Bateman did some excellent on-the-ground reporting on Midwestern alt-righters for outlets including Belt magazine and Vice; he generally encountered a younger cohort than I had on Gab. The kids are out there—it appears we were grasping two different sections of the alt-right elephant. Oliver Lee Bateman, "Among the alt-racists," Belt Magazine, July 29, 2016, http://beltmag.com/alt-racists.

7. Hope Not Hate, "The international alternative right," September 2017, https://alternativeright.hopenothate.com.

8. In addition to the neo-Nazi coordinated abuse I've outlined, there are many other examples of doxxing and death threats, as outlined in Devin Coldewey, "Reddit bans r/altright over doxing," Techcrunch, February 1, 2017, https://techcrunch.com/2017/02/01/reddit-bans-raltright-over-doxing; Amber Cortes, "UW instructor gets doxxed, harassed and threatened after the Milo Yiannopoulos protests," The Stranger, January 27, 2017, www.thestranger.com/slog/2017/01/27/24830371/uw-professor-gets-doxxed-after-milo-yiannopoulos-protests; Sarah Birnbaum, "Journalist says she was the target of an 'alt-right' lynch mob," PRI's The World, February 7, 2017, www.pri.org/stories/2017-02-07/journalist-says-she-was-target-alt-right-lynch-mob.

9. Alex Dackevych, "Hollywood star trolled in Lapland," BBC News, April 17, 2017, www.bbc.co.uk/news/av/magazine-39592281/hollywood-star-trolled-in-lapland.

10. Personal interview, May 2017.

11. "Women and the alt-right," The Economist, February 1, 2017, www.economist.com/blogs/democracyinamerica/2017/02/no-women-s-march.

12. The Atlantic blurred many of the faces of the people watching Spencer's speech—I counted exactly two women in the crowd. Daniel Lombroso and Yoni Appelbaum, "'Hail Trump!': White nationalists salute the president-elect," The Atlantic, November 21, 2016, www.theatlantic.com/politics/archive/2016/11/richard-spencer-speech-npi/508379.

13. In September of that year, Christopher Poole sold his site to the man who set up the original Japanese image board which was 4chan's inspiration. Fernando Alfonso III, "4chan sold to the founder of the original anonymous image board," The Daily Dot, September 21, 2015, www.dailydot.com/unclick/4chan-moot-sold-2channel-hiroyuki-nishimura.

Chapter 9

1. Mark Price, "Salisbury man investigating fake news has history of drug, alcohol charges," The Charlotte Observer, December 5, 2016, www.charlotteobserver.com/news/local/article118902963.html.
2. IMDB.com, "Edgar Maddison Welch," www.imdb.com/name/nm2625901.
3. US v. Welch, Criminal Complaint, December 12, 2016, archived at https://assets.documentcloud.org/documents/3237677/Welch-Edgar-Federal-Complaint-Dec-2016.pdf.
4. As per eyewitness account in Calum Macdonald, "Trust me, I'm a Journo" (podcast)," January 12, 2017, https://itunes.apple.com/gb/podcast/trust-me-im-a-journo/id1190559131?mt=2.
5. US v. Welch, Criminal Complaint.
6. Superior Court of the District of Columbia, Complaint, December 5, 2016, archived at www.scribd.com/document/333348331/Edgar-Welch-Criminal-Complaint-Comet-Ping-Pong#from_embed.
7. Adam Goldman, "The Comet Ping Pong gunman answers our reporter's questions," New York Times, December 7, 2016, www.nytimes.com/2016/12/07/us/edgar-welch-comet-pizza-fake-news.html?_r=0.
8. Wikileaks, Podesta emails. The specific email chain that allowed the hackers in was included in the Wikileaks document dump: https://wikileaks.org/podesta-emails/emailid/34899.
9. Nicole Perlroth and Michael D. Shear, "Private security group says Russia was behind John Podesta's email hack," New York Times, October 20, 2016, www.nytimes.com/2016/10/21/us/private-security-group-says-russia-was-behind-john-podestas-email-hack.html?_r=0.
10. 4chan, "Podesta/Pizza PAC investigation thread 18: ARCHIVE.IS COMPROMISED EDITION," November 3, 2016, archived at http://archive.is/cfV7z.
11. Craig Silverman, "How the bizarre conspiracy theory behind 'pizzagate' was spread," Buzzfeed, November 4, 2016, www.buzzfeed.

com/craigsilverman/fever-swamp-election?utm_term=.kcoqd AGmZ#.pvx5WRqpN.

12. Gregor Aisch, Jon Huang, and Cecilia Kang, "Dissecting the #PizzaGate conspiracy theories," *New York Times*, December 10, 2016, www.nytimes.com/interactive/2016/12/10/business/media/pizzagate.html.

13. The account was suspended by Twitter in March 2017.

14. "Pizza Party Ben," "Ben Shapiro throws epic Twitter tantrum: exclusive footage," Breitbart, May 18, 2016. The "exclusive footage" was a YouTube video with foreign language commentary showing a child having a breakdown, with fake English subtitles mocking Shapiro slapped on top.

15. "Trump's 'jail Clinton' U-turn sparks conservative backlash," BBC News, November 22, 2016, www.bbc.co.uk/news/world-us-canada-38072846.

16. Jes Skolnik, "The fight for all-ages shows," Pitchfork, April 27, 2015, http://pitchfork.com/thepitch/748-the-fight-for-all-ages-shows.

17. Red State Strategy, "James Alefantis answers questions about Pizzagate" (video), YouTube, November 22, 2016, www.youtube.com/watch?v=gKTiUaloDDA.

18. WeSearchr "PizzaGate urban explorers league ultimate challenge," www.wesearchr.com/bounties/pizzagate-urban-explorers-league-ultimate-challenge. The bounty was posted by alt-rightish comedian Sam Hyde, who himself has become the subject of bizarre fake news stories. Throughout 2016 and 2017, when news broke of mass shootings or terrorist atrocities, trolls would take to Twitter and post pictures of Hyde, alleging that he was the perpetrator in an attempt to trick other Twitter users and journalists. The "joke" became something of a cliché after a while.

19. See https://twitter.com/Cernovich/status/805629939458260992.

20. See https://twitter.com/Cernovich/status/805635937573031936.

21. See https://twitter.com/Cernovich/status/801690170701398016.

22. Mike Cernovich, "Mike Cernovich responds to fake new media conspiracy theories about Pizzagate," Danger and Play, December 4, 2016, www.dangerandplay.com/2016/12/04/mike-cernovich-responds-to-fake-new-media-conspiracy-theories-about-pizzagate.

23. Mandy Oaklander, "Here's why people believe in conspiracy theories," Time Health, August 14, 2015, http://time.com/3997033/conspiracy-theories.

24. Caitlin Shure, "Insights into the personalities of conspiracy theorists," *Scientific American*, September 1, 2013, www.

scientificamerican.com/article/insights-into-the-personalities-conspiracy-theorists.

25. Cassandra Fairbanks, "Internet is on fire with speculation that Podesta emails contain code for child sex," We Are Change, November 3, 2016, http://wearechange.org/internet-fire-speculation-podesta-emails-contain-code-child-sex.

26. Mike Wendling, "The saga of 'Pizzagate': The fake story that shows how conspiracy theories spread," BBC News, BBC Trending blog, December 2, 2016, www.bbc.com/news/blogs-trending-38156985.

27. US vs. Welch, Criminal Complaint.

28. "Take the Red Pill" blog, "DAPL Standoff at Standing Rock - A Closer Look - #NoDAPL," November 27, 2016, https://redpillinfowar.com/category/dakota-access-pipeline.

29. See https://twitter.com/cassandrarules/status/792051133963505668.

30. Efe Kerem Sozeri, "How the alt-right's PizzaGate conspiracy hid real scandal in Turkey," The Daily Dot, November 23, 2016, www.dailydot.com/layer8/pizzagate-alt-right-turkey-trolls-child-abuse.

31. The tweets of Posobiec and others fed a conspiracy theory about the conspiracy theory—that Welch's pathetically dramatic display and unhidden two-bit acting career somehow made him the agent of a "false flag" operation designed to discredit all pizzagate "investigators." See Robert Mackey, "Disinformation, not fake news, got Trump elected, and it is not stopping," The Intercept, December 6, 2016, https://theintercept.com/2016/12/06/disinformation-not-fake-news-got-trump-elected.

32. Allegra Kirkland, "What we know about the gunman who was sold on the 'pizzagate' conspiracy," Talking Points Memo, December 5, 2016, http://talkingpointsmemo.com/livewire/what-we-know-edgar-maddison-welch-pizzagate-gunman.

33. See https://twitter.com/cassandrarules/status/811013877202829312.

34. Andrew Marantz, "Trump supporters at the Deploraball," The New Yorker, February 6, 2017, www.newyorker.com/magazine/2017/02/06/trump-supporters-at-the-deploraball.

35. Cernovich, "Mike Cernovich responds…."

36. Monica Davey, Julie Bosman, and Mitch Smith, "Dennis Hastert sentenced to 15 months, and apologizes for sex abuse," New York Times, April 27, 2016, www.nytimes.com/2016/04/28/us/dennis-hastert-sentencing.html?_r=1.

37. Ibid.

38. The alt-righters and conspiracy theorists conveniently ignore real and serious child protection stories put out by the BBC, including

by me and the BBC Trending team. To take just two examples: Anisa Subedar and Will Yates, "The disturbing YouTube videos that are tricking children," March 27, 2017, http://www.bbc.com/news/blogs-trending-39381889; Mike Wendling, "YouTube child protection mechanism 'failing,'" August 5, 2017, http://www.bbc.com/news/blogs-trending-40808177.

39. "Trump aide Michael Flynn Jnr out after 'Pizzagate' tweets," BBC News, December 7, 2016, www.bbc.co.uk/news/world-us-canada-38231532.

40. Rebecca Hersher, "Webpages linked to pizzeria shooting go dark even as prosecution moves forward," NPR.org, December 14, 2016, www.npr.org/sections/thetwo-way/2016/12/14/505577985/web pages-linked-to-pizzeria-shooting-go-dark-even-as-prosecution-moves-forward.

41. Richard Hofstadter, "The paranoid style in American politics," *Harpers*, November 1964, online at http://harpers.org/archive/1964/11/the-paranoid-style-in-american-politics.

42. William F. Buckley, "Goldwater, the John Birch Society, and me," *Commentary*, March 1, 2008, www.commentarymagazine.com/articles/goldwater-the-john-birch-society-and-me.

43. Hofstadter, "The paranoid style…."

44. Eric Hananoki, "Alex Jones deletes video in which he had told his audience to personally 'investigate' 'pizzagate' restaurant," Media Matters for America, December 16, 2016, www.mediamatters.org/blog/2016/12/16/alex-jones-deletes-video-which-he-had-told-his-audience-personally-investigate-pizzagate-restaurant/214846. Conspiracy theorists with a pizzagate mindset will inevitably pick up on a bit of trivia—Media Matters for America is a stridently progressive media watchdog set up by David Brock, the ex-boyfriend of Comet Ping Pong owner James Alefantis. To call this further proof of a vast conspiracy network is in the same sort of territory as dubbing Steve Bannon a secret neo-Nazi based on the testimony of his ex-wife in a divorce filing.

45. Jon Bowne, "Pizzagate: the bigger picture," Infowars, December 1, 2016, www.infowars.com/pizzagate-the-bigger-picture.

46. Alex Jones video archived at http://mediamatters.org/embed/clips/2016/12/16/51552/youtube-alexjones-20161215-pizzagate.

47. Eric Hananoki, "Alex Jones scrubs pizzagate content; complaint reveals new tie connecting shooter to Jones," Media Matters for America, December 13, 2016, www.mediamatters.org/blog/2016/

12/13/alex-jones-scrubs-pizzagate-content-complaint-reveals-new-tie-connecting-shooter-jones/214809.

48. Eric Hananoki and Ben Dimiero, "104 actual headlines from Alex Jones' Infowars," Media Matters for America, February 8, 2017, http://mediamatters.org/blog/2017/02/08/104-typical-a-alex-jones-infowars/215218.

49. Mike Wendling, "Sandy Hook to Trump: 'Help us stop conspiracy theorists,'" BBC News, BBC Trending blog, April 2, 2017, www.bbc.co.uk/news/blogs-trending-39194035.

50. Jon Ronson, *Them: Adventures With Extremists*, Simon & Schuster, 2003.

51. Stephanie Mencimer, "PizzaGate shooter read Alex Jones. Here are some other fans who perpetrated violent acts," *Mother Jones*, December 12, 2016, www.motherjones.com/politics/2016/12/comet-pizza-suspect-shooters-alex-jones.

52. Gordon Duff, "Israeli death squads involved in Sandy Hook bloodbath: Intelligence analyst," Press TV, December 18, 2012, archived at http://web.archive.org/web/20130101005356/http://presstv.com/detail/2012/12/18/278706/israeli-squads-tied-to-newtown-carnage.

53. Infowars, "Donald Trump tells all on the Alex Jones Show," December 2, 2015, www.infowars.com/donald-trump-tells-all-on-the-alex-jones-show.

54. Erica Lafferty, "Mr. Trump, denounce Alex Jones: Sandy Hook principal's daughter," *USA Today*, November 25, 2016, www.usatoday.com/story/opinion/2016/11/25/donald-trump-sandy-hook-alex-jones-column/94335420.

55. See Wendling, "Sandy Hook to Trump," and for another typical example, Joe Concha, "Infowars claims exclusive preview of mass-emailed Trump address," The Hill, February 27, 2017, http://thehill.com/homenews/media/321366-infowars-claims-exclusive-preview-of-mass-emailed-trump-address.

56. Alex Jones, "Alex Jones' final statement on Sandy Hook," Infowars, November 18, 2016, www.infowars.com/alex-jones-final-statement-on-sandy-hook.

57. Ibid.

58. Oliver Darcy, "Right-wing troll Mike Cernovich goes professional with new hosting gig at InfoWars," CNN Money, May 3, 2017, http://money.cnn.com/2017/05/03/media/mike-cernovich-infowars-alex-jones.

59. "Alex Jones," Southern Poverty Law Center, undated, www.splcenter.org/fighting-hate/extremist-files/individual/alex-jones.
60. Jonathan Tilove, "In Travis County custody case, jury will search for real Alex Jones," Austin American-Statesman, April 16, 2017, www.mystatesman.com/news/state--regional-govt--politics/travis-county-custody-case-jury-will-search-for-real-alex-jones/rnbWzMHnFCd5SOPgP3A34J.

Chapter 10

1. Jonah Engle Bromwich and Alan Blinder, "What we know about James Alex Fields, driver charged in Charlottesville killing," *New York Times*, August 13, 2017, www.nytimes.com/2017/08/13/us/james-alex-fields-charlottesville-driver-.html.
2. Bill Morlin, "Extremists' "Unite the Right" rally: A possible historic alt-right showcase?," Hatewatch, Southern Poverty Law Center, August 7, 2017, www.splcenter.org/hatewatch/2017/08/07/extremists-unite-right-rally-possible-historic-alt-right-showcase.
3. Ibid.
4. Alison Reamer and Lauren Lindstrom, "Charlottesville suspect James A. Fields, Jr., revered Hitler as student," The Blade, August 14, 2017, www.toledoblade.com/local/2017/08/14/Charlottesville-suspect-James-A-Fields-Jr-revered-Hitler-as-student.html.
5. Ibid.
6. Alison Reamer, "Mother of James Fields called authorities for help with violent son," The Blade, August 14, 2017, www.toledoblade.com/Police-Fire/2017/08/14/Mother-of-James-Fields-called-authorities-for-help-with-violent-son.html.
7. Laura Lindstrom, "Mother of Maumee man accused of driving into crowd shocked," The Blade, August 13, 2017, www.toledoblade.com/local/2017/08/13/Mother-of-James-Alex-Fields-accused-of-driving-into-Charlottesville-crowd-shocked.html.
8. Libby Nelson and Kelly Swanson, "Full transcript: Donald Trump's press conference defending the Charlottesville rally," Vox, August 15, 2017, www.vox.com/2017/8/15/16154028/trump-press-conference-transcript-charlottesville.
9. Rosie Gray, "'Really proud of him': Alt-right leaders praise Trump's comments," *The Atlantic*, August 15, 2017, www.theatlantic.com/politics/archive/2017/08/really-proud-of-him-richard-spencer-and-alt-right-leaders-praise-trumps-comments/537039.

10. Catherine Shoicet and Michael Pearson, "Garland, Texas, shooting suspect linked himself to ISIS in tweets," CNN, 5 May 2015, http://edition.cnn.com/2015/05/04/us/garland-mohammed-drawing-contest-shooting.
11. Southern Poverty Law Center, "Active anti-Muslim Groups," Intelligence Report, Spring 2015, www.splcenter.org/fighting-hate/intelligence-report/2015/active-anti-muslim-groups.
12. Nicole Hensley and Reuven Blau, "Two gunmen shot dead by cops after opening fire outside controversial 'Prophet Muhammad' art exhibit in Texas," New York Daily News, May 4, 2015, www.nydailynews.com/news/crime/people-shot-texas-prophet-muhammad-art-exhibit-article-1.2208953. The AFDI had expected trouble, and reportedly spent $10,000 on 40 additional extra security officers for the event.
13. See http://boards.4chan.org/pol/thread/129575171/im-done.
14. Scott Johnson, "Father of 20-year-old accused of wanting to bomb 9/11 memorial says, 'We had no idea,'" News4Jax, September 11, 2015, www.news4jax.com/news/florida/clay-county/father-of-20-year-old-accused-of-wanting-to-bomb-9_11-memorial-says-we-had-no-idea.
15. US vs. Joshua Ryne Goldberg, Criminal Complaint, September 10, 2015, www.justice.gov/opa/file/769556/download.
16. Reddit r/Nolibswatch, "More of Joshua Goldberg's bullshit on reddit: He was behind the accounts /u/Death_To_SJWs, /u/Europe_Hates_Niggers and /u/MoonMetropolis and regularly called himself out with different accounts. Bizarre," September 12, 2015, www.reddit.com/r/NolibsWatch/comments/3knaoj/more_of_joshua_goldbergs_bullshit_on_reddit_he.
17. Reddit, r/WikiInAction, "Terrorist troll Joshua Goldberg had a Wikipedia account, he was (fittingly) recently blocked for 'trolling, disruption or harassment' and rape/death threats," September 14, 2015, www.reddit.com/r/WikiInAction/comments/3kyeb6/terrorist_troll_joshua_goldberg_had_a_wikipedia.
18. Mike Wendling, "What should social networks do about hate speech?," BBC News, BBC Trending blog, June 29, 2015, www.bbc.co.uk/news/blogs-trending-33288367.
19. Personal email, June 24, 2015.
20. Personal email, June 25, 2015.
21. Milo Yiannopoulos, "Brianna Wu chatted to 'terrorist troll' Joshua Goldberg after he outed her as transgender," Breitbart, September 12, 2015, www.breitbart.com/big-government/2015/09/12/brianna-

wu-chatted-to-terrorist-troll-joshua-goldberg-after-he-outed-her-as-transgender.

22. Milo Yiannopoulos, "Daily Kos founder claims contributor at Daily Kos is a 'Breitbart writer arrested for terrorism,'" Breitbart, September 12, 2015, www.breitbart.com/big-government/2015/09/12/daily-kos-founder-claims-contributor-at-daily-kos-is-a-breitbart-writer-arrested-for-terrorism.

23. Joshua Goldberg, writing as Tanya Cohen, "Here is why it's time to get tough on hate speech in America," Thought Catalog, January 5, 2015, http://thoughtcatalog.com/tanya-cohen/2015/01/here-is-why-its-time-to-get-tough-on-hate-speech-in-america.

24. Mike Masnick, "That crazy story about making 'hate speech' a crime? Yeah, that's satire," Tech Dirt, January 7, 2015, www.techdirt.com/articles/20150106/17571729615/best-satire-about-attack-free-speech-that-you-could-ever-read.shtml.

25. Joshua Goldberg, "How social justice warriors are creating an entire generation of fascists," Thought Catalog, December 5, 2014, http://thoughtcatalog.com/joshua-goldberg/2014/12/when-social-justice-warriors-attack-one-tumblr-users-experience.

26. R.S. Benedict, "Right-wing reporter Milo Yiannopoulos tied to terrorist troll," Unicorn Booty blog, October 25, 2015, https://unicornbooty.com/right-wing-reporter-milo-yiannopoulos-tied-to-terrorist-troll.

27. News4Jax, "Man accused in terror plot to remain in medical facility," December 9, 2016, www.news4jax.com/news/competency-hearing-set-for-man-accused-in-terror-plot.

28. News4Jax, "Man accused of plotting to bomb 9/11 memorial found competent for trial," April 29, 2017, www.news4jax.com/news/joshua-goldberg-found-competent-to-stand-trial.

29. Twitter conversation, May 2017.

30. The acronym NEET means "Not in education, employment or training"—the meaning of the rest of the slang is unfortunately pretty obvious.

31. 4chan, "Joshua Goldberg was he /ourguy/?," December 7, 2017, https://yuki.la/pol/101928653.

32. Paul Joseph Watson, "New York Times parrots debunked Poplawski smear," Infowars, April 7, 2009, www.infowars.com/new-york-times-parrots-debunked-poplawski-smear.

33. Anti-Defamation League, "Richard Poplawski: The making of a lone wolf," April 8, 2009, www.adl.org/news/article/richard-poplawski-the-making-of-a-lone-wolf.

34. Anti-Defamation League, "Richard Poplawski: Selected on-line postings, 2007–2009," 2011, www.adl.org/sites/default/files/documents/assets/pdf/combating-hate/Richard-Poplawski-Comments-Categorized.pdf; and Dennis Roddy, "An accused cop killer's politics," Slate, April 10, 2009, www.slate.com/articles/news_and_politics/politics/2009/04/an_accused_cop_killers_politics.html.

35. Mencimer, "Pizzagate shooter read Alex Jones…"

36. Noah Rothman, "Report: Tamerlan Tsarnaev 'took an interest' in Alex Jones' 'Conspiracy Theory Website' Infowars," Mediaite, April 23, 2013, www.mediaite.com/online/report-tamerlan-tsarnaev-took-an-interest-in-alex-jones-conspiracy-theory-website-infowars.

37. Tom Kludt, "The story behind Alex Jones' unlikely Pizzagate apology," CNN, March 30, 2017, http://money.cnn.com/2017/03/30/media/alex-jones-apology-pizzagate-james-alefantis.

38. Roof's manifesto was taken down from his website but archived at http://web.archive.org/web/20150620135047/http://lastrhodesian.com/data/documents/rtf88.txt.

39. Joel Brown, "Dylann Roof, the radicalization of the alt-right, and ritualized racial violence," Sightings blog, University of Chicago, January 12, 2017, https://divinity.uchicago.edu/sightings/dylann-roof-radicalization-alt-right-and-ritualized-racial-violence.

40. *Minnesota vs. Allen Lawrence Scarsella*, Criminal Complaint, November 30, 2015, http://stmedia.startribune.com/documents/S12AK115113013170.pdf.

41. "Allen Scarsella texts and instant messages—trial exhibits," archived at www.documentcloud.org/documents/3458518-Allen-Scarsella-Texts-and-Instant-Messages.html.

42. Minnesota Public Radio, "Scarsella gets 15 years for shooting 5 at Jamar Clark protest," April 26, 2017, www.mprnews.org/story/2017/04/26/jamar-clark-protest-shooter-scarsella-gets-15-years.

43. 4chan, "Minneapolis chimpout (Jamar Clark)," April 30, 2017, archived at https://archived.moe/pol/thread/123535737.

44. Kate McKenna and Jonathan Montpetit, "Suspect in mosque shooting a moderate conservative turned extremist, say friends, classmates," CBC News, January 31, 2017, www.cbc.ca/news/canada/montreal/quebec-city-mosque-alexandre-bissonnette-profile-1.3959581.

45. Eric Boehlert, "Canada's 'alt-right' mosque shooter, and what he means for right-wing media," Media Matters for America, February 1, 2017, www.mediamatters.org/blog/2017/02/01/canada-s-alt-

right-mosque-shooter-and-what-he-means-right-wing-media/215207.

46. Les Perreaux and Eric Andrew-Gee, "Quebec City mosque attack suspect known as online troll inspired by French far-right," *Globe and Mail*, January 30, 2017, https://beta.theglobeandmail.com/news/national/quebec-city-mosque-attack-suspect-known-for-right-wing-online-posts/article33833044/?ref=http://www.theglobeandmail.com&.

47. Brian Tashman, "Alex Jones: Quebec attack was a false flag," Right Wing Watch, People for the American Way, January 31, 2017, www.rightwingwatch.org/post/alex-jones-quebec-attack-was-a-false-flag.

48. *State of Washington vs. Elizabeth Joy Hokoana, State of Washington vs. Marc K Hokoana*, Criminal Complaints, April 18, 2017, https://assets.documentcloud.org/documents/3676970/Charging-Documents-State-v-Hokoana.pdf.

49. Steve Miletich, "Couple plead not guilty to charges in UW shooting during Milo Yiannopoulos speech," *Seattle Times*, May 3, 2017, www.seattletimes.com/seattle-news/crime/couple-pleads-not-guilty-to-charges-in-uw-shooting-during-milo-yiannopoulos-speech.

50. Susan Svrluga, William Wan, and Elizabeth Dwoskin, "There was no Ann Coulter speech. But protesters converged on Berkeley," *Washington Post*, April 27, 2017, www.washingtonpost.com/news/grade-point/wp/2017/04/27/theres-no-speech-planned-but-protesters-are-converging-on-berkeley-today/?utm_term=.6e3da15a51c0.

51. Daniella Silva, "White man who allegedly went to NYC to hunt black men says he meant to kill younger, more successful person: Report," NBC News, March 26, 2017, www.nbcnews.com/news/us-news/white-man-who-allegedly-went-nyc-hunt-black-men-says-n738751.

52. Shayna Jacovs, Graham Rayman, and Larry McShane, "Hate-fueled Baltimore man saw first victim as 'practice' to 'kill additional black men' in Times Square," *New York Daily News*, March 23, 2017, www.nydailynews.com/new-york/white-supremacist-killer-planned-carnage-times-square-article-1.3006719?cid=bitly.

53. Ashley Southall, "White suspect in black man's killing is indicted on terror charges," *New York Times*, March 27, 2017, www.nytimes.com/2017/03/27/nyregion/timothy-caughman-james-harris-jackson-terrorism.html.

54. Kelly Weill, Katy Zavadski, and James Laporta, "James Jackson liked alt-right videos, claimed he was a genius in army intelligence," The Daily Beast, March 23, 2017, www.thedailybeast.com/articles/2017/03/23/james-jackson-liked-alt-right-videos-claimed-he-was-a-genius-in-army-intelligence.html.
55. Amanda Marcotte, "Accused Portland killer Jeremy Christian's excuses sound an awful lot like alt-right rhetoric," Salon, June 9, 2017, www.salon.com/2017/06/09/accused-portland-killer-jeremy-christians-excuses-sound-an-awful-lot-like-alt-right-rhetoric.
56. Corey Pein and Nigel Jaquiss, "Who radicalized Jeremy Christian? Alt-right extremists rush to distance themselves from MAX slaying suspect," Williamette Week, May 31, 2017, www.wweek.com/news/2017/05/31/who-radicalized-jeremy-christian-alt-right-extremists-rush-to-distance-themselves-from-max-slaying-suspect.
57. Deeyah Khan, "How normal men become radicalised jihadis," Telegraph, November 27, 2015, www.telegraph.co.uk/men/thinking-man/how-normal-men-become-radicalised-jihadis.

Chapter 11

1. Blow-by-blow accounts of the incident can be found in Louis Jacobson, "Donald Trump's 'Star of David' tweet: a recap," Politifact, July 5, 2016, www.politifact.com/truth-o-meter/article/2016/jul/05/donald-trumps-star-david-tweet-recap; and Anthony Smith, "Donald Trump's Star of David Hillary Clinton meme was created by white supremacists," Mic, July 3, 2016, https://mic.com/articles/147711/donald-trump-s-star-of-david-hillary-clinton-meme-was-created-by-white-supremacists#.oTFbUnpI4.
2. Josh Feldman, "Let it go: Donald Trump uses Frozen sticker books to argue his tweet wasn't anti-Semitic," Mediaite, July 6, 2016, www.mediaite.com/online/let-it-go-donald-trump-uses-frozen-sticker-books-to-argue-his-tweet-wasnt-anti-semitic.
3. Caroline Simon, "5 times Donald Trump has engaged with alt-right racists on Twitter," Business Insider, July 9, 2016, http://uk.businessinsider.com/donald-trump-alt-right-2016-7?r=US&IR=T.
4. Ben Kharakh and Dan Primack, "Donald Trump's social media ties to white supremacists," Fortune, March 22, 2016, http://fortune.com/donald-trump-white-supremacist-genocide. Fortune's analysis wasn't perfect—it highlighted Trump campaign staffers who followed top "white genocide" influencers, a somewhat poor proxy for white nationalist sympathies (after all, it would include me and

many critics and journalists not aligned with the alt-right). But the retweeting point was strong and the overall trend is clear—this was part of the social media ecosystem that the campaign was swimming in.

5. Jon Greenberg, "Trump's pants on fire tweet that blacks killed 81% of white homicide victims," Politifact, November 23, 2015, www. politifact.com/truth-o-meter/statements/2015/nov/23/donald-trump/trump-tweet-blacks-white-homicide-victims.

6. Charles Johnson, "We found where Donald Trump's 'black crimes' graphic came from," Little Green Footballs, November 22, 2015, http://littlegreenfootballs.com/article/45291_We_Found_Where_Donald_Trumps_Black_Crimes_Graphic_Came_From.

7. Politico, "Transcript: Hillary Clinton's full remarks in Reno, Nevada," August 25, 2016, www.politico.com/story/2016/08/transcript-hillary-clinton-alt-right-reno-227419.

8. Ibid.

9. For instance, Red State Strategy, "Prankster yells 'PEPE' when Hillary Clinton mentions ALT RIGHT in her Reno, NV speech," YouTube, August 25, 2016, www.youtube.com/watch?v=-p4P-MbMrv8.

10. The protester was not asked whether he thought the Sandy Hook massacre was a hoax. Charlie Nash, "We spoke to the guy who yelled 'Pepe' during Hillary Clinton's alt-right speech," Breitbart, August 26, 2016, www.breitbart.com/tech/2016/08/26/spoke-guy-shouted-pepe-hillarys-alt-right-speech.

11. By far the biggest spike of "alt-right" in popularity as a search term during 2016 came in the two weeks after the election, when queries were roughly double those of the week of Clinton's Reno speech. When it comes to general public interest, no other time period comes even remotely close, at least as far as Google search results are concerned. See https://trends.google.com/trends/explore?date=2015-01-01%202017-05-07&q=alt-right; and https://trends.google.com/trends/explore?date=2016-08-01%202016-08-30&q=alt-right.

12. The feeling was given intellectual heft by a much-cited essay, "The Flight 93 election" by Michael Anton, who was later given a job as a White House advisor. Using the pseudonym Publius Decius Mus, he wrote: "2016 is the Flight 93 election: charge the cockpit or you die. You may die anyway … if you don't try, death is certain." In the essay, Anton slam leftists and "Social Justice Warriors," reserving special ire for "Conservativism Inc." which "reeks of failure," although he scorns "alt-right pocket Nazis" as "manna from heaven

for the Left." Michael Anton, writing as Publius Decius Mus, "The Flight 93 election," *Claremont Review*, September 5, 2016, www. claremont.org/crb/basicpage/the-flight-93-election.

13. Matthew Lyons, "Ctrl-Alt-Delete: The origins and ideology of the alternative right," Political Research Associates, January 20, 2017, www.politicalresearch.org/2017/01/20/ctrl-alt-delete-report-on-the-alternative-right/#sthash.ODAzReRw.ghUnd8gp.dpbs.

14. Matthew Heimbach, "The Trump Train and the Southern strategy: The only hope for the GOP," Traditionalist Youth Network, October 2015, www.tradyouth.org/2015/10/the-trump-train-and-the-southern-strategy-the-only-hope-for-the-gop.

15. Steve Peoples, "Trump convention message cheers white supremacists," Associated Press, July 25, 2016, www.usnews.com/news/politics/articles/2016-07-25/trump-convention-message-cheers-white-supremacists.

16. See https://twitter.com/realdonaldtrump/status/653856168402 681856?lang=en.

17. Issie Lapowsky, "Here's how Facebook *actually* won Trump the presidency," Wired, November 15, 2016, www.wired.com/2016/11/facebook-won-trump-election-not-just-fake-news.

18. Charlie Northcott and Mike Wendling, "US Election 2016: Trump's 'hidden' Facebook army," BBC News, BBC Trending blog, November 15, 2016, www.bbc.co.uk/news/blogs-trending-37945486.

19. Craig Silverman and Lawrence Alexander, "How teens in the Balkans are duping Trump supporters with fake news," Buzzfeed, November 3, 2016, www.buzzfeed.com/craigsilverman/how-macedonia-became-a-global-hub-for-pro-trump-misinfo?utm_term=.ouxa9JnLb#.ilJoe3qW6.

20. Twitter is the most visible and easily manipulated social network, as tweets are by default publicly available and Twitter's list of top trends drives news agendas to a degree out of proportion with its actual user base. Facebook, for instance, is about six times larger, however has much more restrictive privacy settings and no publicly available list of hashtag-based trends. See Farhad Manjoo, "How Twitter is being gamed to feed misinformation," *New York Times*, May 31, 2017, www.nytimes.com/2017/05/31/technology/how-twitter-is-being-gamed-to-feed-misinformation.html?_r=0.

21. Statistics website FiveThirtyEight tracked the spike in searches, matched it to poll figures, and found some circumstantial evidence Wikileaks may have contributed to Clinton's loss, but acknowledged

"we really can't say much more than that." Harry Enten, "How much did Wikileaks hurt Hillary Clinton?," FiveThirtyEight, December 23, 2016, https://fivethirtyeight.com/features/wikileaks-hillary-clinton.

22. Mike Wendling, "Conversations with a hacker: What Guccifer 2.0 told me," BBC News, BBC Trending blog, January 14, 2017, www.bbc.co.uk/news/blogs-trending-38610402.

23. Perhaps the number one takeaway from my conversations with Guccifer 2.0 was linguistic—the would-be hacker's command of the English language varied oddly, in communications with me and with a journalist from Vice, and in his publicly available blog posts. Vice also established that his grasp of Romanian was more than a bit shaky. Lorenzo Franceschi-Bicchierai, "We spoke to DNC hacker 'Guccifer 2.0'," Motherboard, Vice, June 21, 2016, https://motherboard.vice.com/en_us/article/dnc-hacker-guccifer-20-interview.

24. This interpretation conveniently skirts around Russia's significant ethnic diversity and large Muslim population. See Wikipedia, "Islam in Russia," https://en.wikipedia.org/wiki/Islam_in_Russia.

25. David Weigel, "Trump moves praise for Putin closer to the mainstream of the GOP," *Washington Post*, September 9, 2016, www.washingtonpost.com/politics/trump-moves-praise-for-putin-closer-to-the-mainstream-of-the-gop/2016/09/09/ccf2853c-7693-11e6-8149-b8d05321db62_story.html?postshare=46314735150008779&tid=ss_tw&utm_term=.5d4cb87225e5.

26. Casey Michel, "Meet the Moscow mouthpiece married to a racist alt-right boss," The Daily Beast, December 20, 2016, www.thedailybeast.com/articles/2016/12/20/meet-the-moscow-mouthpiece-married-to-a-racist-alt-right-boss.html.

27. RIA Novosti, "Russian analyst predicts decline and breakup of U.S.," November 24, 2008, archived at https://sputniknews.com/world/20081124118512713.

28. Owen Matthews, "Alexander Dugin and Steve Bannon's ideological ties to Vladimir Putin's Russia," *Newsweek*, April 17, 2017, www.newsweek.com/steve-bannon-donald-trump-jared-kushner-vladimir-putin-russia-fbi-mafia-584962.

29. Politico, "Transcript: Hillary Clinton's full remarks in Reno, Nevada."

30. 4chan, "Should I move to Russia or stay here?," December 10, 2016, archived at https://yuki.la/pol/102290016.

31. Journalists working for the BBC and other organizations in Moscow are routinely given the tagging treatment, and even I was tagged in

one of the embassy's most popular baiting tweets. See Adam Taylor, "How the Russian Embassy in London uses Twitter to undermine the West," *Washington Post*, April 12, 2017, www.washingtonpost. com/news/worldviews/wp/2017/04/12/how-the-russian-embassy-in-london-uses-twitter-to-undermine-the-west/?utm_term=.18 c629ec6e33.

32. Megha Mohan and Mike Wendling, "Macron Leaks: The anatomy of a hack," BBC News, BBC Trending blog, May 9, 2017, www.bbc. co.uk/news/blogs-trending-39845105.

33. Ryan Broderick, "Trump supporters online are pretending to be French to manipulate France's election," Buzzfeed, January 24, 2017, www.buzzfeed.com/ryanhatesthis/inside-the-private-chat-rooms-trump-supporters-are-using-to?utm_term=.mgVkAlKQ1#. ajDO50aQ2.

34. Ingrid Melander, "France's Le Pen launches election bid with vow to fight globalization," Reuters, February 5, 2017, www.reuters.com/ article/us-france-election-fn-idUSKBN15K0R1.

35. Gabriel Gatehouse, "Marine Le Pen: Who's funding France's far right?," BBC Panorama, BBC News, April 3, 2017, www.bbc.co.uk/ news/world-europe-39478066.

36. Mohan and Wendling, "Macron Leaks."

37. One online security firm ascribed those faked documents to Andrew Auernheimer. Brian Feldman, "Dubious Macron Leaks linked to infamous Neo-Nazi hacker-troll weev," *New York Magazine*, May 16, 2007, http://nymag.com/selectall/2017/05/ dubious-macron-leaks-linked-to-infamous-hacker-troll-weev.html.

38. Alexandre Capron, "How we debunked rumours that Macron has an offshore account," The Observers, France 24, May 5, 2017, http:// observers.france24.com/en/20170505-france-elections-macron-lepen-offshore-bahamas-debunked.

39. However, another plausible explanation is that the hackers did not necessarily want Le Pen to win—or Trump for that matter—but simply that they wanted to discredit Macron or put a cloud over the early stages of his presidency. From that perspective, the operation might well have been a success. Richard Wolf, "Clinton campaign chief: Did Trump, Russians collude?," *USA Today*, December 18, 2016, www.usatoday.com/story/news/politics/onpolitics/2016/ 12/18/clinton-campaign-chief-did-trump-russians-collude/ 95584106.

40. The term was coined—and the phenomenon identified—by 4chan and Anonymous expert Gabriella Coleman. See Gabriella Coleman,

"The public interest hack," Limn, February 2017, http://limn.it/the-public-interest-hack.

41. There was no indication that the DNC or Podesta emails were fabricated, although the Macron campaign later said that they had prepared for a hack and had even sown fake documents among the campaign's authentic emails. Sean Gallagher, "Macron campaign team used honeypot accounts to fake out Fancy Bear," Ars Technica, May 10, 2017, https://arstechnica.com/security/2017/05/macron-campaign-team-used-honeypot-accounts-to-fake-out-fancy-bear.

42. Abby Ohlheiser, "'We actually elected a meme as president': How 4chan celebrated Trump's victory," *Washington Post*, November 9, 2016, www.chicagotribune.com/bluesky/technology/ct-meme-president-4chan-trump-wp-bsi-20161112-story.html.

43. 4chan, November 9, 2016, archived at https://yuki.la/pol/97245682.

44. Nicky Woolf, "Donald Trump's 'alt-right' supporters express dismay at disavowal," *Guardian*, November 23, 2016, www.theguardian.com/us-news/2016/nov/22/alt-right-supporters-donald-trump-backlash-disavow-reddit-4chan.

Chapter 12

1. Lombroso and Appelbaum, "'Hail Trump!': White nationalists salute the president-elect."

2. Katie Reilly, "Read Hillary Clinton's 'basket of deplorables' remarks about Donald Trump supporters," *Time*, September 10, 2016, http://time.com/4486502/hillary-clinton-basket-of-deplorables-transcript.

3. Allan Smith, "Alt-right movement descends into civil war after leading figure is booted from Trump inauguration event," Business Insider, December 27, 2016, http://uk.businessinsider.com/alt-right-civil-war-twitter-cernovich-milo-alaska-2016-12?r=US&IR=T.

4. Some of the tweets were collected by *New York Magazine* writer Jesse Singal, and included "hilarious" jokes such as Gionet talking about the "JQ" and leaving a waitress a tip of exactly $14.88 (a reference to "1488"—see chapter on language), https://twitter.com/jessesingal/status/813515155069931520.

5. Brakkton Booker, "Alt-right infighting simmers around inaugural 'DeploraBall,'" NPR.org, January 1, 2017, www.npr.org/2017/01/01/507395282/alt-right-infighting-simmers-around-inaugural-deploraball.

6. Marantz, "Trump supporters at the Deploraball."

7. Brooke Singman, "'Deploraball' guests met by protesters in chaotic scene," Fox News, January 20, 2017, www.foxnews.com/politics/2017/01/20/deploraball-guests-met-by-protesters-in-chaotic-scene.html.

8. Lucian Wintrich, "White supremacist Richard Spencer tries to enter DeploraBall—GETS TOSSED TO STREET," The Gateway Pundit, January 20, 2017, www.thegatewaypundit.com/2017/01/white-supremacist-richard-spencer-tries-enter-deploraball-gets-tossed-street.

9. Marantz, "Trump supporters at the Deploraball"; Issie Lapowski, "At the Deploraball, Trump's online army wonders: What now?," Wired, January 20, 2017, www.wired.com/2017/01/deploraball-trumps-online-army-wonders-now.

10. Claire McNear, "Amongst the belles of the Deploraball," The Ringer, January 20, 2017, https://theringer.com/amongst-the-belles-of-the-deploraball-1e01f3e327e3.

11. Tessa Stuart, "Inside the DeploraBall: The Trump-loving trolls plotting a GOP takeover," *Rolling Stone*, January 20, 2017, www.rollingstone.com/politics/features/inside-the-deploraball-trump-loving-trolls-plot-gop-takeover-w462082.

12. Lapowski, "At the Deploraball."

13. Deploraball website, "Deploraball: the debrief," February 6, 2017, archived at http://web.archive.org/web/20170219011935/http://deploraball.com/post/deploraball-the-debrief.

14. Personal interview, May 2017.

15. Yet another example of the strict dichotomous thinking on the alt-right, with many channers and Twitter personalities unable to countenance the possibility that both ISIS and Assad could be very bad things indeed.

16. See https://twitter.com/richardbspencer/status/850163031568941057.

17. See https://twitter.com/richardbspencer/status/850187638376202240.

18. Tina Nguyen, "Alt-right goes 'apoplectic' over Trump's decision to bomb Syria," *Vanity Fair*, April 7, 2017, www.vanityfair.com/news/2017/04/alt-right-donald-trump-syria.

19. Josh Horwitz, "Now that Trump has attacked Syria, his ardent supporters are divided on what to think," Quartz, April 7, 2017, https://qz.com/952781/now-that-trump-has-attacked-syria-his-ardent-supporters-are-divided-on-what-to-think. Ben Schreckinger, "Trump's Troll Army Isn't Ready for War in Syria,"

Politico Magazine, April 7, 2017, www.politico.com/magazine/story/2017/04/trump-alt-right-syria-war-214998.

20. 4chan, April 11, 2017, archived at https://yuki.la/pol/120617583.

21. Personal communication.

22. Ben Schreckinger, "The alt-right comes to Washington," *Politico Magazine*, January/February 2017, www.politico.com/magazine/story/2017/01/alt-right-trump-washington-dc-power-milo-214629.

23. Matthew Sheffield, "The alt-right eats its own: Neo-Nazi podcaster 'Mike Enoch' quits after doxxers reveal his wife is Jewish," Salon, January 16, 2017, www.salon.com/2017/01/16/cat-fight-on-the-alt-right-neo-nazi-podcaster-mike-enoch-quits-after-doxxers-reveal-his-wife-is-jewish.

24. Alan McEwen and Stephen Jones, "Racist vlogger who became global YouTube sensation unmasked as jobless ex-student who lives with dad," *Mirror*, January 9, 2017, www.mirror.co.uk/news/uk-news/racist-vlogger-who-became-global-9588308.

25. German Lopez, "Meet the 16-year-old Canadian girl who took down Milo Yiannopoulos," Vox, February 24, 2017, www.vox.com/policy-and-politics/2017/2/24/14715774/milo-yiannopoulos-cpac-pedophile-video-canada.

26. Richard Spencer, "What to do about Milo: a strategic assessment," AltRight.com, May 2, 2017, https://altright.com/2017/05/02/what-to-do-about-milo-a-strategic-assessment.

27. See https://twitter.com/RealAlexJones/status/874395072539897856: "I'm calling for @megynkelly to cancel the airing of our interview for misrepresenting my views on Sandy Hook."

28. See www.mgtow.com/no.

29. For real: www.mgtow.com/the-water-fountain.

30. 4chan, May 17, 2017, archived at https://archive.4plebs.org/_/search/tnum/125849390.

31. 4chan, "Emmanuel Macron elected next French president," May 10, 2017, archived at http://archive.4plebs.org/_/search/tnum/124891474.

32. "Far-right smear campaign against Antifa exposed by Bellingcat," BBC News, BBC Trending blog, August 24, 2017, www.bbc.co.uk/news/blogs-trending-41036631.

33. 4chan, "The left is really starting to get on our tactics," August 24, 2017, archived at https://archive.4plebs.org/pol/thread/138889541/#q138889541.

34. Angela Nagle, "Goodbye, Pepe," The Baffler, August 15, 2017, https://thebaffler.com/latest/goodbye-pepe.

35. Schreckinger, "The alt-right comes to Washington."
36. Anonymous, "TRIGGERED SNOWFLAKES!," *The Portland Mercury*, May 19, 2017, www.portlandmercury.com/i-anonymous-blog/2017/05/19/19022807/triggered-snowflakes.
37. Brianna Sacks, "Trolls tricked conservatives into holding a massive rally to defend a Texas monument," Buzzfeed, June 12, 2017, www.buzzfeed.com/briannasacks/trolls-tricked-hundreds-of-conservatives-to-hold-a-rally-to?utm_term=.xn1B50aKV#.clJdJELaq; Hannah Henderson with Mike Wendling, "The hoax about desecration of US Civil War graves," BBC News, BBC Trending blog, June 30, 2017, www.bbc.co.uk/news/blogs-trending-40444786.

Index

Index

framing/plants attempts 127,
218–19
in Portland, Oregon 221
Richard Spencer and 1–3, 2–3
violence against 189, 190–1,
210; Charlottesville 44, 46,
73, 140, 174–5
PUAhate.com 60–1, 237n5
Putin, Vladimir 202–3, 205

Quebec City mosque attack
189–90
Quinn, Zoe 63–4, 238n16

r/KotakuInAction 66–7
racism see also Nazism; white ethno-nationalism
denial of 121–2
fake statistics and 195
online 21–2, 42, 49, 55, 79–80,
121–2, 180, 181
"scientific" 19, 22, 36, 56–7, 85,
230n18
segregation, calls for 13, 22,
24–5, 86, 120, 123–4
self-confidence issues and 61,
80–1
of Spencer 21–7
terrorism/murders and 43–7,
189, 191
trolling of individuals 139–40
white genocide conspiracy
theory 44–6, 50, 74, 77–8,
115, 122, 153, 195
of Yiannopoulos 117–18
radicalization 190, 192
Radix Journal 25–6
Ramsey, Paul Ray 123, 136–7
rape 69–70, 98–9
"rapefugees" 98–9
"red pill" metaphor 29–32, 59, 63

"red pill" moments 144, 146, 147,
151
Reddit 57–9, 66
as bridge from extreme to
mainstream media 57–8, 59,
81
deleting of extremist sections
181
Gamergate and 64, 66–7
r/KotakuInAction 66–7
r/The_Donald board 57–8, 79,
226n21
racist boards on 180, 181
Tumblr and 97–8
refugees 98–9, 111–12
regressive left 99–100
Reker, Henriette 138
Republicans 19, 210, 220
resistance to alt-right 134–5,
171, 214–15, 220–2 see also
protesters
Return of Kings website 68–71
The Right Stuff blog 82–3
Rodger, Elliot 60–1
Roof, Dylann 45, 86, 137–8, 188
Roosh V (Daryush Valizadeh)
68–71
Russian involvement 127, 157,
161, 201–5

Sanders, Bernie 91, 92
Sandy Hook attack 169–73, 196
Scarsella, Allen 189
Scavino, Dan 195
Schwartz, Dana 80–1
Seaman, David 161
Seattle protester attack 190
secession 123–4, 198
segregation, calls for 13, 22, 24–5,
86, 120, 123–4, 153
self harm, encouragement of 140